Beiträge zur
Dialogforschung

Band 20

Herausgegeben von Franz Hundsnurscher und Edda Weigand

Dialogue Analysis and the Mass Media

Proceedings of the International Conference Erlangen, April 2–3, 1998

Edited by
Bernd Naumann

Max Niemeyer Verlag
Tübingen 1999

Die Deutsche Bibliothek – CIP-Einheitsaufnahme

Dialogue analysis and the mass media : proceedings of the international conference, Erlangen, April 2–3, 1998 / ed. by Bernd Naumann. – Tübingen : Niemeyer, 1999
(Beiträge zur Dialogforschung ; Bd. 20)

ISBN 3-484-75020-0 ISSN 0940-5992

Printed in Germany.
Gedruckt auf alterungsbeständigem Papier.
Druck: Gulde-Druck GmbH, Tübingen
Buchbinder: Nädele Verlags- und Industriebuchbinderei, Nehren

Table of Contents

Preface

CMC – Computer Mediated Communication – is one of the catchwords of modern society. The concept of what is now called "Internet" arose in America in the 60ies as part of military research in the times of the Cold War. Soon the enormous advantages for general communication via electronic networks became evident and the scope of the Internet grew rapidly. In the meantime CMC has, indeed, become an electronic highway where millions of participants exchange messages day after day. Because new means of communication never replace older ones, CMC has not replaced traditional exchanges, face to face, by letter, by telephone, or by fax, but it has complemented them. CMC has added a new dimension, it has been incorporated by the existing modalities and thus changed and restructured the whole system of traditional communication.

On the occasion of many conferences and meetings, the members and guests of the International Association of Dialogue Analysis (IADA) have been analysing the ways of oral and written communication, for about fifteen years by now and seen from many perspectives. The 1998 conference of the Association, which was held in Erlangen, dealt with aspects of dialogic communication in the Mass Media in general, and with aspects of CMC in particular. The conference was – as usual – highly international in character: Participants came from (according to numbers) Germany, Czechia, the Netherlands, Romania, Italy, the United States, and from Switzerland. Conference languages were English, French, German, and Italian – but there were no contributions offered in French and Italian. Most participants preferred to read their papers in English (12 papers), some used German (6 contributions). There were two sections at the conference, one dealt with the new means of electronic communication, mainly with E-mail communication and with Internet Relay Chat (IRC), the other with dialogues on television and the radio, or with specific aspects of Mass Media communication.

There were two opening papers at the conference. The first one, by Naomi Baron from Washington (pp. 1-34), outlines the history and the dimensions of multimedial communication with regard to dialogue analysis in general, one of her overall results: "Teletechnologies can redefine relationships between participants in social discourse, particularly with regard to social distance and control" (p. 31). The second paper (pp. 35-54) deals with the media as "part of complex dialogic processes"; it expands on what Edda Weigand (Münster) has been calling "dialogic action games" in her recent publications with regard to the Mass Media. She ends with a vision of a fully electronic society: "For television, reality has become a matter of opinion and presentation, for IRC reality might become a matter of virtuality. We hope that language and human dialogic action will not be lost in the dreams that might arise from these huge amounts of data of virtual worlds" (p. 52).

The papers on aspects of CMC show, that there are still many problems unsettled, that still much work needs to be done. It is an exciting subject, because it is relatively new, and you do not permanently walk in beaten tracks. The paper by Hoffmannová and Müllerová (pp. 55-64) on E-mail communication opens the "electronic section". It deals with the question whether an E-mail can be called a private letter or not. It can, the authors claim, and what is more, it combines the advantages of a face-to-face dialogue, a telephone conversation, and of a traditional letter: "Trotz Aufrechterhaltung einiger Textstützen, die das Genre Brief auszeichnen, haben wir aus diesen Briefen eher den Eindruck einer unmittelbaren, natürlichen Unterhaltung, der Realisierung des Bedürfnisses, mit jemandem zu plaudern, gewonnen" (p. 63). The papers by Schulze (pp. 65-82), by Geers (pp. 83-100), and by Grosch (pp.101-112) deal all with IRC texts. Schulze: "The paper will discuss how the total absence of paraverbal and nonverbal relational (and social) cues is fostering the evolution of a repertoire of text-based surrogates for these" (p. 65). Geers analyses chatlogs of no less than 7654 utterances in many interesting details. His general idea: "IRC stellt eben nicht einen einzigen, medial bestimmten Gesprächstypen dar, sondern bezeichnet ein Kommunikationsmedium, das Kommunikation auf bisher unbekannte Weise ermöglicht und beeinflußt" (p. 98). Grosch deals with the modalities of turn-taking in IRC texts: "Die in der Artikelüberschrift aufgeworfene Frage, ob Turn-Verteilung in IRC-Kommunikation letztlich eher eine Frage der medialen Rahmenbedingungen oder aber der sozialen Regulierung sei, läßt sich nach den vorherigen Ausführungen nur mit einem 'Sowohl-als-auch' beantworten" (p. 109). Čmejrkovás contribution (pp. 113-126) looks at oral and written elements in CMC in the context of the Prague School of linguistics. "In contrast to face-to-face oral exchange in which the speakers find themselves in social contact, in 'face-to-face scripturality' the participants of CMC feel they are very close to each other on the computer network, however, they are in social isolation" (p. 125). With the more general orientated contribution by Rothkegel (pp. 127-136) ends the section on CMC. She pleads for a closer integration of the electronic media in the humanities: "Insofern als ein Hypertext ein Text ist, können linguistische Text- und Dialogmodelle genutzt werden, nach denen Informationsauswahl und Informationsfluß in Abhängigkeit der anvisierten Interaktionsziele analysiert bzw. gestaltet werden können.... In einem weiteren Horizont ergibt sich mit den neuen Medien – vor allem mit Hyper- und Multimedia – eine neue Perspektive für die Integration von Geisteswissenschaften und Informationstechnologie" (p. 134).

The other papers are on more dispersed subjects. It is not possible to sum them up in a few words, because there is no common denominator. Westheide (pp. 137-148) deals with interactive language learning by means of multimedia, Freddi (pp. 149-158) with dialogic aspects of multimedia translation. Bazzanella (pp. 159-170) writes on linguistic aspects of an Italian Talk Show, on "Address Inversion" (she defines it as "a special pattern of nominal address, where the message corresponds to the sender" p. 161) and on "Teknonymy" ("the use of a kin term appropriate to a different kin relationship", p. 162). De Graaf and Hoogenboezem (pp. 171-178) write about the dialogues used in the play 'Homeless' produced in the context of a theatre project in the Netherlands. They are mainly interested in the asymmetries of the exchanges: "Sometimes, asymmetric relationships can give rise to very interesting dialogues and may develop into more equal relations" (p. 178). Daneš (pp. 179-186) deals with vocal phenomena in round table political debates in Czech television and on how to transcribe them. Diewald (pp. 187-200) looks into the rôle of modal particles in spoken exchanges; one of her general results: "Die Modalpartikeln bringen zum Ausdruck, daß die Äußerung, in der sie stehen, nicht initial ist, sondern an ein in der kommunikativen Situation vorgegebenes Element, den pragmatischen Prätext, anknüpfen" (p. 197). Maier's paper (pp. 201-212) pursues the idea, that the individuals who take part in public debates represent general social groups or institutions, which results in specific characteristics of fragmental dialogues. Vântu (pp. 213-220) analyses the functions of headlines in print media, and Manu-Magda (pp. 221-230) deals with linguistic exchanges between social groups in Romania.

The contribution by Dieter Genske and Ernest Hess-Lüttich (pp. 231-248) is not the one Hess-Lüttich had read at the conference. He decided to hand in another one (together with Dieter Genske), which opens a new approach and a new kind of text, he claims: It brings together "media studies, intercultural communication, conversation analysis, environmental studies, sanitary engineering, public relations analysis" (p. 231), a hitherto unread mixture, indeed. Since this lies somewhat outside the scope of our conference and of the contributions collected in this volume, their paper is placed at the end of the volume.

The conference was sponsored by the IADA, by the University of Erlangen-Nuremberg, and by the Siemens Company. To all of them I say thank you for having made the realization of this conference possible. I have to expand my thanks also to all who have helped to organize the meeting, most of all to Ute Szczepaniak, who arranged the manuscripts for printing.

Erlangen, 27 February, 1999

Bernd Naumann

Naomi S. Baron

History Lessons: Telegraph, Telephone, and Email as Social Discourse

Imagine yourself at a dinner party. The meal is finished and preparations are underway for the evening's entertainment. The program will be a concert, sung by a leading diva of the day before an admiring crowd. The guests settle into their seats, and each one is given a device through which to enjoy the music.

The audience is not at the concert hall. Nor does it hear the performance carried by television or radio, or even played on a phonograph. Instead, each guest is handed a telephone. For when the telephone was first invented, long before it emerged as a medium for general social discourse, it was seriously marketed as a device for broadcasting public lectures and performances.

Unlike Athena springing well-formed from the head of Zeus, new technologies may take decades to reach maturity, both in technical sophistication and in functional range. Steam engines were developed for pumping water out of mines, transistors were seen as a panacea for improving hearing aides, and television was initially heralded as an educational device.

This essay explores the evolution and inter-relationship between three teletechnologies: the telegraph, the telephone, and email. The ultimate goal of such a comparison is to better understand the nature of contemporary social discourse – and its future developments – by retrospective comparison with earlier non-face-to-face teletechnologies.

Our approach will be both historical and linguistic. We will argue

- First, that the forms and functions of new communicative technologies are typically conceived of in terms of older technologies.
- Second, that the "mature" linguistic identity of a communication modality may take years to develop.

- Third, that economic issues (rather than just technological development or perceived social need) may play a central role in determining functional shifts in a communicative medium.
- Fourth, that many of the same linguistic variables regarding social dynamics and format are relevant in understanding telegraphy, telephony, and email as forms of social discourse.

We begin (Part 1: Technology and Social Discourse) by looking broadly at how technology has historically been used to facilitate social discourse (and, in the process, has influenced what we say and write). Part 2 (Evolution of the Telegraph, the Telephone, and Email) outlines the historical emergence of each of the three modalities, looking both at the original functions and intended usership of each teletechnology and how the medium subsequently evolved. In Part 3 (Linguistic Analysis), we compare the telegraph, the telephone, and email as means of linguistic communication. Drawing upon what we have learned, Part 4 (History Lessons: *Ceci tuera cela*?) ponders the future of particular teletechnologies as media for social discourse.

1. Technology and Social Discourse

Language as Social Discourse

Human language is, at base, a form of social exchange. Linguistic signs, grammatical constructions, and rules of communicative competence all emerge as socially acquired conventions. Whether writing or speaking (even ostensibly to ourselves, in monologue or diary entry), our linguistic formulations assume an interlocutor.

Speech has historically been the medium *par excellence* of social discourse. With the development of writing (at different times in the histories of many societies), a new medium of discourse became available. Admittedly, writing constrains the interlocutor's opportunity for response – especially if the sender is distanced in space or time. Yet in fairness, even speech does not always guarantee right of response, as in the case of royal edicts or other hierarchical circumstances.

Technologies of Language

One-on-one face-to-face spoken communication does not rely on technological assistance to convey messages from one party to another. However, all other forms of communication potentially do. The means of conveyance may be simple – a megaphone, pen-and-ink, a carrier pigeon – or complex – a printing press, a typewriter, a computer.

All writing entails technology, in that writing necessarily implies the use of tools for its creation (Haas 1996, xi). However, technology can also be used to extend speech through time or space, as with telephones or phonographs.

Language technologies are divisible into two basic categories. The first, **tangible/ tactile**, are those whose output products are physically manifest to the producer. They include:

(a) handwriting
(b) printing
(c) the typewriter
(d) the phonograph
(e) tape recorders
(f) computers as stand-alone machines (for word processing)

The second, **teletechnologies**, are those whose output is transmitted through space (either with or without the benefit of wires or cables) for reception by a distant interlocutor. These include:

(a) the telegraph
(b) the telephone
(c) radio
(d) television
(e) the fax machine
(f) computers as networked machines (for computer mediated communication, especially email)

Some of these technologies obviously relate to written language: handwriting, printing, the telegraph, the typewriter, the fax, computers as word-processors. Other technologies are universally associated with speech or other auditory signals (such as music): the phonograph, tape recorders, the telephone, radio, and television. However, as we shall see throughout this essay, language technologies don't necessarily serve the functions for which they were structurally designed (Nye 1997).

Is Technology Neutral?

If, as Nietzsche said, "Our writing materials contribute their part to our thinking", how might technology, more generally, affect spoken and written messages? There is a growing literature (see, e.g., Baron 1989, 1998b; Eisenstein 1979; Haas 1996; McLuhan 1964/1994) on the ways in which communicative media shape linguistic messages. Most of the interest to date has focused on how a particular technology (e.g., stylus on clay, the printing press, the telegraph) influences the linguistic structure of the message itself (e.g., iconic vs. arbitrary symbolic representations, relevance of consistency in orthography, stylistic conventions). Other discussions have considered possible effects of writing and literacy upon cognition (see e.g., Olson 1995 and Baron 1997 for a review of the issues). This essay extends the discussion to the influence of language technologies on social discourse relationships. In particular, it explores how the relationship between interlocutors is affected by the conveyance technology and how that relationship alters with maturation of the technology itself.

2. Evolution of the Telegraph, the Telephone, and Email

The evolution of a technology is the product not only of scientific or engineering feats but of personal biography, social conditions, and often sheer serendipity. As we look at the emergence of the telegraph, the telephone, and email as communication technologies, our goal is to highlight developments relevant to the theses we hope to establish. To this end, we will lay out our discussion of each technology in terms of

- the basic *chronology of events* in the invention of the communicative medium
- the *original functions and intended users*
- subsequent *evolution of the medium* with respect to technology, cost issues, functions and usership

The Telegraph

Chronology of Events

The idea of sending messages at distances without physically transporting them is as old as smoke signals and drum beats. However, the modern separation of communication from transportation (to use James Carey's phrase – Carey 1983, 313) began in late eighteenth-century France, with the Chappe visual telegraph. As schoolboys, the three Chappe brothers had devised a semaphore to exchange messages with each other because they were at different schools and not allowed to visit in person (Coe 1993, 6). The Chappe telegraph was adopted in 1793 by the revolutionary government to maintain centralized authority across France. In fact, in 1837, a law was passed imposing

> jail sentences of from one month to one year, and fines of from 1,000 to 10,000 Francs on anyone transmitting unauthorized signals from one place to another by means of the telegraph machine or any other means (Attali & Stourdze 1977, 99).

Such concerns later dissuaded Czar Nicholas of Russia, who was very interested in Morse's electric telegraph, from building a system that potentially could be used subversively against his government (Coe 1993, 31). Similar worries about controlling the flow of information were to arise in the twentieth century in the case of the telephone. Adolph Hitler retarded telephone development in pre-war Germany by imposing large taxes (Pool 1983, 86, citing Dilts 1941, 47), and Joseph Stalin vetoed Trotsky's plan for establishing a telephone system in the new Soviet state. Stalin argued that a phone system would "unmake our work. No greater instrument for counter-revolution and conspiracy can be imagined" (from Trotsky's *Life of Stalin*, cited in Boettinger 1977a, 203).

Credit for inventing the electric telegraph goes to Samuel F.B. Morse, a respected nineteenth century-portrait artist. Morse had gone to Europe in late 1829 to enhance his skills. Like many educated men of his era, he was fascinated by emerging ideas about electricity. While in France, he visited the Chappe semaphoric telegraph and soon became obsessed with developing an electric telegraph. On his voyage back to America in fall, 1832, he sketched out a design for such a telegraph. Over the next five years, Morse improved upon his model, liberally incorporating as his own the ideas of friends and acquaintances (including Alfred Vail's telegraph key and Vail's transmission system, which came to be known as Morse Code).

In 1837, Morse initiated the process for patenting the telegraph, and the first successful telegraphic transmission was made in early 1838. However, it was not until 1844 that Morse tapped out the famous message "What hath God wrought!" (selected by Annie Ellsworth, daughter of the US Commissioner of Patents, from the Book of Numbers – 23:23) on the first long-distance telegraph line, built between Washington and Baltimore, and paid for by the US Congress.

Original Functions and Intended Users

Morse had originally designed the telegraph for synchronous two-way communication between individual interlocutors (see Blondheim 1994, 208-209 note 13). In fact, as a form of publicity, Morse's assistants arranged chess tournaments between clubs in Washington and Baltimore to demonstrate the communicative potential of the new technology (Blondheim 1994, 209). However, these real-time exchanges did not prove practical.

Evolution of the Medium

Over the next century, the telegraph evolved from a curiosity to a vital communication medium. Its new functions included serving as a conduit for news and commerce, providing railroad communication, and facilitating targeted interpersonal exchanges between individuals.

One of the earliest widespread uses of the telegraph was to revolutionize the writing and distribution of news in America. Before the telegraph, newspapers spent vast sums dispatching reporters to ports in the northeastern US and Canada to be the first to learn the news carried by ships coming from Europe. The news was then relayed by horse, pigeon, or even chartered boat to Boston or New York, so that editors could scoop the competition.

Initial technological limitations of the telegraph were responsible for profound reorganization in the way news was gathered and disseminated. Because the original telegraph lines between cities could only carry one message at a time, there was fierce competition between reporters as to who would get to the telegraph office first to file a story. This competition led to the establishment of a fifteen-minute time limit being imposed on any individual users of the telegraph (Blondheim 1994, 62-63). In fact, the first collective news-gathering consortium – what was to become the Associated Press – was formed to break the logjam and enable hundreds of newspapers to receive the same stories at the same time (Blondheim 1994; Schwarzlose 1989, 1990; Thompson 1947). The impact of the Associated Press on American newspapers cannot be underestimated. By the early 1850s, at least two columns of AP news appeared in nearly every major American newspaper (Blondheim 1994, 6). By the 1880s, more than 80% of the copy in newspapers published in the Western territories of the US consisted of AP dispatches (Blondheim 1994, viii).

If information was time-critical to newspaper editors, it was equally time-sensitive to titans of commerce. American fortunes could be made or lost, depending upon who first learned the news of political or economic developments in Europe. Nationally and regionally, agricultural business decisions could now be based on rapid access to crop information from around the country. Carey (1983, 316) speculates that

> [i]t was not ... mere historic accident that the Chicago Commodity Exchange, to this day the principal American futures market, opened in 1848, the same year the telegraph reached that city.

While the telegraph clearly facilitated commerce, it also altered previous social conventions about relationships between potential interlocutors. As Carey observes,

> Before the telegraph, business relations were personal; that is, they were mediated through face to face relations, by personal correspondence, by contacts among people who, by and large, knew one another as actual persons .... Through the telegraph ... social relations among large numbers of anonymous buyers and sellers were coordinated (Carey 1983, 306).

The railroad was somewhat slower in adopting the telegraph. Before the appearance of teletechnologies, railroads had no regular way of notifying a train running on a single-track line that another train was headed on a collision course. As the railroad grew, such accidents became a serious problem. A typical make-shift solution was that adopted by the Boston and Worcester Railroad, which

> kept horses every five miles along the line ... [that] raced up and down the track so that their riders could warn engineers of impending collisions (Carey 1983, 314).

Finally, what about the use of the telegraph for interpersonal exchange between individuals? For most of its history, this function has largely been limited to emergencies, congratulations, and bad news, reflecting the high cost of sending telegrams.

Among the well-to-do, the telegraph afforded the potential for casual social exchange. As early as 1858, the British humor magazine *Punch* (1858, vol. 35, p. 254) mused over what might happen if the telegraph were available in private homes:

> With a house telegraph it would be a perpetual tête-à-tête. We should all be always in company .... The bliss of ignorance would be at an end (reprinted in Briggs & Briggs 1972, 203).

A similar vision did, in fact, materialize two decades later. In 1877, the Social Telegraph Association was created in Bridgeport, Connecticut. The Association

> installed instruments in subscribers' homes that could be connected, through a central switchboard, to one another so that subscribers could "speak" to one another through the Morse Code once they had been taught how (Aronson 1977, 18; from Rhodes 1929, 149).

(Looking ahead, we might dub the Social Telegraph Association the indirect ancestor of computer listservs, which connect up social affinity groups for the exchange of written messages.)

Novelty notwithstanding, the telegraph never caught on as a common vehicle of social exchange. Besides the expense and the need to learn Morse Code, the telegraph was inconvenient to use (telegraphic equipment was not commonly installed in private homes) and there was no simultaneity of transmission and reception. All of these problems would be solved by the telephone.

The Telephone

Chronology of Events

Much as Morse's electric telegraph was indebted to the Chappe brothers' earlier semaphore system, Alexander Graham Bell's telephone was originally envisioned as a harmonic version of the telegraph. His initial goal had been to send multiple signals – at different frequencies – along the same telegraphic line.

While Bell is credited with inventing the telephone, he had keen competition for the title from Elisha Gray, who filed his own patent but a few hours after Bell's had arrived on February 14, 1876. In fact, Gray – who later did create a harmonic telegraph – might have completed his invention before Bell, were it not for two critical factors.

First, Gray (unlike Bell) did not appreciate the commercial potential of the telephone. As Gray wrote to his patent lawyer in 1875,

> Bell seems to be spending all his energies on [the] talking telephone. While this is very interesting scientifically, it has no commercial value at present, for they can do more business over a line by methods already in use [i.e., the telegraph] than by that system (Hounshell 1975, 152, cited in Pool *et al.* 1977, 145).

Second, Bell's personal background afforded him a radically different perspective on telecommunications than Gray's. While Gray had extensive experience in telegraphy, Bell was known as a speech expert – a teacher of elocution, a propagandist for his father's notation for "visible speech", an advocate of teaching the deaf to speak, and a student of human physiology, who was to incorporate the bones of an actual human ear into one of his early experimental telephones. What's more, Bell was a musician with an exceptionally keen ear. For Bell, the telephone was less a tool for conveying messages than a device for transmitting voices:

> The telephone may be briefly described as an electrical contrivance for reproducing, in distant places, the tones and articulations of a speaker's voice, so that conversation can be carried on by word of mouth between persons in different rooms, in different streets, or in different towns (Alexander Graham Bell, address to "The Capitalists of the Electric Telephone Company", Kensington, March 25, 1878; printed in Pool *et al.* 1977, 156).

The actual invention of the telephone was the result of an intensive collaboration between Bell and Thomas A. Watson, a machinist who worked at Charles Williams' electrical supply shop on Court Street in Boston, implementing the designs of inventors such as Bell. During a final flurry of activity, Bell and Watson were working at a fever's pitch in rented rooms on Exeter Place in Boston. On the fateful night of March 10, 1876, Watson was positioned in one room and Bell in another when the famous message

"Mr. Watson, come here. I want you!"

could be heard across the line. Note that Bell did not utter these words to signal a scientific accomplishment but rather because he had spilled sulfuric acid on himself and needed Watson's assistance in handling the mess (Boettinger 1977b, 66).

Original Functions and Intended Users

Bell the inventor was also Bell the entrepreneur. His imagination in crafting the device itself was well matched by his creative thinking about the uses to which the telephone might be put. His major stumbling block during the telephone's infancy was inadequate capital, a problem later solved by Gardiner Hubbard (his future father-in-law) and Thomas Sanders (whose deaf son Bell had tutored).

Bell originally conceived of the telephone as a "hard-wired" device for connecting two specific locations. Early users included business owners who could communicate between their homes and places of manufacture (or sales). Other early users were physicians who, in addition to having the money necessary to pay for the service, could use the telephone to transmit prescriptions to pharmacists (the third major group of early subscribers).

Initial difficulties in developing the technology to allow clear two-way conversation (necessitating simultaneous transmission and reception) led Bell to improvise a novel function for the telephone as a one-way device for broadcasting lectures and musical performances. In fact, as a means of supporting himself in the early days of his invention, Bell took to the lecture circuit with his trusted assistant Watson. In demonstrations of "Professor Bell's Speaking and Singing Telephone" (Fischer 1992, 36), Bell might offer up a soliloquy from Shakespeare, while Watson performed a vocal medley, including religious favorites and patriotic tunes (Aronson 1977, 19-21; Watson 1913, 31-32). This "radio" concept of the telephone was actually used fairly widely at the end of the nineteenth century in both the United States and Europe for transmitting music, speeches, sermons, and lectures (see Marvin 1988, 209-216).

Evolution of the Medium

By the end of 1876, Bell and his backers were hard pressed to raise ample moneys to further Bell's invention. Gardiner Hubbard took the extraordinary step of offering the patent on the telephone to the Western Union Telegraph Corporation for the modest sum of $100,000. William Orton, president of Western Union, turned Hubbard down, purportedly with the rhetorical query, "What use could this company make of an electrical toy?" (Aronson 1977, 15-16)

Over the next century, Bell's "electrical toy" revolutionized human communication, thanks to technological and organizational innovations, and to highly creative packaging. In addition to continual improvements in the transmission and reception capacities of the device itself, major landmarks in telephone history included the telephone exchange (making it possible to connect any caller with any other subscriber on the network), laying of the transatlantic cable, and later, introduction of automatic dialing

But the ideas of Bell and his associates for building a market were equally vital to the success of the telephone (Fischer 1992, 62-65). In the early days, they included the introduction of pay telephones, message units (as opposed to unlimited service), and party lines, all of which lowered the cost of telephone use, thereby affording access to a far wider circle of users. Marketing schemes in later years – from telephone extensions to caller ID to call-waiting – are simply continuations of the century-old marketing face of Bell Telephone.

The idea of creating public need for a technology is hardly new. In the case of the telephone, an early advertising circular was issued on October 27, 1877 by Ponton's Telephone Central Service of Titusville, Pennsylvania, a Bell licensee. Ponton listed some of the many applications for a telephone, including putting the user in instant communication with the grocer, butcher, and baker, "along with 176 other occupations" (Kingsbury 1972, 74). More generally, Bell's publicists sought to suggest to the new subscriber "what to do with his telephone ... and to make him ashamed to consider such a thing as ever again doing without it" (cited in Fischer 1992, 63, 332 note 5, from Alfred Vail's testimony, December 9, 1909, in New York State, *Report of the Committee*, p. 398). Such efforts curiously foreshadowed advertisements for another new technology: the computer. In its early days, Apple Computer ran a series of ads entitled, "What Can You Do with a Computer?" that laid out an array of possible uses for the machine to potential buyers.

Growth in the uses of telephony have always been a curious mix of need (real or manufactured), economics, and social control. In England, for example, government support for the post office undercut demand for the telephone. The penny post assured the citizenry an inexpensive way of communicating with one another. Who, therefore, needed the telephone? In 1895, the British Postmaster General proclaimed, "Gas and water were necessities for every inhabitant of the country. Telephones were not and never would be" (Perry 1977, 75). In 1902, the *Times* of London concluded that the telephone

> is not an affair of the million. It is a convenience for the well-to-do and a trade appliance for persons who can very well afford to pay for it .... An overwhelming majority of the population do not use it and are not likely to use it at all, except to the extent of an occasional message from a public station (Perry 1977, 75).

A year earlier, the Chancellor of the Exchequer, Michael Hicks Beach, had declared, "telephone communication is not desired by the rural mind" (Perry 1977, 76).

But when it came to the rural *American* mind, Beach was flat-out wrong. One of the most important functional expansions of the telephone, i.e., from business to social interaction, was initiated not by Bell himself but by the multiplicity of exchanges that sprouted up, particularly in the rural mid-west and western United States, after Bell's first patent expired in 1893. Local communities, often pooling their meagre finances and stringing up connections along barbed wire fences, created local telephone exchanges to link isolated farm houses.

The telephone afforded "a sense of community life" (Fischer 1992, 99) to farm families, especially wives, during the early decades of the twentieth century. In some far-flung communities, residents would pick up party lines at pre-arranged times to engage in the kind of socializing that was not regularly possible face-to-face. Switchboard operators (typically operating out of their own homes) were vital for sharing news, getting help in times of emergency, and basic human contact. With the spread of long-distance service across the country, the telephone became an instrument for maintaining social ties with distant friends and relatives.

It was not until after World War I that the general urban population began using the telephone as a social instrument rather than strictly as a device for conducting practical business or handling emergencies (see Fischer 1992, 225-226; Singer 1981). While this shift was initiated by grass roots users, the successors of Ma Bell capitalized upon it, with mottos such as "Reach out and touch someone" or "The next best thing to being there."

This shift in telephone usage, from an emphasis on the practical to at least an equal emphasis on the social, was to be replicated more than half a century later, when universal dependence on the telephone began giving way to the growing appeal of electronic mail.

Email

Chronology of Events

The history of electronic mail (email) demonstrates the effects of linking a powerful technology (the computer) with a telecommunications system (the telephone), but relying on written language (as with the telegraph) to exchange messages. Email grew out of research projects during the height of the Cold War aimed at developing a decentralized network of computers that could be used to transmit information across the US in case of nuclear attack. The idea was to ensure that a strike on one target would not cripple the nation's ability to distribute defense data elsewhere in the country. By the late 1960s, initial research by the RAND Corporation and MIT had evolved into ARPANET (the Advanced

Research Projects Agency Network), run by the US Department of Defense, which eventually became the backbone for the Internet of the early 1990s.

ARPANET had been designed to facilitate the transfer of data files between computers and to enable remote log-in to other machines, not for individuals to exchange personal electronic messages. However, some casual experiments in the early 1970s by ARPANET researchers revealed that the same technology that worked for data transfer and remote log-in could also be used for personal messaging. This realization, along with Murray Turoff's development of computer-based group decision-making and the independent emergence of computer bulletin-board systems in the late 1970s, provided both the technology and the initial impetus for email (see Rheingold 1993 and Baron 1998a for a fuller discussion).

In talking about electronic messaging, it is important to distinguish between messages shared with a number of individuals simultaneously (as in computer-based conferencing) and those sent to a specific individual (generally called email). Collectively, exchange of information via computer (either broadcast or point-to-point) has come to be known as computer mediated communication (or CMC) (see, for example, Herring 1996). The distinction between broadcast and point-to-point communication will become important in Part 3, when we compare the linguistic characteristics of the telegraph, the telephone, and email.

Original Functions and Intended Users

Like the telephone and telegraph before it, email's functional origins were more pragmatic than social. In the academic world of the 1970s and 1980s, access to email was largely in the hands of faculty and researchers connected with the scientific community, many of whose professional activities were funded by the US Department of Defense. While it was possible, in those early days, to send individual messages to colleagues on personal issues, usage was limited to those with ready access to the technology, along with the patience necessary to formulate and send messages on computer systems that were hardly user-friendly.

In the business world, email was introduced on local area networks in the 1980s to enable employees to communicate about business matters within the organization. Although some employees used the email system to send personal messages, social functions were generally subordinated (see Sherblom 1988).

Email also appeared in the private sector as an outgrowth of public service community bulletin boards (perhaps the most famous being the WELL, based in California – see Rheingold 1993) and subsequent commercial services such as Compuserv and Prodigy, through which computer-afficianados could do public postings or establish private mailboxes. However, it was not until the explosion of networked computing in the 1990s that the range of functions and number of users of email underwent radical transformation.

Evolution of the Medium

As with the telephone, expansion in the use of the computer as a communication device was driven by improvements in the technology, falling costs, and clever marketing. Falling prices of hardware (at least relative to computing power) made computers more attractive to a larger usership, aided by the development of more user-friendly software. As the prices of modems fell in proportion to their speed of transmission, the possibility for individuals to connect up with other machines (and users) became increasingly attractive.

Two critical developments in the 1980s laid the groundwork for exponential expansion of email in the 1990s. The first was the decision by a growing number of universities to wire their campuses, enabling students, faculty, and staff to communicate by computer directly with one another as well as with the outside world. Student users, in turn, became advocates of the technology to their larger circle of family and friends off-campus. The second development, the emergence of the Internet, along with the creation of user-friendly search engines, provided ready access to a seemingly limitless font of information and potential social connections. Now you could easily reach anyone with an email address, regardless of his or her network provider.

America Online (AOL) is only the best known of the commercial providers that have capitalized upon the new infrastructure and public awareness of the possibilities of networked computing. In the late 1990s, email (and computer mediated communication more generally) have revolutionized the presuppositions and expectations of a growing proportion of ordinary citizens about appropriate technologies for communication.

Computer-based communication appears to be filling many functions served by the telephone over at least the past 75 years. First, as a source of information and instrument of commerce, many people turn to the computer to learn airline schedules or a museum's opening hours, place an order for a book, flowers, or even an automobile. Second, the computer has proved to be a conduit for community discourse. Like the rural telephone exchanges of the early twentieth century, computer listservs and Inter-Relay Chat Groups (IRCs) make it possible for clusters of people with related interests to come together virtually, sometimes even in real time. (Note: In the US, it has been interesting to watch the initial commercial success of telephone chat lines in the early 1990s be undermined by the growth of computer chat groups in the mid 1990s. Computer chat groups not only are less expensive but also provide greater anonymity by camouflaging one's voice and even one's sexual identity.)

Third, email is increasingly replacing the telephone (not to mention the traditional letter) for one-to-one social discourse. Given pricing and ease of access, even people with no computer experience are finding that email is often both less expensive and more convenient than traditional phone calls. There are no long-distance charges, you can send however lengthy a message you wish at any time of day or night, and "telephone tag" is eliminated. Some even argue that "universal access" to email is as much a necessity – and right – as universal access to telephone service (Anderson *et al.* 1995).

3. Linguistic Analysis

The individual – and intertwined – histories of the telegraph, the telephone, and email provide a foundation for exploring the essential question of this essay: how do these three teletechnologies compare as forms of communication?

Our analysis is laid out in two main sections. The first, **social dynamics**, looks at each technology with regard to the *social nature of the transmission*, the issue of *privacy*, and *social etiquette* regarding content. The second section, on **format**, considers *durability* and *composition issues*.

Social Dynamics

Social Nature of the Transmission

How do the social dynamics of the relationship between interlocutors shape the actual message being transmitted and the attitudinal response of its receiver? A first consideration is the nature of the transmission:

- Is it intended as a *monologue* (one-way transmission of information from the sender to the recipient) or as a dialogue?
- Is it information exchanged between two individuals (*point-to-point*) or shared with a wider audience (*broadcast*)?

The dichotomies *monologue vs. dialogue* and *point-to-point vs. broadcast* intersect with one another to form a four-way grid. Each of the three teletechnologies can be (or at least has been) used within each sector of the matrix, i.e.,

i. Point-to-Point Monologue
ii. Point-to-Point Dialogue
iii. Broadcast Monologue
iv. Broadcast Dialogue

i. Point-to-Point Monologue

The telegraph evolved as a medium for point-to-point monologue *par excellence*, whereby a single individual sends a message to another individual without anticipating a response. From the time the French revolutionary government adopted the Chappe visual telegraph, telegraphy has largely been a system for informing rather than conversing. The telephone did not become a medium for dialogue until a critical mass of people had private telephones, the quality of transmission and service improved (see Pierce 1977, 173), and, in cases such as France, government control was loosened (see Attali & Stourdze 1977). As for email, the nature of transmission is usually dialogic, although point-to-point monologue is common when a message is sent down the organizational chain, e.g., from a manager giving directives to an employee.

ii. Point-to-Point Dialogue

Perhaps not surprisingly, the telegraph, the telephone, and email were initially conceived of as media for point-to-point dialogic communication between individuals. In the case of the telegraph, much as the Chappe brothers had originally designed their semaphores to converse with each other across distances, Samuel Morse is said to have envisioned the telegraph as a form of conversation,

> linking wives with their distant husbands, allowing children to communicate with their parents, and encouraging lovers to exchange sentiments over the wires (Blondheim 1994, 34, 221 note 18).

This vision (though never practically realized) is strikingly similar to current email systems, especially those offering synchronous communication.

The telephone was designed as – and has remained – primarily a medium for point-to-point dialogue. In fact, in 1877, Bell wrote to his wife Mabel that "When people can ... chat comfortably with each other by telephone over some bit of gossip, every person will desire to put money in our pockets by having telephones" (Bruce 1973, 210).

Email also emerged as a point-to-point dialogic device, though only as an afterthought from several early designers of ARPANET. Although other (broadcast) forms of transmission dominated for nearly two decades, point-to-point dialogue has become the modern function of email *par excellence*.

Finally, it is curious to note that even the radio was initially designed not as a broadcast device but for replacing the telegraph as a medium for point-to-point communication (Czitrom 1982, 67). This early notion of the radio as a "wireless telegraph" is reminiscent of Bell's original goal of creating a new form of telegraphy (the harmonic telegraph) and

Thomas Edison's original conception of the phonograph as a medium for point-to-point communication, whereby an individual could

> record spoken messages that would be transmitted by phone [at an originating telegraph office] to a recorder at another office where the addressee would come to hear it (Boorstin 1973, 379, cited by Pool 1983, 31).

iii. Broadcast Monologue

Additional functions appeared very early in the evolution of both the telegraph and the telephone, rendering them (at least for a time) also broadcast monologic devices. As we saw in Part 2, the telegraph became a broadcast monologic device when newspapers confronted the logjam of only one reporter at a time being able to file a story on the local telegraph wire.

The early broadcast functions of the telephone reflect the ingenuity of Bell and his backers to generate much-needed revenues. As we noted earlier, the telephone was used at the end of the nineteenth century for broadcasting both speech and music. In France, for example, the president of the Republic "inaugurated a series of telephonic soirées" by establishing telephonic connections between the Elysee Palace and the Opera, the Theatre Francais, and the Odeon Theatre (Marvin 1988, 209). However, the most enduring experiment with the broadcast telephone was the Hungarian service known as *Telephon Hirmondo*, which served all the functions of a daily newspaper (news stories, stock exchange reports, advertising) along with musical programming. For over 25 years, *Telephon Hirmondo* offered its Budapest subscribers full-service programming of the sort we have come to associate with radio and later television (see Marvin 1988, 223-228).

Other, more specific broadcast functions of the telephone were also introduced in the US. Where switchboard operators had earlier provided such information as the time or the weather (along with local gossip), recorded time and weather information was later made available to callers, both as a public service and as a way of increasing revenues. More recently, AT&T began offering its individual subscribers (for a fee, of course) the option of sending voice mail to a telephone distribution list, a service also available in many organizations.

Analogously, contemporary email can also be used as a broadcast monologic device. The email distribution list enables users to send identical messages simultaneously to a specific number of individuals from whom one does not anticipate a response.

iv. Broadcast Dialogue

Finally, the telegraph, telephone, and email are all devices capable of dialogic broadcast. Although it never became commercially successful, the "social telegraph" joined together groups of communicants. In the initial 75 years of the telephone, first switchboard operators and then party lines rendered much telephone communication at least open to semi-public broadcast. And with the development of networked computing, computer mediated communication made possible computer-based conferencing (within a known group of interlocutors) and open-ended dialogic broadcasts (through listservs, chat lines, MOOs, and MUDs).

Privacy

The second component in our analysis of the social dynamics of teletechnologies is privacy: to what extent do the telegraph, the telephone, and email ensure confidentiality, invade personal space, or encourage self-disclosure between interlocutors?

i. Confidentiality

In spoken or written discourse between individuals, privacy of the communication is typically assumed unless the interlocutors choose to make the content of their exchange public. How has the introduction of the telegraph, telephone, and email affected these presuppositions?

Telegraph operators have generally been assumed to be like butlers of old: observing much and saying nothing, a position underscored by the telegraph companies' insistence that dispatches were privileged communiqués (Marvin 1988, 69). Yet socially, it took some time before the system gained public confidence. An article in an 1876 issue of *Chambers Journal* ("Curiosities of the Wire", London, September 2, p. 566) related how an elderly woman became indignant when a telegraph operator insisted upon opening the sealed envelope containing the message she wished to send. The woman proclaimed, "'do you suppose I'm going to let all you fellows read my private affairs? I won't send it at all' and ... bounced out of the office in high dudgeon" (told in Marvin 1988, 25).

The telephone, since its inception, has afforded few guarantees of confidentiality. George Bernard Shaw (who himself was briefly employed by the Edison Telephone Company of London – Brooks 1977, 210) complained about the "stentorian efficiency" with which the first London telephones broadcast private messages (Briggs 1977, 61). Interestingly, the commercial success of handsfree telephones with loud speakers is only quite recent. Marketing efforts for such devices were underway as early as 1918, but made few inroads, since the telephone was viewed as "a more private device that does not interrupt everything else going on by filling the room with sound" (Pool 1983, 33, 38 note 52).

The switchboard and party lines later compromised any hopes of telephone confidentiality. Especially in small towns, users came to recognize that "if you don't want someone to know it, don't say it on the telephone" (Fischer 1992, 71). Even with the subsequent development of automatic telephone switching and fully private lines, the potential for wiretapping precludes absolute guarantee of telephone confidentiality. (Note that wire tapping by telephone linemen had been a concern as far back as 1877 – see Marvin 1988, 68).

Email confidentiality is similarly compromised both by legal issues and user inadvertence. As a number of lawsuits have demonstrated (see Sipior & Ward 1995), email sent using employers' computer systems are generally judged to belong to the employers and thus accessible to them. Less contentious – though equally problematic – are instances in which users compromise their own confidentiality, either by accidentally sending a message intended for a specific individual to a larger distribution list or by posting to a public discussion a message that is judged incendiary. As one former lawyer advised,

> Do not put anything in writing [in posting to an email discussion list] ... that you would not want to see on the front page of the newspaper or read to a federal grand jury (Durusau 1996, 12).

ii. Invasion of Personal Space

Beyond the issue of objective confidentiality is the question of whether a teletechnology invades one's personal space. Less than a decade after the introduction of the telegraph, *Punch* had quipped that if telegraph lines were installed in private houses,

> We should come near that most miserable of all conceivable conditions, of being able to oversee and overhear all that is being done or said concerning us all over London! (*Punch* 1858, vol. 30, p. 244; cited in Briggs & Briggs 1972, 203).

While this reality never came to pass for the telegraph, the telephone was a different story.

To appreciate the impact of the telephone on one's personal space, we need to recall how social and business exchanges functioned in the second half of the nineteenth century. Friends and business associates didn't simply drop in, but timed their visits during "calling hours", with such visits typically announced in advance through a letter delivered by messenger or at least with a printed card, identifying one's name and station in life. While one might sometimes be welcoming a stranger into one's home (remember Sherlock Holmes), the stranger's identity was known in advance and such visits were regulated by the resident.

With the coming of the telephone, the previous balance between public and private was redefined. Privacy increased in that much business that used to require face-to-face encounter (e.g., many of the house calls made by physicians, many business transactions) could now be handled by telephone. Yet at the same time, anyone with a telephone was literally "on call" to anyone who might wish to ring, at any time of day or night. Patients who would only send for the doctor in case of true emergency did not hesitate to phone under less dire circumstances. Gentlemen and business owners who were used to having their visitors screened were soon complaining that

> any person off the street may for a trifling payment ... ring up any subscriber and insist on holding a conversation with him (*Scotsman*, Dec. 9, 1884; quoted in Marvin 1988, 103).

Predictably, secretaries (and butlers) were soon installed to monitor incoming telephone calls as they had earlier sized up incoming visitors. However, unlike a face-to-face presentation, where you could quickly evaluate the visitor's social or organizational standing and decide whether or not to grant an interview, there were fewer cues with simply a voice at the end of the line. One runs the risk, when answering the phone oneself, of having to take on all comers.

One does, of course, always have the option of ignoring the ring of the phone. But few of us find it easy to do so (Pool 1983, 142), even if we are in someone else's home or office (Singer 1981, 61, 63). We interrupt face-to-face conversation, jump up in the middle of the night, or drop what we are doing to answer a ringing telephone, even when we have no idea who might be calling or whether it might be a wrong number. However much we rationalize our behavior (e.g., by arguing the call might signal an emergency), most of us are culturally conditioned to assume that if we have a telephone, we are fair game for interruption by any stranger who finds our number. (Unpublished telephone numbers, answering machines, and caller ID represent attempts to cope with the problem.)

In light of our experience with the telephone, it is interesting to watch the degree to which users allow email to invade their personal space. While some businesses have replaced much inter-office phone communication with email (with concomitant expectations about rapid response to incoming email messages), most users see email as a medium that protects their private space far more than the telephone. Email affords us the freedom to access the system any time or place we choose. Moreover, email provides visual and vocal anonymity (ignoring, of course, recent developments that allow transmission of audio and video signals).

The fact that email offers such anonymity is reflected in the common practice among many professionals of listing email addresses where they would hesitate to give telephone numbers. While it is true that email access invites the same kind of intrusion by uninvited strangers that early telephone subscribers bemoaned a century ago, it seems easier to ignore or delete an unwanted email than to hang up on an unwanted caller.

iii. Personal Disclosure

We have seen that while the telephone and email invite intrusions into our personal space, they also provide us physical distance from interlocutors, be they known or unknown. The telephone shields our physical appearance (enabling us, for example, to give a radio interview while still in our nightclothes). Email also removes any auditory cues. As the famous Peter Steiner cartoon in the *New Yorker* has it,

"On the Internet, nobody knows you're a dog."

Or, put another way, with email, we are what we write.

Social psychologists have written at length (e.g., Short *et al.* 1976; Rutter 1987) about the ways in which the lack of visual cues (e.g., when using the telephone) markedly increases the degree to which interlocutors are willing to make personal disclosures (e.g., passing judgments, expressing feelings, divulging health concerns) that they would hesitate to reveal face-to-face. A growing number of studies of computer mediated communication (e.g., Sproull & Kiesler 1986; Weisband & Kiesler 1996) are reporting similar findings with subjects communicating through computers.

Social Etiquette

A third aspect of the social dynamics of using teletechnologies for communication is the rules of social etiquette, either implicit or explicit, governing the kinds of messages that should appropriately be sent via a medium. The issues arising for telegrams, telephone calls, and email messages are much the same that obtain in traditional face-to-face or written communication, e.g., what kinds of messages should be delivered face-to-face, through a handwritten note, or a telephone call; how do participants in the exchange identify themselves and address one another; what about inappropriate language?

i. Medium and Subject Matter

Let's begin with choice of medium and subject matter. Consider, for example, conveyance of condolences or personal thanks. Until almost yesterday, American etiquette demanded a handwritten note (if not a personal visit). I remember, for example, the socially proper handwritten notes that Jacqueline Kennedy Onassis used to send to Brown University in the early 1980s regarding the progress of her son, who was an undergraduate (I was an administrator at Brown at the time). Given her years of experience as a journalist and editor, Onassis knew how to type – but "correctly" chose not to. Today, most people have abandoned handwritten efforts in favor of the greeting card or, as we shall see, email.

Since their inception, the telegraph, the telephone, and email have all undergone evolution with regard to social etiquette. Consider, first, the telegram. When the telegraph was first introduced, its "social" functions were largely restricted to very timely information – often conveying bad news. However, as the medium evolved, new socially accepted functions were introduced, from Christmas greetings to singing telegrams (see White 1939; Oslin 1992).

With the introduction and widespread adoption of the telephone, the question of social appropriateness became more of an issue, given the ease with which people could place calls and converse with interlocutors (compared with the relative inconvenience and formality of the telegram). In the early decades of the telephone, arbiters of etiquette had much to say about what kinds of social communication should or should not take place by telephone. For example, both in England (see Perry 1977, 78) and in the US (see Fischer 1992, 183-187), the telephone was not seen as an appropriate medium for either conveying or accepting an invitation. In the words of one etiquette book, "the person invited [by phone], being suddenly held up at the point of a gun, as it were, is likely to forget some other engagement" or feel obligated to accept (see Fischer 1992, 184, from Hall 1914, 53-54).

The social history of email bears strong resemblance to that of the telephone. While books of email etiquette have appeared sporadically (e.g., for business correspondence), they have done little to shape the evolution of email social practices. Not only do we issue (and accept) invitations via email, but we use the medium to thank people for job interviews, send personal condolences, and solicit assistance.

Why has email adopted such an expansive (and *laissez-faire*) set of conventions for social communication? Because of the private nature of the medium. Since we construct (and send) email in social isolation, and since we see the medium as ephemeral (see below), we feel less constrained by social conventions that govern face-to-face exchange or written communication in "polite society". While most middle-class American college graduates are aware of such social arbiters as Emily Post or Miss Manners (whether or not we heed their dicta), few of us even know of, much less bother to read, books on email etiquette. Rather, we begin by imitating the behavior of peers but ultimately follow convenience and personal bent.

ii. Smalltalk

Human linguistic exchange entails not only delivering information but engaging in social interaction. When we meet face-to-face, even in formal circumstances, we often begin with social chit-chat (e.g., about the weather, recent political events, or acquaintances we have in common) before getting down to business. Similarly, after concluding our business, we often return to social pleasantries ("Let's get together for dinner some time") before parting.

What happens with teletechnologies? In the case of the telegram, there is no room for social smalltalk. With the telephone, however, the situation is more ambiguous. Compared with face-to-face encounters, the telephone is more efficient. John Pierce, paraphrasing Alex Reid, argues that

> a business phone call is different from a face-to-face encounter because it needs no social element; one does not have to ask about health, family, or the weather. A phone call can thus be more economical than and preferable to a face-to-face meeting. (Pierce 1977, 174).

However, it is important to note that this conclusion was based on data collected in England, not the US, and that these data are now 25 years old. Contemporary telephone usage, at least in the US, often incorporates more conversational, social pleasantries (even when the caller is pressed for time or uninterested) to avoid the appearance of rudeness. Those who are abrupt on the phone are likely to be abrupt face-to-face, at least when transacting similar business.

What about email? As with the contemporary business telephone, email provides a rapid system for getting work done without getting bogged down in making smalltalk. This tendency to cut to the chase is particularly clear when it comes to forms of address.

iii. Forms of Address

Social conventions by which communicants identify themselves and address others shift markedly with time and cultural setting. Such cultural distinctions are evident, in fact, not only in teletechnologies but in traditional modes of correspondence. Consider, for example, differences in communication etiquette between the United States and the United Kingdom. In America, business establishments always imprint their identity in the upper left-hand corner of envelopes. In England, following different privacy conventions, comparable establishments insist on sending their correspondence in plain, unmarked envelopes (many of which are still hand-addressed). As an American used to receiving mounds of junk-mail, I have had to train myself to be on the look-out for quarterly statements from a British bank where I have an account. And I literally almost discarded, unopened, a long-awaited book contract from a British publisher because it arrived in a battered, unmarked manila envelope of the sort that constantly bombard my mailbox from American publishers' give-away programs.

In the case of teletechnologies, the issue of forms of address is seen most clearly in the case of salutations and signatures. When every word counts (as with telegrams), these are kept to a minimum, dispensing with such social niceties as "Dear" and "Sincerely". Telephone etiquette is a little more complex, depending upon local cultural conventions (which, in turn, may reflect the level of reliability of the telephone system) and one's relationship, on the social hierarchy, to the interlocutor. Not everyone starts a conversation with "Hello" or ends it with "Goodbye". (In fact, Alexander Graham Bell's initial telephone opening was "Ahoy"; the word "Hello" was deemed impolite at best and vulgar at worst, and was still resisted by some authorities on etiquette up through the 1940s – see Fischer 1992, 71, 186).

In email, salutations and signatures tend to be sparse or even absent. This pattern reflects, in part, the relative informality of email (much as we don't keep saying "Hello" or "Goodbye" to family members or colleagues we see at home or at the work place intermittently throughout the day). But the pattern also derives from the fact that the names of the sender and the addressee appear at the top of the email, making additional greetings and closings redundant. Nonetheless, email conventions have begun to evolve to open messages with "Hi" (even addressed to people one doesn't know) and, at least in some circles, to close with "Best" or "Cheers." Sometimes these emerging conventions are tempered by one's position on the social hierarchy (e.g., employer or employee – see Sherblom 1988) or by email function (e.g., a formal job application versus a note to a friend).

iv. Rudeness and Profanity

Finally, what about the use of rude or profane language? As most of us know, email has, for decades, been notorious for its general rudeness and the apparent ease with which its users have resorted to profanity. In fact, ARPANET (so the story goes) routinely had to purge the message stream of the most egregious cases. As usership has expanded, and as the email community becomes more comfortable exchanging messages without the benefit of auditory and vocal cues, the use of profanity and, perhaps, rudeness in general, may be abating (see Baron 1998a).

What many of us may not know is that the same issues of rudeness and profanity generated similar concerns in the early days of the telephone. Complaints about the use of swearing on the telephone were common. Telephone companies were known to cut off service to offenders and to support legislation that fined or even jailed those abusing the system (see Fischer 1992, 70, 333-334 note 21).

Format

Beyond issues relating to social dynamics, teletechnologies differ in their physical format. Our discussion of message format will focus on questions relating to durability and composition (including message length and editing).

Durability

As their names imply, the tele**graph** and **email** are transmitted in writing, while the tele**phone** conveys an acoustical signal. Hence, the telegraph and email yield physical records of the communicative transaction, while the telephone does not.

What have users perceived the advantages – or disadvantages – of durability of representation to be?

The telegraph industry emerged, by default, as a conveyor of durable messages because that was the medium the technology of the time allowed. Not until Bell (and his competitors) developed the "speaking telephone" was the option available for sending ephemeral auditory messages across distances. However, once the telephone emerged as an alternative teletechnology, the telegraph industry began making a virtue out of necessity. In 1877 (just a year after the appearance of the telephone), Johnson's *New Universal Cyclopedia* touted the advantage of telegraphy over telephony: telegrams constituted written records (cited in Aronson 1977, 16-17, 37). Interestingly, in the early days of email, business-oriented manuals stressed the existence of a written record as one of email's virtues (e.g., Siegman 1983, 9).

How did early users of the telephone view the issue of durability? Some businessmen hesitated to replace the telegraph with the telephone because of the lack of a written record (Fischer 1992, 41). In fact, some telephone proponents were so concerned about the lack of written records as to propose secretarial services that transcribed telephone messages and delivered them in a written format familiar from telegraphy. (Recall that Edison initially conceived of the phonograph as a machine for producing and conveying durable auditory messages, as a replacement for the telegraph.)

Yet from its inception, many telephone users have celebrated the medium's lack of durability. The telephone was an ideal instrument for the empire-building robber barons of the late nineteenth century:

> it was simple to operate and left no written record, a decided advantage when the message often involved the violation of laws and values against monopolies (Aronson 1977, 28).

Or, as H.G. Wells wrote in 1902,

> The businessman may sit at home [on the telephone] ... and tell such lies as he dare not write (cited in Pool 1983, 142, from H.G. Wells, 1902. *Anticipations*, p. 66).

Composition Issues

Closely related to the issue of durability are questions regarding composition: How long are messages? And are they edited before being sent?

i. Message Length

How long, comparatively, are messages sent on the telegraph, telephone, and email? The answer is a function of cost, technology, and resulting social expectations.

Given the relatively high costs of sending telegrams (along with concomitant difficulties, at least in the early days of telegraphy, in getting easy access to multiple telegraph lines), private telegrams have generally been quite short. When the telephone was initially introduced, its messages were also brief, directly following the model of the telegram (Fischer 1992, 81). As we have already seen, the telephone was not initially a "social" instrument, and its messages were very goal-directed. Introduction of message-unit service (along with the high cost of long-distance calls) further constrained the length of early telephone messages. Only with the twentieth-century redefinition of the telephone as a replacement for face-to-face socializing (along with growth in the availability of telephones and continuing decline in costs) did the length of messages come to approximate that of face-to-face dialogue.

Computer mediated communication, like its predecessors, was initially designed for conveying short, goal-directed information. Murray Turoff, the most important force behind what came to be computer based conferencing (which, in turn, helped drive the development of email – see Baron 1998a), insisted that messages should be confined to a single screen-worth of text. (Given the CRT displays of the 1970s, this edict meant very few lines indeed.) In the 1980s, businesses advocated the same single-screen limitation (e.g., Shapiro & Anderson 1985, 23). Only in the 1990s, as email usership has skyrocketed and costs of hardware and transmission have plummeted, has message length begun to increase. However, since most email today is still composed by typing – which is more time-consuming than speaking, average email length does not approach that of telephone discourse.

ii. Editing

The issue of message length leads to the broader question of editing. While "editing" with telegrams and the telephone is largely a matter of shortening one's message, editing issues become more complex in the case of email.

Technically, email is a written medium. Yet its social usage conventions are often closer to those of social telephony or face-to-face discourse than to traditional written prose (see Baron 1998a). As a result, users often neglect to carry out the simplest of editing tasks they would normally perform on a memorandum or even handwritten note. Such editorial nonchalance reflects both the casual nature of the medium and the psychological mind-set (however wrong empirically) that the medium is, like the telephone, ephemeral.

As computer software becomes more sophisticated and as the uses of email continue to expand, the issue of editing is assuming additional dimensions. Many of the newer word processing programs provide the same spell-check and grammar-check options for creating email messages as for producing "written" documents. It will be interesting to see whether people take advantage of such features. For years, many users of word processing programs have simply ignored the editing features available to them. Recently, software programs have even introduced automatic spelling and grammar devices that alert you to errors as you type. However, much as automobile passengers found "automatic" seat belts to be annoying – and disconnected them, users of word processing and email programs don't necessarily appreciate these correct-as-you-go features, preferring post-editing, self-editing, or, particularly in the case of email, no editing at all.

Counteracting this approach to email as an ephemeral medium (that doesn't require editing) is the opposite tendency in a number of business and academic environments for email to replace the more traditional functions of letters and memoranda. To the extent that such a transition occurs, message-senders are likely to transfer to these "formal" email contexts the editing conventions with which they function in preparing official documents. (Alternatively, the *laissez-faire* conventions of social email could invade more formal correspondence.) Outcomes may well differ across individuals, much as the degree of email editing does today. Many users of email buck the prevailing trend of editorial laissez-faire, exercising the same care with messages that happen to be sent electronically as with those formulated or conveyed by more traditional means.

4. History Lessons: *Ceci tuera cela*?

At the outset of this paper, we proposed four theses about telegraphy, telephony, and email as communicative modalities:

- First, that the forms and functions of new communicative technologies are typically conceived of in terms of older technologies.
- Second, that the "mature" linguistic identity of a communication modality may take years to develop.
- Third, that economic issues (rather than just technological development or perceived social need) may play a central role in determining functional shifts in a communicative medium.
- Fourth, that many of the same linguistic variables regarding social dynamics and format are relevant in understanding telegraphy, telephony, and email as forms of social discourse.

All four of these theses have been substantiated through our historical (Part 2) and linguistic (Part 3) analyses of the telegraph, the telephone, and email. The question now is, Can these historical (and linguistic) perspectives help us predict patterns of social discourse in the twenty-first century?

Forecasts in the past have often overestimated the impact of new technologies on existing modes of communication. By placing these forecasts themselves in historical perspective, we may increase our chances of accurately reading the tea leaves not only about the future of the telephone and email, and but also about their place alongside traditional writing and face-to-face spoken discourse. To aid in this enterprise, we will consider earlier predictions about the outcome of **competing forms of communication**, look at how new teletechnologies may **affect the nature of earlier communicative media**, and then close with some final thoughts about the possible **legacies of technology for social discourse.**

Competing Forms of Communication

Predictions that new communication technologies will replace older ones have a long history. Contemporary discussions of the future of the book (e.g., Nunberg 1996; Eisenstein 1997) typically take as their point of reference Victor Hugo's novel T*he Hunchback of Notre Dame*, in which

> the archdeacon first points to the great cathedral and then stretches out his right hand toward a fifteenth-century printed book and announces "*Ceci tuera cela*"; "*This* (the printed book) will kill *that* (the cathedral, which had served for centuries as an encyclopedia in stone)" (Eisenstein 1997, 1055).

These same concerns about the effect of print on previous forms of social discourse also arose with the development of newspapers. Elizabeth Eisenstein (1997, 1060) traces the problem back at least to the seventeenth century, when a "writer expressed regret at the loss of conviviality in coffee houses where ... everyone now sat in 'sullen silence' reading newspapers" (from Brewer 1976, 148). Eisenstein goes on to note that in the nineteenth century, Thomas Carlyle, John Stuart Mill, and Oswald Spengler all voiced concern that the newspaper would hasten the demise of the printed book (Eisenstein 1997, 1050-1051).

In the early days of the telegraph, some newspaper men had perceived the telegraph as a threat to traditional journalism. For example, in Virginia, the Alexandria Gazette wrote that since the public could now get its news of the day from the telegraph, newspapers would need to limit themselves to editorial functions (Blondheim 1994, 37). Given the cost and inconvenience of sending telegrams, this threat never materialized.

In the end, it was not books or newspapers or the telegraph but the telephone and email that profoundly challenged previous modes of spoken and written discourse. In the case of the telephone, growth in telephone usage far outstrips increases in the number of letters being sent (Pierce 1977, 165). Similarly, the telephone has continued to erode the use of face-to-face spoken exchange (Fischer 1992, 236-240; Aronson 1971). The potential for such an erosion troubled students of social interaction even in the early years of the telephone. In fact, Robert and Helen Lynd, in their original study of "Middletown", published in 1929, suggested that growth in telephone usage was undermining "neighborliness" (see Fischer 1992, 237). Perhaps not surprisingly, a study of the social effects of a 23 day telephone blackout in Manhattan in 1975 found that during the blackout, face-to-face visiting increased 34% (Wurtzel & Turner 1977, 254).

Much as social critics have long expressed concern that television will doom the book, contemporary discussions ponder whether email portends the end of letters or the telephone, or the diminution of face-to-face exchange. An early email cartoon showed two co-workers chatting in the hallway, with one saying to the other, "I need to review something with you. I'll send you an email" rather than having the conversation then and there. However, if history is any judge, email is unlikely to be the undoing of letters, phone calls, or personal interaction. One reason is that communication modalities are tending to incorporate rather than replace one another: newspapers and books can be read on-line; email can be sent and accessed through voice mail; many formal letters are now sent via computer rather than through the mails. While changes in technology, cost, and fashion may diminish the role of one of these communication modalities in the years ahead, as of now, reports of their death (like Mark Twain's) are greatly exaggerated.

Effects on the Nature of Earlier Communicative Media

Communication technologies not only encroach on the space of earlier means of exchange. They also have the potential to alter the linguistic conventions of their forebears. Consider the case of the telegraph. As a result of restrictions on the amount of text that could quickly be sent across a telegraph wire – along with the growth of nation-wide wire services, a new "telegraphic" style of journalism emerged. This new style gradually began replacing the sometimes rambling, typically regional, often biased reporting of nineteenth-century newspapers:

> [The telegraph] snapped the tradition of partisan journalism by forcing the wire services to generate "objective" news, news that could be used by papers of any political stripe .... The news services demanded a form of language stripped of the local, the regional and colloquial .... If the same story were to be understood in the same way from Maine to California, language had to be flattened out and standardized (Carey 1983, 310).
> (See also Briggs 1977, 49.)

Similarly, this new journalistic style was to have profound impact on American writing style more generally. Ernest Hemingway – himself a journalist during the Spanish Civil War – was strongly influenced by the strictures of "cablese", which helped "him to pare his prose to the bone, dispossessed of every adornment" (Carey 1983, 311). For many decades, Hemingway's style has been touted to American high school and college students as a paragon of simplicity and clarity, further extending the impact of a style originally designed because of technical limitations on the use of telegraphic wires.

Has the telephone exerted any comparable influence on traditional communicative modalities? Sociologist Peter Berger, for example, has argued that the impersonal nature of telephone conversation can indeed carry over into face-to-face spoken exchange:

> [t]o use the phone habitually also means to learn a specific style of dealing with others – a style marked by impersonality, precision, and a certain superficial civility. The key question is this: Do these internal habits carry over into other areas of life, such as nontelephonic relations with other persons? The answer is almost certainly yes (cited in Fischer 1992, 224, from Berger 1979, 6-7).

Given the relative novelty of email, it may be too soon to argue definitively about the impact of email on either spoken or written language. However, several possible influences bear monitoring in the future. In the written domain, it can be argued (see Baron 1998a; Moran & Hawischer 1998) that the grammatical and stylistic features of email are prime candidates to spill over into traditional written prose. In the spoken domain, there is, paradoxically, the potential for the opposite effect. Among some of us who use email and voice mail interchangeably (e.g., depending upon the communicative preferences of our interlocutor), there is almost a wistful desire to edit voice mail before sending it, much as we have the potential to edit email.

Technological Legacies: Distance and Control in Social Discourse

Over the course of this paper, we have seen that while the telegraph has had only limited effect on contemporary written discourse (i.e., fostering a simple, objective writing style) the telephone and email have more broadly influenced traditional conventions of spoken and written discourse. Two social variables help explain the influence of the telephone and email. The first is *social distance* and the other is *personal control.*

The telephone and email increase social distance between interlocutors and afford one or both parties greater control over the communicative interaction than is possible in face-to-face exchange. The value of this ability to create – and control – personal space is reflected in the fact that, at least in much of the US, people desire to put some distance between themselves and their acquaintances (Fischer 1992, 240). For example, a study done in California reported that "people generally said they would not like their friends to live next door, but would rather have them within easy driving distance" (data from Silverman 1981; cited in Fischer 1992, 367). The telephone and email provide psychological "easy driving distance." In fact, while AT&T has advertised the telephone as "the next best thing to being there", it can be argued that many people find the telephone (and, by extension, email), *better* than being there.

For decades, the telephone has offered a privacy shield that both protects and empowers interlocutors. Increasingly, email is also offering control to users in domains where they previously felt vulnerable or excluded. College-aged students are beginning to report friends who break up relationships on email so they don't have to confront one-another face-to-face. Middle-level managers send email to people higher up the organizational ladder regarding matters over which they would hesitate to call or visit in person. In fact, some people use email to impose upon people they don't know, just because email addresses are publicly available (like the linguistics student from another university who emailed me – and several other linguists around the country – for help with his homework).

How do the controlling powers of email compare with those of traditional writing (in particular, letter writing)? In principle, letters would seem to offer their senders and recipients maximum control. The sender can choose what to write to whom, and when, constructing a message that bears neither auditory nor vocal cues. The recipient can choose whether or not to reply and, if pressed, can always claim the letter never arrived.

Yet given the convenience of the technology, one might argue that email offers even greater communicative control than letter writing. Email is more anomic than a letter – there are no revealing choices to be made about stationary, about whether to hand write or type. Even decisions about choice of salutation or closing can be avoided by simply omitting them. Perhaps even more important is the convenience factor. The effort involved in sending an email is minimal compared with preparing and posting a letter. While sending a letter expresses not only the content contained therein but the sender's level of commitment to conveying the message, email affords the sender a privacy shield that conceals the sender's stake in the communication.

In closing, what "history lessons" have we garnered from our comparative analysis of the telegraph, the telephone, and email? One lesson clearly is that in the early days of a technology, it may be ill-advised to make definitive pronouncements about the directions that technology will take. The telegraph, for example, never developed into a medium for social chit-chat, while the telephone yielded from a potential career as a broadcast device to a medium for one-to-one social dialogue *par excellence.*

Second, communication technologies are less likely to replace one another than to complement or integrate earlier media. With the exception of the telegram, new communicative channels (from the book through the newspaper, telephone, fax, and email) tend to support rather than rival older forms of social discourse, often dividing up (or redefining) functions (e.g., incorporating fax capabilities into computers; accessing email through voice mail).

Third, new language technologies not only introduce additional venues for communication but also reshape existing forms of social discourse. Such influence may appear in the realm of speech (e.g., the impact of the telephone on face-to-face encounters) or writing (e.g., the effect of telegraphy on traditional written prose and the potential influence of email on personal and business writing).

Finally, a fourth lesson is that teletechnologies can redefine relationships between participants in social discourse, particularly with regard to social distance and control. While these relationships are shaped in part by the technologies themselves, other important factors are economic considerations, newly emerging communicative functions, cultural influences, and individual choice. As we round the millennium, it will be fascinating to see how this balance plays out.

References

Anderson, R. et al. (1995): Universal Access to E-Mail: Feasibility and Societal Implications. Santa Monica, CA: RAND.

Aronson, S.H. (1971): The Sociology of the Telephone. International Journal of Comparative Sociology 12, 153-167.

Aronson, S.H. (1977): Bell's Electrical Toy: What's the Use? The Sociology of Early Telephone Usage. – In: Pool, ed., 15-39.

Attali, J. & Stourdze, Y. (1977): The Birth of the Telephone and Economic Crisis: The Slow Death of the Monologue in French Society. – In: Pool, ed., 97-111.

Baron, N.S. (1989): From Print Shop to Desktop: Evolution of the Written Word. – In: J.J. Walsh, ed.: Synchronic and Diachronic Approaches to Linguistic Variation and Change. Washington: Georgetown University Press, 8-21.

Baron, N.S. (1997): Thinking, Learning, and the Written Word. Visible Language 31(1), 6-35.

Baron, N.S. (1998a): Letters by Phone or Speech by Other Means: The Linguistics of Email. Language and Communication, 1-38.

Baron, N.S. (1998b): Writing in the Age of Email. Visible Language 32(1), 35-53.

Ball, D.W. (1968): Toward a Sociology of Telephone and Telephones. – In: M. Truzzi, ed.: Sociology and Everyday Life. Englewood Cliffs, NJ: Prentice Hall, 59-75.

Berger, P. (1979): The Heretical Imperative. Garden City, NY: Doubleday.

Blondheim, M. (1994): News over the Wires: The Telegraph and the Flow of Public Information in America, 1844-1897. Cambridge, MA: Harvard University Press.

Boettinger, H.M. (1977a): Our Sixth-and-a-Half Sense. – In: Pool, ed., 200-207.

Boettinger, H.M. (1997b): The Telephone Book: Bell, Watson, Vail and American Life, 1876-1976. Croton-on-Hudson, NY: Riverwood Publishers Ltd.

Boorstin, D. (1973): The Americans: The Democratic Experience. New York: Random House.

Brewer, J. (1976): Party Ideology and Popular Politics at the Accession of George III. Cambridge: Cambridge University Press.

Briggs, A. (1977): The Pleasure Telephone: A Chapter in the Prehistory of the Media. – In: Pool, ed., 40-65.

Briggs, S. & Briggs, A. (1972): Cap and Bell: Punch's Chronicle of English History in the Making, 1841-61. London: Macdonald & Co.

Brooks, J. (1977): The First and Only Century of Telephone Literature. – In: Pool, ed., 208-224.

Bruce, R.V. (1973): Bell. Alexander Graham Bell and the Conquest of Solitude. Boston: Little, Brown.

Carey, J.W. (1983): Technology and Ideology: The Case of the Telegraph. – In: J. Salzman, ed.: Prospects (The Annual of American Cultural Studies) 8, 303-325. Cambridge: Cambridge University Press.

Coe, L. (1993): The Telegraph. Jefferson, NC: McFarland.

Czitrom, D.J. (1982): Media and the American Mind: From Morse to McLuhan. Chapel Hill: University of North Carolina Press.

Dilts, M.M. (1941): The Telephone in a Changing World. New York: Longman, Green, & Co.

Durusau, P. (1996): High Places in Cyberspace, 1996. Atlanta: Scholars Press.

Eisenstein, E. (1979): The Printing Press as an Agent of Change. Cambridge: Cambridge University Press.

Eisenstein, E. (1997): From the Printed Word to the Moving Image. Social Research 64(3), 1049-1066.

Fischer, C.S. (1992): America Calling: A Social History of the Telephone to 1940. Berkeley: University of California Press.

Grosvenor, E.S. & Wesson, M. (1997): Alexander Graham Bell. New York: Harry N. Abrams.

Harlow, A.F. (1936): Old Wires and New Waves: The History of the Telegraph, Telephone, and Wireless. New York: D. Appleton-Century Co.

Haas, C. (1996): Writing Technologies: Studies on the Materiality of Literacy. Mahway, NJ: Lawrence Erlbaum.

Hall, F. Howe (1914): Good Form for All Occasions. New York: Harper & Brothers.

Herring, S., ed. (1996): Computer Mediated Communication: Linguistic, Social, and Cross-Cultural Perspectives. Philadelphia: John Benjamins.

Hounshell, D.A. (1975): Elisha Gray and the Telephone: On the Disadvantages of Being an Expert. Technology and Culture 16(2).

Kingsbury, J.E. (1972): The Telephone and Telephone Exchanges. New York: Arno Press.

Marvin, C. (1988): When New Technologies Were Old. New York: Oxford University Press.

McLuhan, M. (1964/1994): Understanding Media. First edition, New York: McGraw-Hill; second edition, Cambridge, MA: MIT Press.

Moran, C. & Hawisher, G.E. (1998): The Rhetorics and Languages of Electronic Mail. – In: I. Synder, ed.: Page to Screen: Taking Literacy into the Electronic Age. London: Routledge, 80-101.

Nunberg, G., ed. (1996): The Future of the Book. Berkeley: University of California Press.

Nye, D.E. (1997): Shaping Communication Networks: Telegraph, Telephone, Computer. Social Research 64(3), 1067-1091.

Olson, D. (1994): The World on Paper. Cambridge: Cambridge University Press.

Oslin, G.P. (1992): The Story of Telecommunications. Macon, GA: Mercer University Press.

Perry, C.R. (1977): The British Experience 1876-1912: The Impact of the Telephone During the Years of Delay. – In: Pool, ed., 69-96.

Pierce, J. (1977): The Telephone and Society in the Past 100 Years. – In: Pool, ed., 159-195.

Pool, I., ed. (1977): The Social Impact of the Telephone. Cambridge (MA): MIT Press.

Pool, I. (1983): Forecasting the Telephone: A Retrospective Technology Assessment. Norwood, NJ: Ablex.

Rheingold, H. (1993): The Virtual Community: Homesteading on the Electronic Frontier. New York: HarperPerennial.

Rhodes, F.L. (1929): Beginnings of Telephony. New York: Harper & Brothers.

Rutter, D.R. (1987): Communicating by Telephone. Oxford: Pergamon.

Schwarzlose, R.A. (1989, 1990): The Nation's Newsbrokers, vols. 1 and 2. Evanston, IL: Northwestern University Press.

Shapiro, N.A. & Anderson, R.H. (1985): Toward an Ethics and Etiquette for Electronic Mail. Santa Monica, CA: RAND.

Sherblom, J. (1988): Direction, Function, and Signature in Electronic Mail. Journal of Business Communication 25(4), 39-54.

Short, J., Williams, E., & Christie, B. (1976): The Social Psychology of Telecommunications. London: Wiley.

Siegman, J.H. (1983): Electronic Mail Services. Media, PA: Seybold Publications, Inc.

Silverman, C.J. (1981): Negotiated Claim. PhD dissertation, Department of Sociology. University of California, Berkeley.

Singer, B.D. (1981): Social Functions of the Telephone. Palo Alto, CA: R & E Research Associates.

Sipior, J.C. & Ward, B.T. (1995): The Ethical and Legal Quandary of Email Privacy. Communications of the ACM 38(12), 48-54.

Sproull, L. & Kiesler, S. (1986): Reducing Social Context Cues: Electronic Mail in Organizational Communication. Management Science 32, 1492-1512.

Thompson, R.L. (1947): Wiring a Continent: The History of the Telegraph Industry in the United States 1832-1866. Princeton, NJ: Princeton University Press.

Watson, T.A. (1913): The Birth and Babyhood of the Telephone. Chicago: American Telephone and Telegraph Co.

Weisband, S. & Kiesler, S. (1996): Self Disclosure on Computer Forms: Meta-Analysis and Implications. Proceedings of the Conference on Human Factors in Computing Systems (CHI 96), Vancouver, BC, 3-9.

White, R.B. (1939): Telegrams in 1889 and Since. Princeton, NJ: Princeton University Press.

Willey, M.M. & Rice, S.A. (1993): Communication Agencies and Social Life. New York: McGraw Hill.

Wurtzel, A.H. & Turner, C. (1977): Latent Functions of the Telephone: What Missing the Extension Means. – In: Pool, ed., 246-261.

Edda Weigand

Dialogue in the Grip of the Media

1. The media as a factor of modern life

Life has changed fundamentally since we no longer live in small villages, talk to a few people and can observe reality and shape our opinions directly in a circumscribed small area. Today we are citizens of the world, globalization, internationalization has taken effect. Even if we are not actively engaged in this process, we want at least to be informed, listen to the world news and shape our opinions about what is happening every day around the world. We need technical means that place the world and the people of the world in front of us. That is the point where the *media come in. They are means of overcoming space and time* and enable us to interact with persons on the other side of the globe.

At this point, however, we should be aware that there is no longer *reality* as such; reality instead is reported, mediated and *constructed by the media* especially on television. What are facts? Facts in the media are events selected and reported by journalists. We become aware of them through the eyes of other persons. Facts stand in networks, in complex relations to other facts. We are therefore continuously faced with complex events and controversial questions. News transmissions do not only report news but more and more mediate and present them from the viewpoint of different people.

The *media are part of complex dialogic processes*. They have come in because dialogue in its natural form as face-to-face dialogue in a speech situation is unable to fulfil the demands of global or mass interaction. The question arises: what is the price that dialogue has to pay to enable it to become mass or global interaction? Dialogue is necessarily under pressure from the media to allow communication which goes beyond the limits of the speech situation. Thus dialogue necessarily loses some characteristics of its natural form and gains other potentials.

First, I will sketch some characteristics of *dialogue in its natural form* which we will then use as a *background for our analysis of dialogue in the media.* We will *contrast two forms* of mass media, the traditional one of television and the new and more spectacular one of electronic media. Media in recent years have been increasingly investigated either from a technical or cross-cultural perspective or considering their effects on our opinions and life images (cf. e.g. Höflich 1996, Hess-Lüttich 1992, Merten/Schmidt/Weischenberg 1994). In contrast, we will *look at the media as a component of dialogic action* and ask how the principles of dialogue are changed by technical means.

2. Dialogues as action games

I will shortly introduce *the model of dialogic action games* which I will use to analyse dialogue in the media (cf. Weigand 1997). In the centre of the action game, which is a complex cultural unit, there are human beings trying to achieve their interactive purposes with communicative means. Focussing on the unit of the action game is, in my opinion, a necessary consequence of including some features we have previously neglected, for instance, in the rule-governed pattern model of dialogue grammar. The model of action games goes beyond rules and conventions and is based essentially on *principles* which can be seen as techniques of our communicative competence for tackling the problem that social interaction is mainly based on cases of probability. Preferences and habits, presumptions and suggestions play an important role (cf. Dascal 1994 and Weigand 1998). We have to acknowledge that it is in principle *different* human beings interacting, bringing in different communicative backgrounds and personal experiences that necessarily result partly in different understandings. Our communicative competence is able to deal with this problem by accepting open points and the risk of misunderstanding.

I will shortly describe a few major principles, the *Action Principle, the Principle of Communicative Means and the Dialogic Principle*, because it is mainly these principles which we will find changed to a certain degree by the grip of the media. I understand the *Action Principle* as the principle of trying to achieve communicative purposes by communicative means. Thus the functional structure of every speech act consists of a communicative function or purpose related to a specific state of affairs, as Searle (1969) has indicated in his formula F(p). It seems to be a characteristic of the Action Principle that we really have the intention which underlies the communicative purpose of the speech act and do not only play the game that Searle perhaps had in mind when he introduced his *sincerity condition*. This is the point that comes under pressure in dialogues on stage such as on television.

According to the *Principle of Communicative Means*, we do not only use verbal utterance forms based on our ability to speak but simultaneously and not separably use other means and abilities as well such as the abilities to see and to think. In the case of electronic media, we notice some interesting changes which are necessary in order to tackle the problem that it is not sufficient to key in what is said. Also the means that can be *seen* in the natural speech situation have to be transformed into the written medium.

It is a specific characteristic of communicative action that it is dialogically oriented. With the exception of the declarative speech act, there is no other individual speech act which is communicatively autonomous but the minimal action game is based on action and reaction. Action and reaction are correlated by the very characteristics of the initiative speech act itself. An initiative speech act makes a pragmatic claim, for instance, to truth, as the representative speech act, or a claim to volition as the directive speech act. Thus it aims, by its inherent characteristics, at a reactive action that fulfils this claim in a positive or negative way by accepting or rejecting it. Making and fulfilling a pragmatic claim constitutes *the Dialogic Principle* which changes Searle's global illocutionary types into dialogically oriented types (cf. Weigand 1991). In essence, the Dialogic Principle is based on what Austin (1962, 115) had already postulated: '*So performance of an illocutionary act involves the securing of uptake* ...' In the end, it is this central Dialogic Principle which governs coherence and understanding. The Dialogic Principle comes under pressure when interaction is no longer restricted to a small group but is supposed to be multiple or mass interaction.

The *term medium* is used in different sense. In a narrow sense, it is restricted to the feature of using *the voice versus written visible signs*. This feature however normally goes hand in hand with other features, for instance, using the voice normally goes hand in hand with presence in the speech situation and with spontaneous immediate reaction. Thus we arrive at a large sense of the medium as a constellation of features. *Technical means* have changed these natural constellations of features totally. By technical means, it becomes, for instance, possible to participate in a dialogic action game by means of video-conferencing. In this large sense, Naumann (1997, 171) has characterised the medium of Internet Relay Chat, a specific type of electronic media, as oral even if for technical reasons it uses the typed form. Also the users who type their utterance feel that they are speaking, not writing. Talking about the media in our modern life we are talking about complex technical means, about *multi-media* that allow us to overcome time and space in the age of globalization and mass interaction.

Thus the priority of the feature voice *versus* written sign has lost significance (cf. Weigand 1993). For the action game as a complex whole another feature has become more important, the feature whether *immediate reaction* is possible or not and how it becomes possible. We will *focus* on this aspect in the framework of the mass media.

3. Dialogues on stage on television

There is an interesting development in television which has recently been called 'infotainment'. *Information and entertainment* seem to be necessarily mixed, true to the purpose of the institution television which can be related to the ancient 'docere et delectare'. Recently however there seems to come in a further purpose as a consequence of what is modern reality. Modern reality is global reality. It consists in large part of a network of opinions. We are always and everywhere confronted with controversial questions to be discussed. They are presented on television but not decided nor solved on stage. Pros and contras are displayed in order to shape opinions. *Shaping opinions* has become a new purpose of television in between information about facts and pure entertainment.

Here we notice some *cultural differences*. Whereas the German 'Tagesschau' seems to make a rather rigid division between facts and interviews or opinions, the BBC passes more smoothly from facts to opinions, for instance, in 'Europe direct', and the Italian 'Telegiornale' regularly presents a series of interviews addressed to persons who try to confirm their importance by getting asked for their opinion on television.

From the mixture of the purposes of informing, shaping opinions and entertainment multiple types of dialogic action games on stage arise, even destructive ones, fights, that do not aim at understanding at all but only at *hurting* the other, for instance, the American talk shows in contrast to comedy shows, or German talkshows such as 'Der heiße Stuhl'. Here we have a modern variant of the ancient gladiatorial spectacle.

As a consequence of our reality being a network of different opinions, dialogues on television, especially in Germany, often have topics in form of a question, such as:

> Are the Greens capable of taking part in government?/Sind die Grünen regierungsfähig? (S. Christiansen, ARD)
> Football for all?/Fußball für alle? (Pro und Contra, ARD)
> Islamists in Germany – danger for internal security?/Islamisten in Deutschland – Gefahr für die innere Sicherheit? (Pro und Contra, ARD)
> Revolt against the Pope?/Aufstand gegen den Papst? (S. Christiansen, ARD)

These controversial questions can be answered by yes or no and thus structure the action game as a *debate* (cf. Weigand forthcoming). In addition to this topical feature, dialogues on television are always *dialogues on stage*. 'On stage' means 'to be seen, to be known'. Almost everyone who is seen in the mass media tries to present themselves in the best possible way, they play a *role*. Also the participants in a controversial talk are playing a role, either on the pro or on the contra side, but this time not assigned by themselves for reasons of publicity but according to the guidelines of the transmission, which are valid also for the presenters themselves.

In dialogues on stage there is always someone who tells the actors, at least to a certain extent, what they have to do. This type of 'ordered' action, of action on stage according to a *role* given by the actors themselves or by the structure of the game, is the opposite of *spontaneous* action. In contrast to the theatre, on television the role has to fit the person. Guests are invited according to the role they might take. In this point dialogues on stage are similar to institutionalized dialogues such as business negotiations or instructions in which the institution determines the roles of the interlocutors.

We will shortly analyse an extreme example of such a pro and contra game on stage which manifests clearly the structuring lines. It is the programme *Football for all?/Fußball für alle?* of November, 22, 1997, of the German talkshow 'Pro & Contra' which is announced by: '*Two pro, two contra, form your own opinion!*' It represents a totally pre-calculated event on stage which leaves nothing to spontaneity. Every participant, from the presenter to the audience, has their *role* to play according to the pre-established structure of the game. Speaking time, order of turns and even their purposes are pre-arranged. The guests are experts or persons who are directly involved in the topic. We have an audience in the studio and the viewers at home. The purpose of the whole game, namely shaping opinions, becomes manifest by the fact that the audience in the studio votes before, during and after the debate. Thus some sort of mass interaction takes place: Immediate reaction is possible but regulated according to roles. The role of the audience in the studio is restricted to voting and to answering a few questions from the presenter. The viewers at home remain passive but could in principle – as we know from other talk shows – participate actively via telephone even if it is not guaranteed that the call will get through.

This rigid pattern is reflected by the structure of the programme of which I will mention only the main points:

- The audience in the studio and at home is welcomed by the presenter.
- The advocates give their pleas and are questioned by the experts, two for each side.
- The presenter joins in with a question addressed to the experts.
- The presenter poses a few questions to the audience in the studio.
- The audience votes three times, before, during, and after the debate.

The debate and its previously determined structure becomes something like an institution similar to a court but now pleas and questioning take place in a show on stage. Also the more complex parts, the questioning of the experts by the advocates, are totally pre-determined. The roles dominate and tell the actors what they have to do. Thus, for instance, the supporting advocate questioning the supporting expert has to fulfil the role of giving him the opportunity to present supporting arguments and to counter opposing arguments, whereas the opposing advocate questioning the supporting expert has to fulfil the role of countering supporting arguments and of presenting strong opposing arguments. Let us have a short look at this part of the game translated into English (for the German authentic text see appendix 1):

> *Supporting advocate* Herr Fünfgeld, I would like very much to first of all give you the opportunity of again saying something in reply to the accusation that the public broadcasting system is also pay-TV. COUNTERING OPPOSING ARGUMENTS
>
> *Supporting expert* I wouldn't say that. In Germany we have a dual broadcasting system. ... those who have a radio or TV set have to pay licence fees. But not only for football. That's the decisive point. And now I have to give the first answer: for us sport is not primarily entertainment, but a part of our information and that is the fundamental difference ...
>
> *Supporting advocate* Yes. The public broadcasting service, it is said, is charged with providing a basic service. You yourself talked about that just now. Are live international football matches part of that service? PRESENTING SUPPORTING ARGUMENTS
>
> *Supporting expert* Of course! ....

It becomes clear that it is the job of the participants to effectively fulfil their role as they are told by the script of the show in the best possible rhetorical way. Naturally, there are other talk shows which are not so strictly regulated and allow some leeway and spontaneity. But in the end the grip of the media remains. In return, the media display their power to those who have managed to be invited.

Mass interaction and dialogic uptake has become possible on stage at the price of management and control. This price affects mainly the *Action Principle* of the game. The speech acts are not only produced in agreement with the intentions of the actors but according to roles and that means according to structural decisions taken elsewhere including also commercial persuasive strategies. The game is played for the purpose of shaping opinions and gives the audience the illusion of being included in an important process of public life.

4. Dialogue games on the Internet

Let us now change the scene and look at the seemingly 'infinite' possibilities that are offered to us by the new electronic media. There are in principle two different types of computer mediated communication, off-line via e-mail and on-line, for instance, via Internet Relay Chat which is a computer programme that enables multiple users to engage in synchronous communication across a network (Reid 1991, 9). Communication via e-mail including also so-called 'news groups' has become a very convenient and quick facility for sending messages across the world but it does not provide the possibility of immediate online interaction. We will therefore not deal with the e-mail type but with the more spectacular type of IRC to which also some so-called Internet Conferences belong. Here you seem to key in directly not only to your own monitor but quasi-simultaneously to the monitor of those who are in the channel. Immediate reaction seems to become possible worldwide and is not restricted by stage conditions.

We will have a closer look at what it really means to be able, at least potentially, to communicate and interact directly with all those who are in the channel. Let us approach the complex phenomenon by the following questions:

- Why do interlocutors join the channel?
- What are the rules of interaction when you are in the channel?

The first question about the reason for interlocutors to join the channel can be understood as *question about the types of action games* that take place in so far as we characterize action games primarily according to their communicative purpose. The main reason why interlocutors join the channel seems to be for the purpose of chatting, of having small talk worldwide, of belonging to the group of modern people able to surf the Internet. Next there is the purpose of getting information. When you seek an expert, you may choose a topic-specific channel or hope to find him in a channel that is not topically restricted. Thus we have declarative action games like small talk for the purpose of establishing modern social relations, as well as explorative action games in order to interview an expert. Within small groups which are however not our focus you will find also more complex types such as negotiations, even of great importance on special conference channels, for instance, between representatives of China and Toyota wishing to invest in China. In principle, every type of action game can be played on the Internet, not only declarative and explorative ones but also representative and directive games.

Now to our next question: *What are the rules* you have to observe when you are in the channel? There are various rules you have to know, for instance, that you introduce yourself by a nickname and thus the whole game takes place between anonymous users who may even pretend to be quite another person, for instance, changing sex by using a specific nickname. I will not go into these details of the game but refer amongst others to the 'classic' paper on IRC by Elizabeth Reid (1991) (cf. also Naumann 1997, Werry 1996). We will concentrate instead on the *Dialogic Principle* and on the *Principle of Communicative Means.*

The main interesting aspect of IRC in my opinion concerns the technique of how immediate reaction becomes possible in a channel in which a mass of players has congregated, let's say about hundred and more. *Immediate* reaction does not at all mean immediate in the sense of a subsequent utterance. You have to key in your utterance, press the return key and then wait and see. The utterances will be displayed on the monitor in the linear chronological order in which they are received by the IRC system, if there is no 'lag', a technical problem that sometimes occurs. Overlap and interruption are excluded. The chronological order is reflected in the spatial order of the utterances running relatively quickly over your monitor, at a pace directly proportional to the speed of the chat. So the Internet chatters seem to me a bit like global players sitting at home in front of their computer but virtually around a global table throwing in their utterances and hoping to win, i.e. to see their utterances soon on the monitor so that they are not lost or overlooked.

4.1. The standard game

Can we recognize in this sort of electronic 'roulette' the dialogic core of what Austin has called 'uptake'? Let us analyse an example of standard IRC which has, like all small talk, no specific topic. In a rather frequented channel, sequences like the following result:

(1) [SERVER]	fredFOO!~squires@mne.net has joined this channel
(2) [xilef]	well, i'll go to bed then... quit early on this side of the big water
(3) <howie>	Hiya FredFoo!!
(4) [tony]	beth...im in sonoma
(5) [turt]	mvmidsch is either speaking UUENCODE or has a noisy line!
(6) [SERVER]	debra!debra@well.sf.ca.us has joined this channel
(7) [FathrRich]	San Diego, California.
(8) [fredFOO]	re foo
(9) [Gabriel]	wave
(10) [jburge]	I like sonoma
(11) [debra]	Hello all from S.F. CA
(12) <howie>	hey debra, welcome back
(13) [SERVER]	r134a!~bhaskar@or4.me.uiuc.edu has joined this channel
(14) [beth]	tony, jburge...we've got a decent group here...and early, too...
(15) [ferrell]	Pleasanton, Ca Happy New Year (early)
(16) [tony]	me too....nice square in town.
(17) [jburge]	ya we got the SF guys here
(18) [ACTION]	xilef waves and falls asleep.
(19) [debra]	wow howie you're still here!

(20) [SERVER]	xilef has quit IRC Leaving
(21) [rgk]	a bit earlier, I asked who amongst us thought they might be on the oldest, most obsolete machine. Current holder ot the tile of record was on a 286. Any new champions?
(22) [PineMtn]	I'm near the other one — Sonora
(23) [Blaze]	Hi Foo Boston! Is it busy and fun at The Other Side?
(24) <howie>	but of course :)
(25) [Harry]	hi again Fredfoo – made it over here
(26) [tony]	hey sonora..
(27) [fredFOO]	echo "Happy New Year" | figlet
(28) [SERVER]	poe!pearce@netcom9.netcom.com has joined this channel
(29) [SERVER]	mvmidsch!mvmidsch@well.sf.ca.us has joined this channel
(30) [FathrRich]	Happy New Year!!!!! (Early)_
(31) [siggy]	Debra: I couldn't get on the WELL tonight. Pretty crowded?
(32) [Gabriel]	(has a 286, too...thhppptthh)
(33) [poe]	Hello all
(34) [jburge]	happy new year
(35) [eataPeach]	is the east coast still here? everyone seems to be from the left coast
(36) [tn]	quit
(37) <howie>	good one rgk – for the 'record' what kinds of machines are you all using to connect?
(38) [SERVER]	FathrRich has left this channel
(39) [SERVER]	tn has quit IRC Leaving
(40) [SERVER]	russ!mcclay@tpts1.seed.net.tw has joined this channel
(41) [javaman]	Does a new year come with a guarantee?
(42) [ferrell]	:::pouring everyone a shot::::
(43) [ACTION]	howie is on EST time!
(44) [jburge]	so tony whats go'in on
(45) [peter_ma]	rgk, I have a 40-year-old typewriter, but it doesn't get me on line.
(46) [Gabriel]	<------EAST COAST
(47) [javaman]	I am on the east coast.Norfolk, Va.
(48) [debra]	I've had no problem getting on the well. The muse keeps crashing though.

What you see here as a print-out, is part of an endless text, of a dialogue without beginning or end, that constantly scrolls up (and then off) each user's monitor. Simultaneously, you will have about 15 lines on your monitor. We can identify various groups talking and addressing themselves by their nicknames. We will pick out the group of tony, jburge and beth and address briefly two others.

Our group of three users starts with tony's utterance (4) addressing beth and telling her where he is, namely in Sonoma. This utterance relates to utterances before, not on our print-out, and to utterances behind and is thus simultaneously reactive and initiative, like most of the utterances in the ongoing conversation. Even if addressed to beth, it is taken up by jburge in (10) with a comment on Sonoma. It is also taken up by another comment of beth in (14). Tony's utterance (16) represents a comment to jburge (10), and jburge's utterance (17) probably represents a comment to beth (14). Thus we get the following relations between the corresponding utterances:

(4) [tony]	beth...im in sonoma	↑↓
(10) [jburge]	I like sonoma	↑↓
(14) [beth]	tony, jburge...we've got a decent group here...	↑↓
(16) [tony]	me too...nice square in town	↑
(17) [jburge]	ya we got the SF guys here	↑

All these utterances have the form of a statement. However, they are not all making a claim and are not just being initiative as is characteristic of representative speech acts. Some of them are reactive speech acts, such as (16) and (17), some of them are both, initiative and reactive as well, such as (4), (10), and (14). As representatives they are telling something, informing us about: *im in sonoma, I like sonoma*, thus making a claim to truth which in the case of informative speech acts is not at issue but quasi-presupposed. Informatives aim at a comment, thus, for instance, utterances (10) and (14) being comments on (4) as well as initiative for (16) and (17). In so far as the initiative claim to truth of informative speech acts is to some degree presupposed, there is no strict need of being taken up; a reactive comment is not absolutely necessary. Nevertheless, the relations between these utterances become obvious only when assuming the underlying *Dialogic Principle* which relates in our case INFORMATIVES as a sub-type of REPRESENTATIVES to COMMENTS as a sub-type of speech acts of ACCEPTANCE (cf. Weigand 1989):

INFORM (REPRESENTATIVE) ↔ COMMENT (ACCEPTANCE)

Thus the five utterances are dialogically oriented as a process in time of five subsequent steps:

1 tony to beth
2 reaction by jburge
3 reaction by beth addressed to tony and jburge
4 reaction by tony addressed to jburge
5 reaction by jburge addressed to beth

Let us now have a short look at another chat group consisting only of two persons, siggy and debra, and one talk exchange between (31) and (48):

(31) [siggy]	Debra: I couldn't get on the WELL tonight. Pretty crowded?	↓
(48) [debra]	I've had no problem getting on the Well. The muse keeps crashing though.	↑

This talk exchange is interesting as it demonstrates how far away a reaction might show up on the monitor, even only after the initiative utterance has disappeared. Whereas siggy addresses her/his utterance directly to debra, the reaction is not addressed but is pretty clearly understood as a reaction to (31) by what is said. In this case the reaction does not represent a comment after a representative but a response after an explorative speech act.

We could pick up many other interesting points in this part of our IRC print-out. I will only deal with one further point. In line (18) we have the indication ACTION in capital letters which refers back to line (2) and forward to line (20):

(2) [xilef]	well, i'll go to bed then...quit early on this side of the big water
(18) [ACTION]	xilef waves and falls asleep.
(20) [SERVER]	xilef has quit IRC Leaving

In this way, practical and mental actions are brought in, i.e. what the speaker does and thinks. The visual and cognitive level are transformed in accordance with the technical conditions of the medium. In (1) xilef informs the others that he will go to bed which is realized as ACTION in (18) and confirmed by the SERVER in (20).

Thus we see that it is not only the Dialogic Principle that gets in the grip of the media but also the Principle of *Communicative Means*. IRC has developed interesting means not only for typing practical and mental actions but also for gestures and facial expressions known as smileys or emoticons. These smileys however are consciously and intentionally used, which results in a certain difference to natural face-to-face interaction. For instance, if you want to express a smiling face, you key in a smiley as for example in (24). This smiley is part of howie's utterance which is a reaction to (19) in a talk between debra and howie:

(11) [debra]	Hello all from S.F. CA	↓
(12) [howie]	hey debra, welcome back	↑↓
(19) [debra]	wow howie you're still here!	↑↓
(24) [howie]	but of course :)	↑

There are multiple smileys, not all known to every user. There are also funny abbreviations such as:

rotflo which means: the speaker is 'rolling on the floor laughing' or
CU l8er which means: see you later.

These and other funny means, in part from comic-strip language, emphasize the game character of the chat. Also features of intonation are keyed in such as expressive intonation by sign repetition or loud voice by capital letters as we have in (46). IRC transforms what can be seen, heard, and thought in the natural speech situation to what can be keyed in and read on the monitor and thus manifests the importance of all these levels which are simultaneously and inseparably present in the action game. By keying in what is thought

IRC even goes beyond the natural means. Natural face-to-face interaction however can rely on what can be seen. Inferences therefore might be drawn more easily.

Before we take IRC as a *test case* for models of dialogue analysis, let us have a short look at what lies behind the ambitious notion of on-line *Internet Conferences.* One expects something like a structure, an agenda, and is disappointed. Apparently, the technical conditions of IRC do not allow it to structure a conference with multiple participants. The agenda consists in the topic itself, for instance, the Euro, and in the fact that there is an expert on the conference channel to whom questions might be addressed. Questions and responses however are restricted to the same technical conditions as IRC because an on-line multi-party conference channel functions like an IRC channel. There is thus the danger of not getting a chance to speak, as becomes evident from the following example taken from an Internet conference on the Euro, of December 22, 1997, and translated into English (for the authentic German text see appendix 2):

(1)	<Expert>	Hall, here is Expert, I've just come straight from the broadcast and am available now.
(9)	<xxx >	HELP!!!!
(10)	<xxx >	HELP!!!!
(11)	<xxx >	HELP!!!!
(12)	<xxx >	HELP!!!!
(24)	<xxx >	SILENCE!!!!!!!!!!!!!!!!!!!!!!!
(27)	<xxx >	SILENCE!!!!!!!!!!!!!!!!!!!!!!!
(28)	<xxx >	SILENCE!!!!!!!!!!!!!!!!!!!!!!!
(29)	<xxx >	SILENCE!!!!!!!!!!!!!!!!!!!!!!!
(145)	<yyy>	IT'S CHAOTIC HERE...

What results, is in principle not different from the possibility of asking questions via telephone during or after the broadcast. Neither the on-line Internet conference nor the telephone channel provides a secure opportunity of getting an answer to one's question. There would be the possibility of organizing a conference via e-mail, with an agenda similar to news groups, but then we have left on-line multiple interaction and immediate reaction is no longer possible.

Now let us see what conclusions we can draw from these observations if we take them as a test case for an adequate model of dialogue analysis. On the one hand, the model should take account of what we learned from the Principle of Communicative Means, namely that dialogue cannot satisfactorily be described on the verbal level only. As Naumann (1994a, 431) has remarked in an article on 'Dialogue with the Answerphone', linguistic models of dialogue analysis such as the model of dialogue grammar are mainly interested in elaborating verbal actions. Even if they do not ignore the relevance of non-verbal elements, these factors are considered as accompanying, not as constitutive factors. In contrast, IRC confirms that the verbal level of the text cannot be a separate major level. We have to change the model of dialogue grammar which focuses on texts to a model of action games which focuses on human beings who are different in principle and interact with all their abilities together (cf. also Naumann 1994b). The verbal level of the text represents only one component in the action game.

On the other hand, an adequate model should take account of what we learned from the fundamental role of the Dialogic Principle for what concerns coherence and understanding. What is so striking is the dynamic and seemingly arbitrary nature of dialogue which cannot satisfactorily be represented by a pre-established pattern of fixed rules such as in the model of dialogue grammar. At first glance, we might think that these running sequences confirm the basic assumption of conversational analysis as was again expressed in a recent publication by Gruber (1996) who maintained that in performance every utterance may follow a preceding utterance: 'Denn in der 'Praxis' kann eben jeder Sprechakt nach jedem kommen' (p. 44). Such an assumption however reflects only the superficial impression and does not at all come to the point of what constitutes coherence and understanding. In the end, it is the Dialogic Principle and the constant attempt to find a dialogically connected utterance that gives coherence to these sequences. We therefore need a Model of Principles that, on the one hand, allows open points and differing understandings, but, on the other hand, tells us how we orient ourselves by principles if we cannot rely on fixed rules but only on a network of probabilities.

From the perspective of IRC, we now understand the importance of some features of natural interaction which we have often neglected, such as the feature of eye-contact, by which we may request an uptake of our utterance in the natural speech situation. In IRC, we can use only the technique of explicitly addressing the utterance which however is not sufficient. It is much easier for the user of IRC to escape than in the natural speech situation because it could always be the case that he had simply overlooked an utterance. If there are only a few users in the channel, the problem of uptake will not arise seriously. On the level of multiple users, however, uptake is not guaranteed; it is in the end given by chance.

Whereas in our example of a dialogue on television, the sequence of utterances depends on previous management of the controversial topic according to roles, now it depends on technical conditions resulting from the strictly linear time order. The users, mostly young academic people, are conscious of this condition, they know that uptake is not fully secured. Nevertheless or even precisely because of this, they play the game. According to the central thesis by Reid (1991, 5 and 48), 'IRC is essentially a playground' for the virtual community of 'electropolis', even if 'the games are not always funny'. 'Speed of response and wit are the stuff of popularity and community on IRC' (p.23). In so far as the users of IRC deconstruct social boundaries and 'construct their own community and culture', they are seen by Reid (p. 6) as a postmodern phenomenon. Playing the game and thus being a member of the community may become more important than exchanging specific messages. Only an open model as the Model of Dialogic Principles can deal with such a game and its feature that not everything fits but is based in the end on probability and virtual freedom.

One might object that in natural interaction uptake is also not fully secured nor does everything fit. Developing the Model of Principles was in fact a consequence of admitting that natural interaction in the end is based on probability. Nevertheless, I think we can expect and even request on the basis of an obligation that our utterances receive a dialogical uptake in natural games. We therefore consider a refusal to respond a strong communicative 'affront'. In IRC however requesting an obligatory uptake contradicts the technical conditions. The Dialogic Principle therefore is at risk.

4.2. The great moments of the game

Having analysed parts of normal IRC, we will now briefly look at one of the great moments of IRC, namely the famous chats that took place during the *Gulf War* in 1991. The main difference between the standard and the famous chats results from the fact that there is one central and dominating topic to which nearly all utterances are related: the beginning of the war, the first bombs dropping on Baghdad, as was reported on the radio channels. The chatters are listening to different radio programmes and are informing themselves about the news. Another important difference results from the fact that there are users in the channel who are quasi-witnesses of the historical event, namely users from Israel. These famous Gulf War chats are thus based on a shared feeling of excitement that embraces all the sequences of utterances, the feeling of being in the midst of an important historic event and of being able to observe it quasi-live.

Again many utterances are representatives which tell the news. What is not so important is receiving a specific comment, because they all refer to the same central event. Besides, there are other short talk exchanges, exploratives and answers, directives and corresponding consents, and greetings which can be described as declaratives. We take as an example a small part from the continuously running sequences (http://www.leo.org/pub/omp/general/networking/irc/doc/report-desert-storm.tar.Z. [28. 3. 1998]):

(1)	<Mix>	are you scared Boy?
(2)	<Lipstick>	CNN saoid he didnt hear any hits on aircraft.
(3)	<Arkie>	186 users.

(4) <BOY>	HELLO ALL ..
(5) <Anipa>	Oh they didn't nuke the links :)
(6) <Icarus>	The greatest server shutdown in the world ..... !
(7) <Anipa>	Welcome back,
(8) <Frank>	Max: tuleeko jotain ?
(9) <xaM>	tekstitv
(10) <Neuro>	CNN
(11) <tsh>	{h, toihan tuli jo cnn:lt{
(12) <viu>	Frank: ei juuri mit{{n
(13) <tsh>	ajat sitten
(14) <pi>	maailma tulee takaisin ..
(15) <Neuro>	MK: Anythinh happening in Israel?
(16) <tsh>	katos ;). gm tuli jo :)
(17) <Arkie>	so much for working tonight. :)
(18) <Mosiah>	89!
(19) <tsh>	argh
(20) <Goofa>	□{Our aircraft isn't in there.
(21) <BOY>	MIx: yes ..
(22) <kimberli>	bye all
(23) <lynx>	□ no finnish please □
(24) <Goofa>	Yet.
(25) <umfonta6>	wide range of dropping
(26) <Will>	this channel is slightly crowded
(27) <HollowMan>	this sucks
(28) <xaM>	wow
(29) <tsh>	oh shit...
(30) <Tylenol>	WAR STARTS!!!!
(31) <MK>	Not yet. Only air craft in air
(32) <Mosiah>	93
(33) <nova>	"nothin has landed very near the hotrel (where the cnn guys are)"
(34) <Faustus>	People in Isreal: can you see anything happening? I guess not.....
(35) <Lipstick>	Ooof!
(36) <MidHacker>	When did war start? and specify timezone
(37) #Breeze#	white house press report in 2 minutes
(38) <Datawolf>	the joint chiefs have confirmed, ther is war.
(39) <Alexander>	Hi Swan!
(40) <Arkie>	good evening, swan.
(41) <noone>	94
(42) <Blitz>	91....gosh wonder why the net shut down----channel overload
(43) <Mix>	We're scared for you too Boy...
(44) <CaptainJ>	BOMBS HAVE BEEN DROPPED (CNN)
(45) <Will>	mosiah, you are being bombed? wgherere are you?
(46) <Arkie>	hi, sylvia.
(47) <BigCheese:+peace>	92? Yowch!
(48) <Goofa>	Channel 2 is making too big of a deal about this.
(49) <spam>	Breeze white house press report in 2 minutes
(50) <Alexander>	95!!!!!!!!!!!!!!!
(51) <Tylenol>	YES
(52) <Arkie>	mosiah is in usa evidently

(53) <CaptainJ>	POSSIBLE TARGET – COMM CENTER IN BAGDAD (CNN)
(54) <Will>	please, speak english so we can all understand
(55) <tsh>	midhac: 20 minutes ago
(56) <xaM>	lynx: sorry, we were speaking finnish during the net split.
(57) <tsh>	or 30
(58) <BOY>	Fau: we can see nothing.

We pick out a few interesting points.

- The important news is emphasized with capital letters, for instance, in (30), (44) and (53):

(30) <Tylenol>	WAR STARTS!!!!
(44) <CaptainJ>	BOMBS HAVE BEEN DROPPED (CNN)
(53) <CaptainJ>	POSSIBLE TARGET – COMM CENTER IN BAGDAD (CNN)

- Some utterances report numbers which indicate the users on the channel, such as 186 users according to utterance (3).
- Interest and concern are concentrated on Israel, as becomes manifest from some explorative-response exchanges:

(1) <Mix>	are you scared Boy?
(21) <Boy>	MIx: yes ..
(43) <Mix>	We're scared for you too Boy ...
(15) <Neuro>	MK: Anythinh happening in Israel?
(31) <MK>	Not yet. Only air craft in air.
(34) <Faustus>	People in Isreal: can you see anything happening I guess not ...
(58) <Boy>	Fau: we can see nothing.

- There is also an interesting directive talk exchange referring to some Finnish utterances:

(23) <lynx>	□ no finnish please □
(56) <xaM>	lynx: sorry, we are speaking finnish during the net split.

I think it has become evident already from these few points that we are dealing with an action game between multiple users who in principle can act and react immediately, but in reality have to wait and accept the chronological order of the in-going utterances. Utterances that belong together as initiative and reactive are torn apart, their coherence is in danger of getting lost, but the speakers precisely watch the flow of the utterances and in most cases put together what belongs together according to the Dialogic Principle. Thus coherence is given by the users in their attempt to understand the running sequences by referring to the Dialogic Principle.

We may compare this situation with face-to-face talk in a large group of people. The interlocutors normally are engaged only in small groups at a time, passing from one small group to another. They hear others talking in the background, but they have to disregard these voices and concentrate on the utterances of their own group and on the persons who have caught their eye. In the Internet, users have to disregard the utterances that belong to other groups and have to concentrate on utterances which are explicitly addressed or connected by the Dialogic Principle. Depending on the number of users, the distance between the initiative and reactive utterance can become very large and in the end no reaction at all might follow. Perfect users however might simultaneously participate in different groups. This type of multiple simultaneous talk is in principle possible also in natural conversation, presumably however only to a minor extent.

5. Conclusion and future perspectives

In this paper, we have concentrated on three major principles of dialogue that apparently get changed to a certain degree by the mass media. Dialogue in the media, supported by technical means, can be seen as contrasting with natural face-to-face interaction. In order to describe it more precisely, we would have to refer to a larger text corpus and to other principles of Dialogue such as Rhetorical Principles or Principles of Entertainment.

Modern life is based on the mass media. To appear and talk or be referred to on television assigns importance and power. Acting on television means playing to act, acting on stage according to a role. It is this feature of the role by which the Action Principle of natural spontaneous interaction is modified in the grip of television. Action becomes presentation.

Quite another game is played on the Internet. Here we have the chance of acting on-line without being on stage, even hidden behind a nickname, and of interacting with multiple users across the whole world, with witnesses of historical events. In contrast to action games on stage, it is the very aim of the users to be spontaneous and original. There are however other technical conditions that change and modify action games on the Internet in contrast to natural interaction. It is, on the one hand, the linear chronological order of the utterances that makes coherence and the Dialogic Principle difficult and problematic. To have the *chance* of uptake, often seems to be all important. This is the price that has to be paid for achieving multi-party talks with hundreds, even thousands of users worldwide and on-line. You have to accept this condition and therefore to take it in the end as a game. On the other hand, the grip of IRC affects also the Principle of Communicative Means. The complex interrelation of different types of communicative means has to be transformed into the mere level of keying in.

The game of IRC gains its attraction in part from the fact of being a game of highly advanced computer technology that gives the users a specifically elitist flair. Time however passes quickly, and it can be expected that in the next generation almost everyone will be an expert. Then the game will lose its point. Certainly, it will be changed, the players might appear graphically on the monitor as Avatars as is already possible now. We might think of other changes, to electronic department stores in the commercial area or to video-conferences, to video-instructions and to video-operations via robot in the professional area. In these changes however anonymity will be lost.

The technical aspects are certainly exciting prospects which might be seen as 'the dream of infinite data' (Geers, in this volume). Technologies of communication are, on the one hand, vehicles of optimizing complex organization of everyday commercial life (Höflich 1996, 27). On the other hand, they create virtual worlds not only for concrete commercial purposes but also for arts, fantasy and play. For television, reality has become a matter of opinion and presentation, for IRC reality might become a matter of virtuality. We hope that language and human dialogic action will not be lost in the dreams that might arise from these huge amounts of data of virtual worlds.

References

Austin, J.L. (1962): How to Do Things with Words. London, etc.

Dascal, M. (1994): Speech Acts Theory and Gricean Pragmatics: Some Differences of Detail that Make a Difference. – In: Tsohatzidis, S.L. (ed.): Foundations of Speech Act Theory. Philosophical and Linguistic Perspectives. London, New York, 323-334.

Gruber, H. (1996): Streitgespräche. Zur Pragmatik einer Diskursform. Opladen.

Hess-Lüttich, E.W.B. (ed.) (1992): Medienkultur – Kulturkonflikt. Massenmedien in der interkulturellen und internationalen Kommunikation. Opladen.

Höflich, J.R. (1996): Technisch vermittelte interpersonale Kommunikation. Grundlagen, organisatorische Medienverwendung, Konstitution ‚elektronischer Gemeinschaften' (Studien zur Kommunikationswissenschaft 8). Opladen.

Merten, K./Schmidt, S.J./Weischenberg, S. (eds.) (1994): Die Wirklichkeit der Medien. Eine Einführung in die Kommunikationswissenschaft. Opladen.

Naumann, B. (1994b): Überlegungen zu einem Dialogbegriff als Handlungsspiel. Gestik und Mimik im Gespräch und in der Gesprächsanalyse. – In: Weigand, E. (ed.): Concepts of Dialogue Considered from the Perspective of Different Disciplines (Beiträge zur Dialogforschung 6). Tübingen, 1-14.

Naumann, B. (1997): IRCs – schriftliche Sonderformen von Mehrpersonengesprächen. – In: Weigand, E. (ed.): Dialogue Analysis: Units, Relations and Strategies beyond the Sentence. Contributions in Honour of Sorin Stati's 65th Birthday (Beiträge zur Dialogforschung 13). Tübingen, 161-178.

Reid, E. (1991): Electropolis. Communication and Community on Internet Relay Chat. http://www.ll.mu.oz.au/papers/emr/electropolis.html.

Searle, J.R. (1969): Speech Acts. An Essay in the Philosophy of Language. Cambridge.

Weigand, E. (1989): Sprache als Dialog. Sprechakttaxonomie und kommunikative Grammatik (Linguistische Arbeiten 204). Tübingen.

Weigand, E. (1991): The Dialogic Principle Revisited. Speech Acts and Mental States. – In: Stati, S./Weigand, E./Hundsnurscher, F. (eds): Dialoganalyse III. Referate der 3. Arbeitstagung, Bologna 1990, vol. 1 (Beiträge zur Dialogforschung 1). Tübingen, 75-104.

Weigand, E. (1993): Mündlich und schriftlich – ein Verwirrspiel. – In: Löffler, H. (ed.): Dialoganalyse IV. Referate der 4. Arbeitstagung, Basel 1992, vol. 1 (Beiträge zur Dialogforschung 5). Tübingen, 137-150.

Weigand, E. (1997): The Unit beyond the Sentence. – In: Weigand, E. (ed.): Dialogue Analysis: Units, Relations and Strategies beyond the Sentence. Contributions in Honour of Sorin Stati's 65th Birthday (Beiträge zur Dialogforschung 13). Tübingen, 3-12.

Weigand, E. (1998): Misunderstanding: the Standard Case. – In: Journal of Pragmatics, special issue on misunderstanding, ed. by Marcelo Dascal.

Weigand, E. (forthcoming): Rhetoric and Argumentation in a Dialogic Perspective. – In: Rigotti, E./Cigada, S. (eds.): Rhetoric and Argumentation (Beiträge zur Dialogforschung). Tübingen.

Werry, Ch.C. (1996): Linguistic and Interactional Features of Internet Relay Chat. – In: Herring, S.C. (ed.): Computer-Mediated Communication. Linguistic, Social and Cross-Cultural Perspectives (Pragmatics & Beyond. New Series 39). Amsterdam, Philadelphia, 47-64.

Appendix 1: Fußball für alle? (Pro & Contra, November 22, 1997, ARD)

Pro-Anwalt Herr Fünfgeld, ich würde Ihnen ganz gerne zunächst einmal Gelegenheit geben, auch noch mal was zu dem Vorwurf zu sagen, daß das öffentlich-rechtliche Rundfunksystem auch ein Pay-TV sei. AUSRÄUMEN VON CONTRA-ARGUMENTEN

Pro-Experte Das würde ich nicht sagen. Wir haben in Deutschland ein duales Rundfunksystem. ... diejenigen, die ein Rundfunkempfangsgerät haben, müssen Rundfunkgebühren bezahlen. Aber nicht nur für Fußball. Das ist doch das Entscheidende. Und jetzt muß ich die erste Antwort geben: Für uns ist Sport keine Unterhaltung primär, sondern ein Teil unserer Information, und das ist der grundlegende Unterschied. ...

Pro-Anwalt Ja. Der öffentlich-rechtliche Rundfunk, so heißt es, hat einen Grundversorgungsauftrag. Sie haben das selber eben angesprochen. Gehören dazu auch Fußball-Länderspiele live? AUFRUFEN VON PRO-ARGUMENTEN

Pro-Experte Aber natürlich! ....

Appendix 2: Internet conference on the Euro

(1) <Expert> Hall, hier ist Expert, ich komme direkt von der Sendung und stehe Ihnen jetzt zur Verfügung

(9) <xxx > HILFE!!!!
(10) <xxx > HILFE!!!!
(11) <xxx > HILFE!!!!
(12) <xxx > HILFE!!!!

(24) <xxx > RUHE!!!!!!!!!!!!!!!!!!!!!!!!

(27) <xxx > RUHE!!!!!!!!!!!!!!!!!!!!!!!!
(28) <xxx > RUHE!!!!!!!!!!!!!!!!!!!!!!!!
(29) <xxx > RUHE!!!!!!!!!!!!!!!!!!!!!!!!

(145) <yyy> IST DAS EIN CHAOS HIER

Jana Hoffmannová/Olga Müllerová

Ein Privatbrief auf E-mail: immer noch ein Brief oder eher eine Plauderei?

1. Der E-mail-Text als Brief

Die E-mail-Konversation ist in der Gegenwart so beliebt, daß hierbei entstandene Texte unsere Aufmerksamkeit wecken und immer mehr zum Forschungsgegenstand werden (Vgl. z.B. Čmejrková 1997; Naumann 1998; Uhlířová 1994; Violi 1998; u.a.) Es bilden sich verschiedene **Genre** des E-mail-Dialogs heraus: z.B. Fachdiskussionen und Konferenzen, die sich um Problemlösungen bemühen. Unser Beitrag befaßt sich mit einem anderen Genre: es sind Privatbriefe, mittels denen ein langfristiger Dialog aus der Ferne geführt wird. Die an die Eltern gerichteten E-mail-Briefe einer tschechischen Studentin stellten für sie während ihres USA-Aufenthalts die einzige Verbindung mit dem Zuhause dar. Sie schrieb regelmäßig diese Briefe (fast jeden Tag) und informierte darin die Eltern über ihre Arbeit im Labor, darüber, wie sie die Freizeit verbrachte und das exotische Milieu des amerikanischen Bundesstaates Arizona kennenlernte, über ihren Gesundheitszustand usw.

Bei der Lektüre der Briefe stellten wir uns sofort die Frage, inwieweit sich diese E-mail-Texte noch als **Briefe** klassifizieren lassen. Einige ihrer Merkmale stimmen vollständig mit unserer traditionellen Vorstellung von Briefen und Korrespondenz überein.

1.1 Reaktionen, Antworten auf den vorangegangenen Brief des Partners

Führen wir mit jemandem einen regelmäßigen Briefwechsel, **reagieren** wir immer in unserem Brief auf den vorangegangenen des Partners. Auch die Autorin unserer Texte reagierte kontinuierlich auf die Briefe von zu Hause; die E-mails, die sie von den Eltern erhielt, hatten wir zwar nicht zur Verfügung, aber aus den Briefen der Studentin läßt sich deren Inhalt (und manchmal auch die benutzten sprachlichen Mittel) in bedeutendem Maße rekonstruieren. Die Autorin hielt es wahrscheinlich für ihre ständige Pflicht, auf die Fragen der Eltern zu antworten, und nahm diese Pflicht sehr ernst; die Formulierungen, mit denen sie ihre Antworten einleitet, wirken daher in einigen Fällen fast amtlich und offiziell:

Vati schickte mir ein paar Vorschläge und Fragen, zu denen ich mich äußern kann...
Zu weiteren Anfragen von Vati ergänze ich ein paar Informationen....
Teilweise habe ich so einige von Vatis Anfragen beantwortet und den Rest ergänze ich noch: 1)...2)...3)...
(Alle Beispiele aus tschechischen E-mail-Texten wurden ins Deutsch annähernd übersetzt.)

In anderen Fällen sind die Anfragen der Eltern nur implizit im Text enthalten; daß aber die Tochter darauf antwortet, ist u.a. aus der aktuellen Gliederung und der Wortfolge ihrer Reaktionen klar ersichtlich:

Mit dem Netz gibt es keinerlei Probleme.
Um den 23. Mai herum gibt es nicht viel frei...
Über die hiesige Zeit habe ich keine anderen Informationen als daß sie ständig um neun Stunden im Vergleich zu euch verschoben ist und wann sie sich ändern wird, ahne ich wirklich nicht...

Im Unterschied zu den „E-mail-Konferenzen" überträgt die Autorin keinerlei Passagen aus den Briefen ihrer Eltern in die eigenen Briefe, sie zitiert diese nicht.

1.2 Das Textmuster Brief und seine Komponenten

Unsere E-mail-Texte enthalten jedoch auch eine Reihe weiterer Elemente, die gewichtige Komponenten des **„Textmusters"** Briefs sind. Es sind dies:

1.1.1 Grüße (*Seid gegrüßt, Eltern; Servus, Mutti und Vati);*
1.2.2 Dankesformeln (*danke für den schrecklich langen Brief und die allerneuesten Nachrichten);*
1.2.3 Schlußformeln und Wünsche (*lebt einstweilen wohl und ich wünsche Euch ein schönes Wochenende; grüßt alle Bekannten, die nach mir fragen, und irgendwann wieder tschau);*
1.2.4 Fragen, Interessebekundung für die Geschehnisse zu Hause, auf gegenseitigen Kontakt orientierte Passagen (*wie ist's, hat der Schnee schon angefangen, bei Euch vom Dach zu fallen?; und mein Mütterchen, das kann sich irgendwie lange nicht zum Briefeschreiben entschließen?).*

In Übereinstimmung mit dem Textmuster Brief stehen sowohl diese eher formalen Rahmenelemente als auch die gesamte Gestaltung des Briefes, seine thematische und inhaltliche Struktur, seine Absatzgliederung.

1.3 Metakommunikative Ausdrücke

Beim Verfassen üblicher Briefe kommentieren wir oft einige eher technische Aspekte der Korrespondenz (wie lange es dauerte, bis der Partner den Brief erhielt, wie die Post funktioniert usw.) Auch unsere E-mail-Briefe kommentieren regelmäßig die Fernmeldetechnik (*die Talk-Verbindung hat nicht lange angehalten; meistens muß ich mich an die dreimal einloggen; ich kehre lieber zu e-mail zurück).* Interessant ist, daß in diesen „metakommunikativen" Passagen in hohem Maße gerade die Ausdrücke Brief und Korrespondenz erscheinen (*ich habe einen weiteren Brief angefangen; in der letzten Zeit habe ich diese Korrespondenz ein bißchen vernachlässigt; ihr müßt aber einsehen, daß ich nach so einem anspruchsvollen und direkt erschöpfenden Brief Anspruch darauf habe, mich ein paar Tage vom Briefeschreiben auszuruhen).* Ab und zu haben wir aber den Eindruck, daß das junge Mädchen seinen Kontakt mit den Eltern ein bißchen anders wahrnimmt: es ist, als ob es direkt mit ihnen erzählen würde (*wenn ich so zuhöre, wie Vati Rad fährt....),* z.B. auch per Telefon (*nun bin ich schon wieder an der Strippe).*

2. Zwischen dem Brief und dem spontanen Erzählen

Bis jetzt haben wir gezeigt, wie E-mail-Texte das **Textmuster** des Briefes einhalten; sie sind in Übereinstimmung damit strukturiert und beinhalten dessen zentrale Komponente. Diese Organisation ist aber andererseits desorganisiert, stark gestört durch das **konkrete** Sprachmaterial, mit dem das Modell angefüllt ist. Die E-mail-Verbindung ist schnell und leicht, für viele Schreiber ist heute die Produktion einer E-mail-Mitteilung weitaus natürlicher als ein normaler Brief. Deswegen verhalten sie sich im E-mail-Dialog spontan und fassen diesen Kontakt als ganz zwanglos auf. Es scheint, daß sich die E-mail-Dialoge irgendwo **zwischen** der geschriebenen Korrespondenz und dem gesprochenen Face-to-face-Dialog und dem Telefongespräch bewegen, und daß sich der E-mail-Dialog von allen anderen hier genannten Formen durch die größte Spontaneität auszeichnet.

Beim **Face-to-face-Dialog** befinden wir uns nämlich unter dem permanenten Druck der Situation, der wir uns anpassen müssen, der Rücksichtnahme auf den Partner. So können auch bestimmte Hemmungen entstehen, man steht unter ständiger Selbstkontrolle. Beim **Telefongespräch** entfällt zwar der visuelle Kontakt – wir müssen also nicht auf unsere Mimik, Gestik, Bewegungen achtgeben. Aber ein bedeutendes Bedürfnis nach Selbstkontrolle dauert auch hier an: was wir sagen, können wir nicht mehr zurücknehmen, gefährlich kann auch die Stimmfärbung sein, der ironische Ton, Gelächter, Pausen und verschiedene unbestimmte Geräusche. Dieser Druck entfällt beim **Briefschreiben,** wo wir zwar auch Rücksicht auf den Partner und unsere gegenseitige Beziehung nehmen, der Situationsdruck ist aber nicht so zwingend: einen Brief schreiben wir in Ruhe und in privater Umgebung, wir können alles durchdenken. Das Schreiben eines Briefes empfinden wir aber wohl als einen sehr offiziellen und repräsentativen Akt.

Dagegen verbindet die **E-mail-Kommunikation** offensichtlich die Vorteile **aller** dieser Dialogformen: sie behält die Intimität bei, in der wir die Mitteilung schreiben; sie umfaßt nicht den unmittelbaren Situationsdruck und die damit verbundenen Barrieren; dabei engen uns nicht Gefühle der Offizialität und der Verbindlichkeit ein. Der Schreiber der E-mail-Mitteilung ist „mit seinem Computer allein“, er nutzt diese Privatheit, sie ermöglicht ihm eine beträchtliche Individualisierung des Textes. Die Unförmlichkeit der ganzen Situation führt aber zugleich dazu, daß er mit dem Adressaten der Mitteilung irgendwie spontan, ohne Hemmungen **erzählt**. Dem entsprechen auch die Sprache und der Stil des Textes. Unser Material ist dafür ein lebendiges Beispiel; wir nehmen aber an – und das beweisen auch schon durchgeführte Forschungen – daß auf diese Art nicht nur der E-mail-Dialog zwischen der Tochter und den Eltern verläuft (also zwischen Partnern, die sich untereinander maximal nahestehen), sondern auch der Dialog zwischen Freunden, Kollegen usw.

3. Der E-mail-Text als spontanes Erzählen

Weiter weisen wir wenigstens auf einige Charakterzüge hin, mit denen sich die Briefe des jungen Mädchens dem spontanen Erzählen mit den Eltern annähern.

3.1 Syntax

Die Oszillierung dieser Briefe zwischen geschriebenen und gesprochenen Texten äußert sich u.a. darin, daß wir darin nur wenige Spuren der gesprochenen **Syntax** finden. Vor allem dort, wo die Autorin das Milieu und die Natur beschreibt, benutzt sie verhältnismäßig lange und gegliederte Satzkonstruktionen, häufig treten Mittel der syntaktischen Kondensierung sowie Konstruktionen auf, die auf attributiv gebrauchte Partizipien gegründet sind (*die in Spalten zwischen riesigen Steinen wachsenden gekrümmten Bäume; der unter den Hufen der Pferde aufwirbelnde Staub).* Wir finden hier keinerlei Berichtigung, Rückformulierung noch Anakoluthe, die dem eigentlichen spontanen gesprochenen Text eigen sind.

Andererseits ist allerdings die Syntax des Briefes „gewellt" durch eine Menge von **Fragen** (*Also was...? Also wie...? Also wieviel....?),* **Ausrufen** *(Also bin ich hier! Unbegreiflich!!!)* und unkonventionellen **Appellen** an entfernte Adressaten (*helft bitte; versucht mitzuteilen....).* Eher auf den gesprochenen Dialog weist auch die Menge der erklärenden und kommentierenden **Einschübe** hin, die die Schreiberin an allen möglichen und unmöglichen Textstellen in Klammern setzt; diese sind gerade oft der Träger der Spontaneität, der Individualisierung bis hin zur Vertraulichkeit: *das nächste (eigentlich schon dieses) Wochenende; einer der schönsten (angeblich) hiesigen Cañons; Libor P. (Ihr kennt ihn ja); Edgar (der betreffende Zahnarzt)...* Auch ist einer der wenigen auffälligen Mittel der gesprochenen Syntax im Text die Art und Weise der **Textverknüpfung,** die sehr oft die Ausdrücke *na, so, ansonsten, eigentlich* benutzt *(<u>eigentlich</u> weiß ich nicht; <u>na</u> und das muß ich mindestens noch siebenmal wiederholen; <u>ansonsten</u> grüßt selbstverständlich Hanka).*

3.2 Vergegenwärtigung

Die Schreiberin ist sich dessen bewußt, daß ihre Nachricht schneller, früher die Adressaten erreicht, noch bevor die geschilderten Erlebnisse der Vergangenheit angehören (Čmejrková, 1997, spricht davon, daß die E-mail-Korrespondenz auf das Gefühl der

Simultaneität gegründet ist; Violi, 1998, nennt das „Quasi-Gegenwart"). Deswegen „zieht" sie ihre Eltern direkt in die Situation hinein, sie ermöglicht ihnen, sozusagen unmittelbar ihre Erlebnisse (von Ausflügen usw.) **zu teilen.** Sie erreicht das durch die Anwendung

3.2.1 der **2. Person Singular oder Plural** (*ein paar Dutzende Meilen findest du weder eine Tankstelle noch eine Imbißbude; das Schwimmbad und den Turnsaal kannst du besuchen, wann und wie du willst; vor dir öffnet sich wie aus dem Nichts der Blick....)*;

3.2.2 Mittel der **räumlichen** Deixis, besonders Lokaladverbien, die den Adressaten irgendwie das Milieu „vergegenwärtigen", in dem sich die Tochter bewegt (*es geht hier überall bergauf und bergab; hierher verläuft sich kaum ein hiesiger Tourist)*;

3.2.3 **Temporal**adverbien, Konjunktionen und verschiedene Ausdrücke und Konstruktionen mit temporaler Semantik, die das Gefühl des unmittelbaren, sozusagen ständigen Kontakts erhöhen: *lebt einstweilen wohl; am Montag wieder Servus; ich warte gerade...; es bleiben mir nur noch...; dann laufe ich schon direkt ins Bett; wenn wir schon dabei sind; nur so nebenbei gesagt*;

3.2.4 **wertende und modalisierende** Ausdrücke, die der Autorin behilflich sind, die Adressaten zu überzeugen, auf sie einzuwirken (*es ist wirklich sehr schön; die Täler sind selbstverständlich ganz schön tief)*;

3.2.5 zahlreiche **Interjektionen** – also vielleicht die spontansten Mittel, die besonders an den Formulierungen der Ausrufesätze beteiligt sind: *Phhu!; Hurraa; Hahaha; Juchhe (juchhe, das wird eine Pracht; juchheißa, das war aber eine Pracht!).*

Alle diese Mittel unterstützen deutlich den **Dialog**charakter der Briefe; so dialogisiert sind auch die umfangreichen und zusammenhängenden Textabschnitte, die erzählen oder die Natur schildern.

3.3 Expressivität

Das spontane Herangehen der Autorin an die Artikulierung des Textes führt natürlich zur Wahl zahlreicher **expressiver** Ausdrücke. Dazu gehören die schon erwähnten Interjektionen. Außer diesen möchten wir noch auf **Diminutive** aufmerksam machen, die die Studentin besonders zu lieben scheint; wahrscheinlich gehören sie zu den charakteristischen Zügen ihres **Idiolekts,** eventuell auch zu der Ausdrucksweise ihrer gesamten Familie. Die Benutzung der Diminutive ist allerdings unterschiedlich motiviert:

3.3.1 Nur einige davon bezeichnen wirklich in räumlicher Ausdehnung gesehen **kleine** Dinge (*ein kühleres Lüftchen brachte auch ein paar Wölkchen; in dem schönen kleinen Zimmerchen; voll von Landsträßchen*);

3.3.2 Sie bezeichnen Dinge oder Personen, zu denen die Autorin eine **gefühlsmäßige Beziehung** hat: *Mamilein, Wägelchen, Fahrrädchen*;
3.3.3 Sie werden mit einer gewissen **Nachsicht** oder einer leichten **ironischen** Färbung benutzt: *das ist so ein nettes Alterchen; für hiesige Verhältnisse ist das noch ein Krümelchen* (gemeint ist ein Auto);
3.3.4 Dort, wo die Studentin die Eltern über ihre Forschungsarbeit im Labor informiert, benutzt sie Diminutive als für einen **Laien** verständlichen Ersatz der **Fachtermini:** *in einem Wässerchen schwenken*;
3.3.5 Sie sind für die Kommunikationsweise einer erwachsenen Tochter mit den Eltern charakteristisch, sie verleihen dem Text ein **vertrauliches** Gepräge: *überall ist es voll von Leutchen; ein Stückchen*; tschechische Diminutive *nazdarek, ahojky, zpravicky, darecky, zrovinka, pomaloucku...* Mit Diminutiven behilft sich die Tochter auch dort, wo sie ihre Eltern ein bißchen foppt.

3.4 Schriftsprache und Alltagssprache

Das Briefeschreiben und die Produktion von geschriebenen Texten ist im Tschechischen überwiegend mit der Benutzung der **Schriftsprache** verbunden. Die Spontaneität und die Zwanglosigkeit der E-mail-Mitteilung aber führt bezeichnenderweise dazu, daß die Autoren – in unserem Falle die Studentin – sehr oft zu nicht-schriftsprachlichen Formen greifen, besonders zu den Mitteln der **tschechischen Alltagssprache**: *starost s knedlikama* (Alltagssprache – statt *knedlíky* in der Schriftsprache); *celej* (Alltagssprache – statt *celý* in der Schriftsprache) *den jsem se ulejvala*; *uvidime co z toho vyleze* (Alltagssprache – statt *vyjde* in der Schriftsprache); *fotak* statt *fotoaparat, fotky* statt *fotografie, diaky* statt *diapositivy...* Die Berufs- und Fachkommunikation per E-mail ist auch noch von vielen **Slangausdrücken durchsetzt**. Diese treten auch in unseren Briefen auf, hauptsächlich in den Passagen, in denen die Studentin den Eltern ihre Versuche beschreibt. Diese Abschnitte sind ein anschauliches Beispiel für die Kombination von

- Fachtext mit zwangloser Plauderei („Geschwätz“, „Plappern“, „Quasseln“);
- einer sachlichen, notionalen Ausrichtung einerseits und der sozialen, kontaktpflegenden und emotionellen andererseits;
- Termini mit Slangausdrücken, einschließlich manchmal kaum durchschaubarer Abkürzungen, die in der Biochemie verwendet werden (*mittels RNA Proben werde ich mRNA für Early Trypsin lokalisieren; na und gerade diese mRNA werde ich in diesen Zellen mittels ihres markierten komplementaren Stücks suchen, das sich daran festklebt und sie so markiert; klitzekleine goldene Kügelchen kann man unter EM detektieren...).*

3.5 Grafik

Die E-mail-Briefe bieten also ein solches Maß an Spontaneität und Zwanglosigkeit der Ausdrucksweise an, daß die Texte in der Tat den Charakter eines herzlichen und vertrauten Gesprächs der Autorin mit ihren nächsten Verwandten, der übersprudelnden Mitteilung von Erlebnissen, des unmittelbaren Kontakts aufweisen. Die Schreiberin hat die völlig unbegrenzte Möglichkeit, in den Texten ihre Energie und ihr Temperament zur Entfaltung zu bringen; dadurch überwindet sie nicht nur den Umstand, daß diese Kommunikation (gegenüber dem unmittelbaren persönlichen Kontakt) arm an **nonverbalen und paraverbalen** Mitteln (Blicke, Lächeln, Intonation...) ist, sondern daß auch **diakritische Zeichen** fehlen. Dadurch, daß diese – für das Tschechische so wichtige – Zeichen in der E-mail-Mitteilung fehlen, wird die Vorstellung der **lautlichen Seite** des Textes wesentlich geschwächt (zum Unterschied zu den üblichen Beispielen, wo wir bei der Produktion und Rezeption eines geschriebenen Textes mehr oder weniger dessen lautliche Seite wahrnehmen, die wenigstens potentionell gegenwärtig ist, wo wir den Briefschreiber manchmal im wahrsten Sinne des Wortes „hören"). Durch diese Textreduktion wird u.a. die wirkliche Quantität des Vokals i/í (kurz:lang) verwischt: es ist z.B. nicht völlig klar, ob die Schreiberin bei *musim, tesim se, splouchaji* den schriftsprachlichen Ausdruck (*musím*, d.h. mit langem í) oder den nicht-schriftsprachlichen Ausdruck (*musim*, d.h. mit kurzem i) benutzen wollte; es läßt sich auch schwer die Aussprache des in der Form clovici *(človíci? človíčci?)* niedergeschriebenen Ausdrucks rekonstruieren. Alle diese Einschränkungen überwindet aber die Autorin mit der ihr eigenen Vitalität auch dadurch, daß sie den Adressaten auf dem Weg von der graphischen zur lautlichen Seite direkt hilft: *nach Chiricahua Nat Monument (lies cirikagua mit Häkchen am Anfang)*. Und die Reduktion der Grafik des E-mail-Textes (im Falle der tschechischen Mitteilung) wird auch dadurch kompensiert, daß in die Grafik expressive Elemente hineingetragen werden, wie z.B. die häufige Verdoppelung oder Verdreifachung von Vokalen (*dlouhataansky, obrovitaanske, veelikanske*; statt der normalen Unterschrift *Míša* meistens *Miiii* – wahrscheinlich in Übereinstimmung damit, wie sie in der Familie angeredet wird). Weiter benutzt sie auch Zeichen vom Typ -)))).

4. „Eher eine Plauderei!"

Also auch unsere Sammlung von Briefen einer nur einzigen Schreiberin (es handelt sich um einen Komplex von etwa zwanzig ausführlichen Briefen) bestätigt, daß die E-mail-

Briefe zwischen Monolog und Dialog, zwischen geschriebenem und gesprochenem Text, zwischen sachlicher (manchmal direkt fachlicher) und kontaktpflegender, expressiver Mitteilung oszillieren; und daß sie in diesem Pendeln eher zum Pol der Mündlichkeit, des lebendigen Dialogs, der Spontaneität ausschlagen. Trotz Aufrechterhaltung einiger Textstützen, die das Genre Brief auszeichnen, haben wir aus diesen Briefen eher den Eindruck einer unmittelbaren, natürlichen Unterhaltung, der Realisierung des Bedürfnisses, mit jemandem zu plaudern, gewonnen. In der Psychologie der E-mail-Kommunikation, die wahrscheinlich sowohl einige mit dem Briefschreiben als auch mit dem Face-to-face-Dialog (und für einige Forscher auch mit dem Telefongespräch) verbundenen Hemmungen ausschließt, kann man dadurch wahrscheinlich den Grund für deren wachsende Vorliebe erblicken. (Vielleicht haben wir paradoxerweise aus diesen Texten stellenweise den Eindruck, daß wir uns in der Nähe des **künstlerischen** Texts bewegen: vielleicht deswegen, weil der Text lebendig und dynamisch ist, die sprachlichen Mittel sind bunt und reich differenziert, der Text wirkt als Dialog – und dabei geht es nicht um die mechanische Umschreibung eines gesprochenen Dialogs und der Text enthält keine Charakterzüge der Syntax der mündlichen Äußerung, die in der Regel auch nicht in der sekundären Kommunikation im künstlerischen Text erscheinen.)

Literatur

Čmejrková, S. (1997): Čeština v síti: Psanost, či mluvenost? (O stylu e-mailového dialogu). [Tschechisch in dem Netz: Geschriebenheit, oder Gesprochenheit? (Über den Stil des E-mail-Dialogs).] – In: Naše řeč 80, 225-247.

Naumann, B. (1998): Stirbt die deutsche Sprache? Überlegungen zum Sprachwandel durch IRC (Internet Relay Chat). – In: Čmejrková, S./Hoffmannová, J./Müllerová, O./Světlá, J. (eds.): Dialoganalyse VI. Teil 1, Tübingen: Niemeyer, 249-262.

Uhlířová, L. (1994): E-mail as a New Subvariety of Medium and its Effects upon the Message. – In: Čmejrková, S./Štícha, F. (eds.): The Syntax of Sentence and Text. Amsterdam, Philadelphia: J. Benjamins, 273-282.

Violi, P. (1998): Electronic Dialogue between Orality and Literacy. A Semiotic Approach. – In: Čmejrková, S./Hoffmannová, J./Müllerová, O./Světlá, J. (eds.): Dialoganalyse VI, Teil 1, Tübingen: Niemeyer, 263-270.

Markus Schulze

Substitution of Paraverbal and Nonverbal Cues in the Written Medium of IRC

Abstract

For a long time, dialogue analysis has separated spoken language from written language. This dichotomy is valid in many cases as it is mostly parallel to the distinction of synchronous and asynchronous communication with the associated affinity to graphic and acoustic media, respectively.

During the present decade, many forms of computer mediated communication (CMC) have become widespread. With Internet Relay Chat (IRC), CMC introduced the new form of synchronous, written – or rather typed – many-to-many communication. This novel constellation gives rise to several aspects that require a further differentiation of the strict dichotomy of spoken vs. written language.

This paper will discuss how the total absence of paraverbal and nonverbal relational (and social) cues is fostering the evolution of a repertoire of text-based surrogates for these. Examples will also show that the planning strategies involved in the fast-paced conversations on IRC are not those usually employed for written language.

1. General aspects

1.1. Technical aspects

The acronym IRC stands for *Internet Relay Chat*. It is the name of an Internet-based chat system which was invented in 1988 by Jarkko Oikarinen. Today there are a multitude of IRC clients based on this protocol running on all kinds of computing platforms. IRC provides both the facility for one-to-one communication (1:1) via private messages and the many-to-many mode (m:n) via so-called channels.[1] Communication on IRC is exclusively text-based. Interlocutors edit short messages and then submit them. This is done in a very short time frame comparable to that of spoken dialogues.

The m:n mode of IRC communication is organised in channels or *virtual conference rooms* (c.f. Naumann 1995, p.168)[2] where interlocutors meet to converse. Channels have a name and a motto. Names are often chosen to give a rough impression of the subjects talked about on this channel (like in *star-wars*, *gay.bruxelles* or *webmaster*) while sometimes they remain cryptic – partly because of referring to topics not widely known (like *d666*, *PA3BPAT* or *doNotTestMe*).[3] The motto of a channel – the so-called *topic* – contains either a short description or simply a catchy phrase.

Any user can open a channel and set a name and a topic for it only limited by the etiquette on the net (see e.g. Hambridge 1995). Furthermore special states can be assigned to a channel (e.g. invite only, invisible, moderated etc.). Using channels allows for an approximate choice of the subject of conversation. Beside the many topic-related or ad-hoc-created channels, there are also channels with a regular crowd of users (e.g. the channels *erlangen*, *edinburgh* or *20+*) usually discussing more personal subjects rather than general topics.[4]

At the start of an IRC session, the user has to enter his or her so-called *nickname* (or *nick*). This name is what is seen by other IRC users and the only means to reference interlocutors. Nicknames range from common (first) names over names of fictional characters to bizarre combinations of characters (*Alex*, *Mike*, *Urmel*, *badboy*, *Calamity*, *Lion22*, *effendi^*, *speen*, *hope*, *lippy*, *o^-^o*)

1.2. Who is using IRC?

At any time of day or night there a roughly 100 000 IRC users logged on worldwide. They are distributed among the four major IRC networks which are independent of each other (EuroNet: 25 000, Dalnet: 20 000, EFNet: 37 000 (North America), UnderNet: 22 000).

These numbers are increasing rapidly. When the author first took a look at IRC in 1992 there were only about 1 000 users worldwide on the network that now has split up into EuroNet and EFNet. Apart from the mentioned IRC networks, there are several more, which are either small or have no international relevance.

To get a better overview over the persons using IRC (apart from the subjective impressions from personal use of the medium) the author made a user poll in 1997. Questionnaires were sent out to 400 German IRC users.[5] The questionnaires contained questions about age, gender, profession, perceived anonymity of the medium, typical contents of their IRC chats etc. The author received 104 replies. This poll gives a good impression of the people typically found on IRC but the figures probably will vary substantially with the time of day. Furthermore these numbers might well be different for other countries.

According to this poll, most of the IRC users are students. There are also academics and other professional users of the internet, as well as a growing number of people with private internet access (see figure 1).

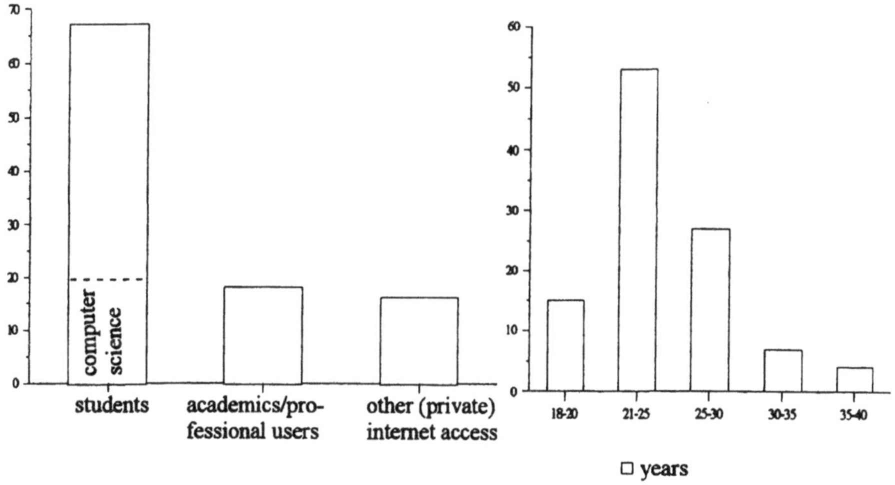

Figure 1: IRC users by profession and by age

The high percentage of students probably strongly influences the age distribution on IRC. The young age of the medium itself also accounts for the young average age of its users,[6] which has a great influence on the language used.

The distribution of male and female users (see figure 2) probably reflects the high percentage of students of technical majors – although there could be further reasons for IRC being used mostly by males.

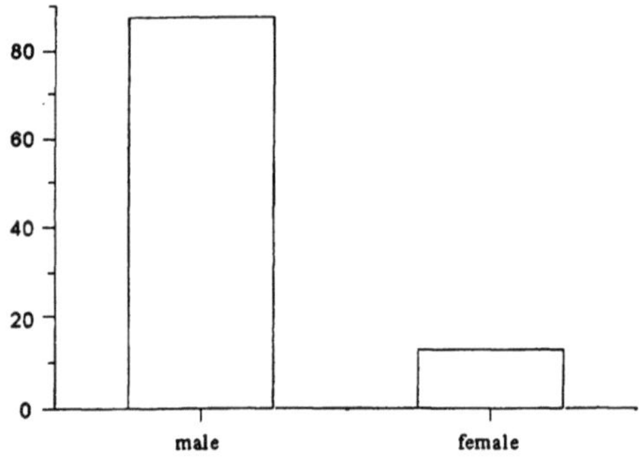

Figure 2: IRC users by gender

1.3. Content and motives of IRC communication

For people not personally acquainted with IRC, the mere thought of communicating via a computer terminal may seem horrid. A brief look into IRC by logging onto it and joining the next-best channel is very well suited to confirm prejudices such as the prevalence of "shrunken dialogues[7], disregard of polite respect and style", as Hess-Lüttich (1997) sees it.[8] Such a brief look into IRC can be compared to going downtown, walking into the next-best bar, pub or night-club and listen to the conversation there.

On IRC there is, of course, also exchange of messages taking place that can hardly be considered communication, as figure 3 illustrates.

<clax> who is from london???????
*** Goddezz has left channel #london
<Medo_> not me
<clax> who?
<clax> who?
*** clax has been kicked off channel #london by IMC ([nc] We heard you the first time [nc])
<Medo_> not me !
*** clax (adr) has joined channel #london
*** jets (adr) has joined channel #london
*** Medo_ has left channel #london
*** clax has left channel #london
<mayol> Rowan cannot speak English!
<Rowan> mayol is a real sucker
*** Rowan has left channel #london
* mayol ain't no sucker
<mayol> rowan is a fuckin' lamer
*** mitzy has left channel #london
<jets> Hi all, I am just showing this channel to my collegue
<trava> hay

<trava> hay
<Slowikus> Hi
*** trava has been kicked off channel #london IMC ([nc] We heard you the first time [nc])

Figure 3: Example for incoherent exchange of messages, taken from channel *London*, 25 users, March, 5th, 1998, 9:00 GMT

This, however, is not unique to the medium of IRC *per se*. One can easily think of a lot of face-to-face (FTF) situations like a late hour at a carnival, a group of youths in a disco, etc. where the sequence of utterances is comparably incoherent.

Hess-Lüttich also mentions typical characteristics of teenage and student slang (op. cit., p. 234). This is not very surprising when the average age of IRC interlocutors (see figure 1) is considered. It rather is evidence for people not changing their use of language when switching from FTF dialogue to communication on IRC. [9]

There are differences, though. IRC is a relatively young medium and there are quite a few users who have no idea what to use it for and how to use it. This is similar to the telephone being tried out for many purposes at first. Many of these it is not suited for, e.g. the transmission of concerts. Also it was not considered very useful at first. A Western Union internal memo of 1876 reads as follows: "This 'telephone' has too many shortcomings to be seriously considered as a means of communication. The device is inherently of no value to us."

The parameters accounting for the coherence and depth of dialogues might slightly differ for FTF communication and IRC. A large number of active interlocutors adversely affects meaningful exchange FTF and on IRC alike, but while virtual chat-rooms offer space for a principally unlimited number of interlocutors, pub tables do not. Furthermore the communication on channels with a regular crowd appears to be more coherent than that on channels where users join and leave by the second and do hardly know each other – if at all.

When the desire for an in-depth discussion of any topic arises, this is mostly taken to the 1:1 mode of private messaging. This is not unlike conversation at parties with two interlocutors noticing a topic of common interest and later discussing this in private.[10]

IRC communication today is almost exclusively a leisure activity. At any time of day or night, there are literally thousands of participants logged onto IRC. Potential communication partners on IRC can be anywhere: in the next building or on the other side of the world. The possibility of at least virtually crossing the distance between Europe and Singapore and sitting down for a chit-chat with people from other countries and cultures is one of the motives of using IRC, of course.

There are others, though, as the existence of local channels such as *erlangen* show. The idea of communication with persons via IRC and its medial distance with presence reduced to verbally transported information might seem very unappealing when compared to the possibility of meeting face-to-face. For a lot of users this initial anonymity is exactly what makes IRC interesting (see also section 1.5).

Another prominent aspect cannot be overlooked (see the examples given in section 2): the fun IRC users have playing with language. The necessity of fast and efficient communication may originally have lead to the invention and use of abbreviations, ideograms (emoticons) and similar means. A closer look at the language used on IRC channels suggests that having to write language rather suitable for spoken communication incites many IRC users to playfully twist the strict rules of written language. On German channels for instance, foreign words are integrated into German morphology ad hoc. This can be seen in figure 4 showing how the English word *idle* (the IRC term for being on a channel but not actively participating in the communication) undergoes German morphological processes. Corresponding creativity in language use has been described for the language of adolescents (see Schlobinski et al. 1993, pp. 27/121).

* Segler muss mal eben (kurz) wechidlen (xhope auch ;>)

...

* xhope idlet kurz wech mompls

...

<xhope> moin oberidler ;>

...

<M|CHA> fordi: na..idlest du wieder rum?...;)

...

<C0untZer0> idunno: muss num bischen idlen, also was tun :)

...

<Pockman> shecat: wechgeidlet

Figure 4: Integration of the lexeme *to idle* into German morphology

1.4. Speed

An important formative factor of IRC is its high speed – a speed otherwise only found in spoken communication:

> It is a written – or rather typed – form of communication that is transmitted, received and responded to within a time frame that has formerly been only thought relevant to spoken communication Reid (1991).

While interlocutors in FTF communication normally do not have difficulties with producing speech with sufficient pace, the production of written messages via a keyboard is inherently slower. Besides most IRC users are no trained typists and thus even slower at keying in what they want to say.

The prevalent speed gives rise to the necessity to formulate and type one's contributions fast and efficiently. This can be seen in the vast majority of contributions in the m:n mode of channel-based IRC communication as the examples in section 2 will show. The impact of the speed on time and potentiality to plan an utterance has already been discussed in Naumann (1995):

> One has to respond in an initial, frequently provoking statement by just one sentence or phrase or uttering and post this immediately. If you fail to do so and prefer to think first and then to compose a longer statement in reply before posting it electronically, the discussion might have gone on in the meantime, and your carefully thought out reply will no longer interest any more.

In order to be able to participate in channel communication in a reasonable way, IRC users have to adopt planning strategies of synchronous spoken communication.

1.5. Medial distance and anonymity on IRC

An interlocutor on IRC is sitting in front of a computer screen typing in messages to other users "visible" only by their nickname. The messages thus exchanged are exclusively text-based. Furthermore, they consist of standardized characters only. This totally rules out the perception of any nonverbal, paraverbal, status and position cues or any context information whatsoever. The transmitted content is purely verbal.

These medial characteristics made psychologists assume IRC – or CMC in general – to be deindividuated and marked by reduced self-awareness and self-control (e.g. Kiesler *et al.*, 1984). These assumptions appear to be contradicted by studies such as described in Myers (1987). Myers considers the (initial) anonymity to be "part of the magic".

The user poll mentioned in section 1.2 also indicates that the initial anonymity is an important part of IRC's appeal. There is the chance to meet and get to know other people without an interfering bias based on superficial traits like appearance, age, clothing, gender, etc. Moreover the anonymity of the medium IRC eases talking about personal matters or subjects that are usually considered taboo (see Reid 1991). Being protected by anonymity makes it possible for many participants to take part in a free exchange of thoughts with other IRC users. This can then be deepened to any extent. Serious discussions are mostly taken to the 1:1 mode of private IRC communication, though.

The anonymity can at any time be lifted to any extent that seems appropriate to the interlocutors involved – or as Seabrook (1994) put it in his widely quoted lines:

> Maybe this is the way lots of people will communicate in the future: meet on the information highway, exchange messages, get to know the lining of each other's mind, then meet face to face. In each other's physical presence, they will be able to eliminate a lot of the polite formalities that clutter people's encounters now, and say what they really mean.

Often IRC users exchange digitized photographs or their telephone numbers – in some cases even wedding rings –, and some meet face-to-face frequently on so-called *relay parties*. This stands in contradiction to the claim made in Naumann (1997, p. 167) saying that it is untypical for interlocutors to know each other on a more than superficial level.

2. Written speech?

Communication on IRC occurs in a graphical medium. Protocols of IRC sessions do, however, look more like transcriptions of spoken communication than anything one would consider a typical piece of written language. The idea that the simple dichotomy *spoken vs written* is not sufficient is not new: "No single dimension adequately accounts for the range of linguistic variation across spoken/written texts" Biber (1986, p. 385). Various approaches have been made at further differentiation of this simple distinction.

Figure 5 shows a classification of different forms of communication based on Lenke and Schmitz (1995, p. 120). It comprises the four attributes synchronous/asynchronous, local/remote, spoken/written, and one-to-one/one-to-many/many-to-many (1:1/1:n/m:n). The attribute pair spoken/written comprises only the aspect of the medial realisation; any other characteristics typically associated with it are not considered.

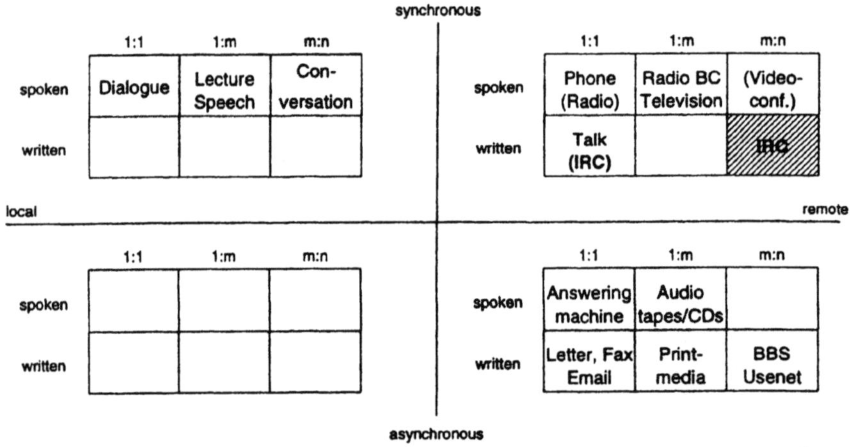

Figure 5: Classification of the form of communication on IRC. The attributes considered are: synchronous/asynchronous, spoken/written, local/remote, and one-to-one/one-to-many/many-to-many.

Noticeably figure 5 shows no forms of local, asynchronous communication. Asynchronous communication always requires the additional expenditure of storing and retrieving any utterances. Furthermore it does not allow direct interaction between interlocutors. In the case of local communication these disadvantages can be avoided. In remote conversation, however, either the secondary medium of written language is used or some technical means for snychronous or asynchronous bridging of distance has to be employed. If there is no restriction making the use of the written medium or technical means necessary, the acoustic medium is chosen for local communication, as figure 5 (left) shows.

For remote communication (right hand side of the diagram in figure 5), a relation between the attributes *synchronous* and *spoken* as well as between *asynchronous* and *written* becomes apparent.

Asynchronous, spoken forms of communication currently have only little relevance today. Documents in the written form can be structured more easily. A table of content and other visual structuring signs provide the possibility of non-linear random-access and browsing of a document. New technological means and further propagation of multimodal documents providing flexible access to non-written content might in fact increase the relevance of asynchronous spoken (or multimodal) communication. Furthermore increasingly widespread computerization of households together with systems like multi-media mail might boost this effect.

Until the introduction of CMC, all synchronous forms of communication took place in the primal spoken form – either without technical aid when local or via technical means when occurring remotely.

IRC was not only the first form of remote, synchronous communication providing the many-to-many mode. It also was the first form of synchronous communication in written form to become widespread.[11]

This accounts for the unique qualities of IRC as a hybrid between the synchronous forms of spoken speech and the asynchronous written medium (Lenke and Schmitz, 1995).

Due to the speed of communication prevalent on IRC, as well as its novelty and uniqueness, persons confronted with IRC at first might not have mechanisms and strategies at hand to produce written language appropriately. This leads to partial adoption and substitution of the well-known strategies and mechanisms of synchronous spoken communication, which allow for the necessary pace.

Koch and Österreicher (1990, p. 5) propose a distinction between medium and conception as illustrated by the examples given in figure 6. While the distinction of *acoustic* and *graphical* medium is strict, the poles of *conceptionally spoken* and *conceptionally written* span a continuum of possibilities.

	accoustic medium		
conceptionally spoken	dialogue	speech lecture	conceptionally written
	transcription comic balloons IRC	book newspaper	
	graphical medium		

Figure 6: Forms of communication by conception a medial realisation

The aspect of conceptual realisation is based on a set of nonverbal parameters having communicative relevance (op. cit., p. 8). These parameters are summarized by the polarity of communicative nearness and communicative distance (op. cit., p. 37).

Using a set of parameters – or rather, linguistic features – to define a dimension of textual variation has some similarities to the statistical analysis made in Biber (1986). Biber applies the multi-feature/multi-dimensional approach of factor analysis to a corpus of 545 texts (spoken and written English) of roughly 2000 words each, taking into account 41 linguistic features. He identifies "three fundamental parameters of textual variations which underlie speech and writing in English." The statistically most significant of these is labeled *Interactive vs. Edited Text.* In Biber (1988) four additional dimensions are identified. The dimension equivalent to *Interactive vs. Edited Text* remains the most important, though.

3. Substitution of cues

The aspect of medial distance (or anonymity) and the question of characteristics of spoken and written language cannot be discussed independently. Section 1.5 has shown that there is a great medial distance on IRC – a graphical medium hiding any social and context cues. Still this anonymity of IRC does not prevent interlocutors from getting to know each other well. Furthermore the interactive dialogues of IRC look more like transcription of spoken dialogues than written exchange. This gives a hint that IRC users do not feel the medial distance during their dialogues.

Höflich (1996, pp. 72) proposes the concept of *social presence*[12] as opposed to the concept of purely medial distance, disregarding context and purpose of communication on the respective medium. A crucial factor is the medial capacity to transmit nonverbal cues.

As mentioned in the introduction, IRC does not allow the immediate transmission of such cues. Instead, a repertoire of substitutions has been emerging on its own. Some of these – like the operator status – are unique to IRC. Some have been used in other contexts before as e.g. Hess-Lüttich (1997, p. 237) points out.

These may either have been "reinvented" because they are intuitively understandable or may have been directly transferred from other media – like e.g. verbal stems, coming from comic balloons via teenage and student slang into IRC.

It is questionable, however, whether IRC users should consciously have transferred these substitutions from literature to use on IRC. Given the iconicity of the means of substitution described in the following subsections it might well be that their use on IRC springs from the same kind of creativity that inspired the authors cited by Hess-Lüttich (p. 237).

3.1. Substitution of nonverbal cues

One common way of substituting nonverbal cues is the built-in action command: This command produces output in the third person form. If someone with the nick of *Ju^el* e.g. types */me nods*, the output will be as shown in figure 7. The second example also shows that presence and absence (from the terminal) is very often explicitly signalled by interlocutors on IRC. Another common way of substituting nonverbal cues are verbs or verbal stems braced by asterisks. These also signal an action virtually performed: *Ginny* grins, *Hopeless* hugs *espirit* hello, and *Pepels* gives a special *hugeli-hug* to someone else. This form of verbally describing nonverbal actions probably is derived from verbs/verbal stems used in a similar way in comics (sigh, yell, moan, etc.).

The second set of examples for this use of verbal stems (taken from the German and the English IRC corpus) shows that there may also be objects, adverbs, etc. inside the asterisks. These examples also show a playfulness of language use that can often be seen on IRC.

* Ju^el nods
* Pepels is back btw

<Ginny> *grin*
<Hopeless> hi espirit *hug*
<Pepels> *HUGELIHUG*

evilglint *headshaking*
honkknuddel *Megaknuddel* *aluganzdollknuddel*

Figure 7: Examples for substitution of nonverbal cues

A third way of substitution of nonverbal cues are the well-known emoticons or smileys that had already been widespread on Bulletin-Board Systems before IRC was invented. Once it is clear that smileys have to be read sideways their meaning is iconic. The following smileys: :-) :-(;-) :-| :-o are recognizable as a smile, a frown, a wink, something between a smile and a frown, and open-mouthed astonishment, respectively without further explanation (see also table 1).

Books like Sanderson (1993) might give the impression that smileys are not iconic. This book, as well as other smiley lists contain a lot of smileys that are not iconic. Mentioning three smileys representing Ronald Reagan, Charlie Chaplin and Goerge Washington – as in Hess-Lüttich (1997, p. 236) – is very amusing, but does not tell anything about the use of smileys on IRC. First, the mentioned smileys were most probably not meant as icons transporting non-verbal information but as riddles (much like so-called droodles). Second, a look into the use of smileys in IRC communication gives quite another impression as can be seen in table 1. Apart from the smileys shown in this table there were none to be found in the IRC corpus. Not more than eight types of emoticons (with several minor variations) were used. More than ninety percent of these are slight variations of the simple smiley or frowney. So in actual communication on IRC there is no *code to break* (Hess-Lüttich 1997, p. 237) to understand the use of emoticons. The occurrence of emoticons with the character of a riddle is confined to smiley collections on the World Wide Web or in books. Vice versa, these lists and books do not have the character of a code-book to be learned before being able to partake in IRC communication – they are meant to amuse in a similar way droodles are meant to.

<table>
<tr><th>Type of smiley</th><th>Subtypes</th><th>Frequency of subtype</th><th>Frequency of type</th></tr>
<tr><td rowspan="5">Smiley</td><td>:)</td><td>1056</td><td rowspan="5">1308</td></tr>
<tr><td>:) :)) ...</td><td>193</td></tr>
<tr><td>: -)</td><td>38</td></tr>
<tr><td>: -)) : -)) ...</td><td>16</td></tr>
<tr><td>:o) :0)</td><td>10</td></tr>
<tr><td rowspan="4">Frowney</td><td>:(</td><td>115</td><td rowspan="4">192</td></tr>
<tr><td>:((:(((...</td><td>66</td></tr>
<tr><td>:-(</td><td>10</td></tr>
<tr><td>:-((</td><td>1</td></tr>
<tr><td rowspan="3">Sticking out tongue</td><td>:P :p</td><td>48</td><td rowspan="3">84</td></tr>
<tr><td>:PP :PPP ...</td><td>29</td></tr>
<tr><td>:oP :op</td><td>7</td></tr>
<tr><td>Drooling</td><td>:P~ :P~~ :P~~~ ...</td><td colspan="2">14</td></tr>
<tr><td>Devilish remark</td><td>:> :-> :->>></td><td colspan="2">13</td></tr>
<tr><td>Slight frown</td><td>:/ :\ : |</td><td colspan="2">11</td></tr>
<tr><td>Open mouthed smile</td><td>:D</td><td colspan="2">10</td></tr>
</table>

Table 1: List of types of emoticons and their frequencies in the English IRC corpus (28345 lines) used for this paper

3.2 Substitution of paraverbal cues

Many paraverbal cues can easily be transcribed and thus transported into the purely verbal medium of IRC. Most of the methods of transcriptions employed on IRC have of course been used many times before in other circumstances, probably mostly because they are intuitively understandable and thus need no further explanation.

Reduplication and upper case are among the most common transcription of paraverbal cues used on IRC. Reduplication is especially suited for use on IRC as the effort for typing it is very low: one has to simply leave the typing finger on the key already hit. Reduplication of a vowel represents dilatation as it would occur in speech. Reduplication of the exclamation mark also lends special emphasis to a remark. This is often used in greetings to show excitement, as can be seen in the examples in figure 8. In the second example *DaMo* and *nedd* greet each other using reduplication (and typing in upper case) thus showing great appreciation of virtually meeting each other.

<lippy> hiii!!!
<May--> HELOOOOOOOOOoo

<nedd> DaMo!!!!!!!!!!!!!!!!!!
<LilStar> DaMo?
<DaMo> If I'm lagged they'll be hell to pay
<DaMo> NEDD ! ! ! ! !! !
<dal> HELLO BITCH2
<Bitch2> hi dal
<Bitch2> dont shout though please

Figure 8: Examples for reduplication and use of upper case.

In the third example in figure 8, *dal* greets *bitch2* with a message typed all in upper case, which is interpreted as shouting. The interpretation of upper case as loudness is done intuitively and probably without much conscious effort, as messages in upper case stand out against the stream of channel communication, which usually is all typed in lower case letters.

Interestingly many IRC users make almost no use of punctuation marks. Instead they often transcribe pauses as they would occur if their messages were spoken. Pauses are transcribed as three (or more) consecutive dots. It can be argued that punctuation marks belong to written language while pauses belong to the primal form of spoken language. Being secondary, the planning strategies of written language are much slower and require more effort than the strategies of the primal spoken form of language (which never had to be learned consciously). Under the pressure of the high speed of communication on IRC interlocutors thus fall back on the strategies of spoken language. Planning a pause for spoken language and transcribing it is a lot faster than planning the right punctuation mark – even if it is a single period compared to three or four consecutive dots, as can be seen in figure 9.

<^CopyCat> and u expect it from me .... i am impressed

<Garpur> hi rif
<RifRaf> how's by you?
[...]
<Garpur> fine... buisier every day

Figure 9: Transcription of pauses on IRC

The transcription of pauses commonly found in IRC communication already gives the impression of interlocutors keying in what they actually would speak. Another indication for this is the transcription of variations in pronunciation: be it colloquial speech or a dialect. In figure 10, we have the examples *Gawd, kinda, ye, yer.*

<Lorry> Gawd, this summary is longer than the original ;)
<scotfife> kinda defeats the purpose dont ye think
<Billabong> yer a little boy! LOL!

Figure 10: Transcription of variations in pronunciation

3.3 Compensation of missing status and presence cues

IRC does not provide the possibility to see whether another (potential) interlocutor whose nick is listed in a channel is really present at his or her terminal and following the communication on the channel. It is not uncommon for IRC users to join a channel and not participate actively in the communication but rather wait for a certain person to show up or an interesting topic to be discussed (IRC jargon calls this: to idle).

Thus IRC users have to first check out if the people listed in a channel are listening and willing to communicate. This has fostered the development of elaborate greeting rituals typical of IRC. Even an IRC-specific neologism to greet upon re-entering a channel (or returning attention to a channel) has evolved.

In the short example in figure 11, MrJack reenters the channel australia, is greeted with *wb* (welcome back) by nedd and answers with *re* (actually a short form of *rehi*).

*** MrJack (adr) has joined channel #australia
<MrJack> back
[...]
<nedd> ,mrjack wb

[...]
<MrJack> re nedd

Figure 11: Example of the IRC-specific neologism *rehi/re* used upon re-entering a channel.

Additionally an IRC-specific status cue has evolved as part of the typical greeting ritual: the so-called *operator status* or simply *op*. The operator status is a built-in mode, that allows a user to change certain attributes of a channel, remove other users etc. While the operator status is seldom used for anything else besides giving the operator status to other users, it could be used to seriously disturb the communication on a channel. Accordingly giving the operator status to another user is a sign of sympathy and trust. In figure 12 *Lifeforce* enters the channel *20+*, is greeted by *Kickoff2* and given an op by *Sheryl*.

*** Lifeforce (adr) has joined channel #20+
<Kickoff2> Hiya Life
[...]
*** Mode change "+o Lifeforce" on channel #20+ by Sheryl

Figure 12: Assigning the operator status as part of a greeting ritual

Recently this has been taken a step further: IRC robots have become widespread as channel guardians and op-givers. They give ops to members of the regular crowd of a channel. In this case, the op has become a status cue visible to and interpretable by all other channel users.

4. Conclusions

Textual variation of spoken and written text cannot be sufficiently described by a simple distinction *spoken vs. written*. To classify texts satisfactorily, several factors must be taken into account. The most important of these, according to Biber, is the continuum of *Interactive vs. Edited Text*. There is no doubt that interactiveness is the most important characteristic of IRC. For IRC users (as well as for readers of IRC protocols) communicating on IRC does not feel like written exchange. The other interlocutors are virtually present and respond immediately. The speed of communication is that of spoken dialogues. This situation gave rise to a common and intuitively understandable repertoire of substitutions for nonverbal and paraverbal cues to make communication easier – that is: more similar to the well-known spoken communication.

This also touches upon the question of communicative distance, which cannot be limited on purely medial characteristics. A concept of perceived anonymity is better suited for an adequate description. Even though IRC users consider the anonymity of the medium to be part of the appeal of IRC, the substitutions for nonverbal and paraverbal cues also lessen the medial anonymity – thus creating a perceived presence (or virtual presence) of interlocutors, a presence which is substantial enough to be the start of friendships or even marriages. Still this perceived presence lacks a few things a face-to-face meeting offers. And so IRC friendships only take their beginning on the medium IRC but seldom stay confined to it.

IRC is a relatively young medium of communication with its own advantages and its own shortcomings. The rapidly growing number of IRC users suggest that IRC has firmly established itself in its own special niche which was unoccupied before. It will neither supplant face-to-face meetings, telephone calls nor letters – much like the latter two never replaced the former but added to the variety.

Notes

1) Probably a mixture of those forms is prevalent – like in FTF m:n conversation where one occasionally will communicate with one's neighbour only.
2) Considering the typical content of IRC communication, the term *chatroom* or *virtual café* might seem more appropriate.
3) Some of the names even remain unintelligible because they were originally written in another character set. E.g.: something written in the japanese code-set jis_x0201 will look like gibberish when displayed with the code-set latin-1 (ISO-88591).
4) Apart from that, there's the technical necessity to use channels for m:n communication. Otherwise thousands of IRC users would be forced to communicate with each other simultaneously. Like in FTF m:n communication, there's an upper limit on the number of persons actively participating in a conversation.
5) The email addresses of the recipients were taken directly from IRC during two different sessions around noon on two different days.
6) The average age has even become younger since the user poll of 1997 according to the subjective impressions of the author – most probably due to cheaper and easier Internet access, which has made *net-surfing* a popular pastime for teenagers.
7) Originally: *Dialoge in Schrumpfform*
8) Hess-Lüttich furthermore mocks at fun being one of the aims of communication on IRC. (op. cit., p. 233) but leaves open if he really deems fun an outlandish motive for involving in a pastime.
9) The prevailing informal address of *Du* and christian name mentioned by Hess-Lüttich is not a prolonged version of the *Du* used by students (*Verlängerte Form des Schüler- und Studenten-Du*) (op. cit., p. 234). It is the very same address persons of the age group 18-25 (which

accounted for 69% of the IRC users answering the user poll) typically use when meeting face-to-face.

10) Unlike the communication on channels which can be logged automatically to serve as data for an IRC corpus, a corpus of private messages is not so easy to obtain and has yet to be presented. Until then the nature of private dialogues can only be guessed at from personal experience. Nonetheless it may not be totally disregarded when discussing the medium of IRC.
11) Talk has been used for a longer time but -besides only providing an inconvenient one-to-one-mode only- never really became widespread. It's users were mostly professional Internet users.
12) Originally: *Soziale Präsenz*

References

Biber, D. (1986): Spoken and Written Textual Dimensions in English: Resolving the Contradictory Findings. – In: Language (Journal of the Linguistic Society of America), June 1986, 62(2), p. 384-414.

Biber, D. (1988): Variation across speech and writing. Cambridge University Press, Cambridge.

Hambridge, S. (1995): Netiquette Guidelines, [online] <http://www.dtcc.edu/cs/rfc1855.html>

Hess-Lüttich, E.W.B. (1997): E-Epistolographie: Briefkultur im Medienwandel. – In: Hepp, A., Winter, R. (eds): Kultur – Medien – Macht: Cultural Studies und Medienanalyse, Westdeutscher Verlag. Opladen.

Höflich, J.R. (1996): Technisch vermittelte interpersonale Kommunikation, Westdeutscher Verlag. Opladen.

Kiesler, S., Siegel, J., McGuire, T.W. (1984): Social psychological aspects of computer-mediated communication. – In: American Psychologist, 39, p. 1123-1134.

Koch, P., Österreicher, W. (1990): Gesprochene Sprache in der Romania, Max Niemeyer Verlag. Tübingen.

Lenke, N., Schmitz, P. (1995): Geschwätz im „Globalen Dorf" – Kommunikation im Internet. – In: Osnabrücker Beiträge zur Sprachtheorie, Bd. 50, p. 117-141.

Myers, D. (1987): Anonymity is part of the magic: Individual manipulation of computer-mediated communication contexts. – In: Qualitative Sociology, 1987, 10(3), p. 251-266.

Naumann, B. (1995): Mailbox Chats: Dialogues in Electronic Communication. – In: Future Perspectives of Dialogue Analysis, Franz Hundsnurscher, Edda Weigand (eds.): Beiträge zur Dialogforschung, Bd. 8, p. 162-184. Max Niemeyer Verlag, Tübingen.

Naumann, B. (1997): IRCs – schriftliche Sonderformen von Mehrpersonengesprächen. – In: Dialogue Analysis, Edda Weigand (ed.): Beiträge zur Dialogforschung, Bd. 13, p. 161-178. Max Niemeyer Verlag, Tübingen.

Parks, M.R., Floyd, K. (1996): Making Friends in Cyberspace. – In: Journal of Communication 46(1), [online] <http://www.usc.edu/dept/annenberg/vol1/issue4/parks.html>

Rehm, G., Huber, M., Krumeich, A., Haase M. (1997): Internetkommunikation und Sprachwandel. – In: Schrift computerbasierter Medien und die Bildung sprachlicher Normen, Rüdiger Weingarten (ed.). Westdeutscher Verlag, Opladen.

Reid, E.M. (1991): Electropolis: Communication and Community, On Internet Relay Chat. University of Melbourne, Department of History.

Sanderson, D.W. (1993): Smileys, O'Reilly. Sebastopol/CA.

Schlobinski, P., Kohl, G., Ludewigt, I. (1993): Jugendsprache. Westdeutscher Verlag, Opladen

Schulze, M. (1998): English IRC-Corpus, [online] <http://www.linguistik.uni-erlangen.de/~max/Tree/irc.html>

Seabrook, J. (1994): E-Mail from Bill. – In: The New Yorker, January 1994, p. 48-61.

Rainer Geers

Der Faktor Sprache im unendlichen Daten(t)raum
Eine linguistische Betrachtung von Dialogen im Internet Relay Chat

1. Einleitung

Der Faktor Sprache stellt sich dem Betrachter der verschiedenen Kommunikationsdienste des Internet als ein grundlegender Baustein dar, um virtuelle Räume zu schaffen. Trotz der Wichtigkeit von Sprache und Kommunikation in globalen Computernetzwerken wendet sich die Linguistik nur zögerlich dem neuen Forschungsfeld der Computer-Mediated Communication, kurz CMC, zu. Und dies, obwohl globale Computernetzwerke und ihre Kommunikationsdienste allseits als eine Erfindung beschworen werden, die die menschliche Kommunikation revolutionieren wird. Linda Harasim (1993) kann in ihrer Einschätzung stellvertretend zitiert werden.

> Global networks are communication networks, media that connect people with other people. Historically, the introduction of new communication tolls has transformed humanity. From the development of oral language to literacy, print, and now new telecommunications, communication technologies have opened new doors for human contact and new avenues for social, intellectual, economic, and political growth. Global networks, the use of computers for international communication, will further enhance and expand how humans connect, communicate, and create community. (Harasim 1993, 3)

Wie Rheingold (1994, 18) zu Recht formuliert, erweist sich die gesamte Geschichte der CMC als eine Entwicklung, in der Menschen Technologien, die für einen bestimmten Zweck entwickelt wurden, für ihre eigenen, vollkommen anderen *Kommunikationsbedürfnisse* adaptierten. Dies trifft vor allem bei der Entwicklung des Internet als ursprünglich militärischem Forschungsprojekt zu, das den atomschlagsicheren Austausch technischer Daten zwischen Computern ermöglichen sollte.

2. Computer-Mediated Communication: Ein neues Forschungsfeld wird entdeckt

Die bisher vorgelegten Forschungen im Bereich der CMC sind äußerst heterogen und entbehren eine gemeinsame theoretische Grundlage. Michael Metz stellt fest.

> (...) there is no cohesive groundwork for studying CMC, and, as a result, there is no fundamental theory which guides CMC resaerch. There are no metatheoretical sources available on CMC, leading research about the research. (Metz 1994, 32)

Er verlangt eine Theoriebildung, die sich der Tatsache stellt, daß CMC ein Medium ist, in dem die gesamte Natur der menschlichen Kommunikation verändert wird. Metz fordert, CMC als einen neuen Kontext interdisziplinär wahrzunehmen und zu theoretisieren, der unter der Perspektive menschlicher Handlungen zu untersuchen ist. Dem Wunsch nach einer disziplinübergreifenden Theoriebildung versucht Höflich (1996) in seinem Buch „Technisch vermittelte interpersonale Kommunikation" für den Bereich der Kommunikationswissenschaft mit einem ersten Impuls nachzukommen. Bevor die Anregung eines interdisziplinären Diskurses aufgenommen wird, müßte jedoch jedes Wissenschaftsfach zuerst in seinen eigenen Grenzen die verschiedenen CMC-formen analysieren.

Nach Fuller (1994) und Chesebro/Bonsall (1989) zerfällt das Feld der CMC in zwei Bereiche, in den Bereich des „Mensch-Maschine" Dialogs und den des „Mensch-Maschine-Mensch" Dialogs, wobei uns der zweite Bereich interessiert. Neben den ursprünglich allein technisch-ingenieurwissenschaftlichen Untersuchungen haben sich mittlerweile nahezu alle wissenschaftlichen Disziplinen, vor allem die Soziologie und Kommunikationswissenschaft, die die Kommunikationsformen des Internets als kulturelle Phänomene untersuchen, der CMC zugewendet. Das Spektrum der CMC-Forschung zeigt eine heterogene Vielfalt. Die Linguistik hingegen beschäftigt sich mit dem Forschungsfeld selten, so daß der Äußerung von Baron aus dem Jahre 1984 immer noch zugestimmt werden kann:

> Linguistic studies of computer mediated communication are still in their infancy, barely reaching beyond the realm of anecdotal observation. (Baron 1984, 128)

Zu selten tauchen Arbeiten wie der Sammelband „Computer-Mediated Communication" von Susan Herring (1996) auf. In Bezug auf den Internet Relay Chat, kurz IRC, erscheint die Forschungsliteratur besonders spärlich. Die Dissertation von Elizabeth Reid (1991) kann neben Artikeln von Lenke/ Schmitz (1995), Werry (1996) und Naumann (1997) genannt werden. Und dies, obwohl alle wissenschaftlichen Disziplinen nach den Worten Reids zur Überprüfung ihrer Grundannahmen in der Auseinandersetzung mit dem IRC gezwungen werden.

> If IRC, and computer-mediated communication in general, is to be fully understood and analysed, the conventions of many disciplines must be deconstructed. Linguistics, communication theory, sociology, anthropology – and history – are challenged by the culture shared by the users of IRC. The divisions between spoken and written, and synchronous and asynchronous forms of language, are broken down. (Reid 1991, n.pag.)

Die Überprüfung dieser Dekonstruktionshypothese kommunikativer Grundaxiome in computervermittelter Kommunikation muß der Fokus eines stärker geführten linguistischen Diskurses sein.

3. Internet Relay Chat: Merkmale einer neuen Kommunikationsform

Mit IRC wird eine im Internet als Zusatzdienst existierende globale Kommunikationsform bezeichnet, innerhalb der sich mehrere Internetnutzer, egal wo auf der Welt sie sich mit ihrem Computer in das Internet eingeloggt haben, zeitlich synchron per Tastatur unterhalten können.

Zwei Dimensionen sind zu unterschieden, zum einen eine technische, in der IRC als Softwareprogramm zu betrachten ist, dessen technische Anlage die Konversationen in ihren Diskursmerkmalen beeinflußt, und zum anderen die Dimension von IRC als Subkultur, einem virtuell geschaffenen Raum, in dem sich Gruppen über die Sprache konstituieren und eine Welt mit eigenen Konventionen und kommunikativen Strukturen ausbilden.

Die Architektur des IRC, die Organisation in Kanälen, gestattet es einer beliebig großen Menschenmenge gleichzeitig miteinander zu kommunizieren. In einem Kanal werden alle Äußerungen, technisch müßte von mit der Returntaste abgeschickten schriftlichen Beiträgen gesprochen werden, untereinander linearisiert. Dies führt dazu, daß jeder Nutzer eines Kanals jede Äußerung lesen kann. Die Konversationen werden schneller, je mehr Anwender sich in einem Kanal zu Wort melden. D.h. die Äußerungen rollen schneller über den oberen Bildschirmrand hinweg, so daß die Beiträge kürzer werden, um gesprächsrelevant zu bleiben.

Da sich in einem Kanal selten alle Teilnehmer gleichzeitig über dasselbe Thema unterhalten, bestehen explizite Adressierungskonventionen. Ein IRCer, der einem anderen etwas sagen will, schickt dessen *Nick*, dessen IRC-Spitznamen, seiner Äußerung voraus. Dadurch können *Chatter* leicht die an sie gerichteten Äußerungen identifizieren. Durch die explizite Adressierung und die Linearisierung aller Äußerungen nach ihrem Absendezeitpunkt ist sowohl das System des Turn-taking, wie es in der face-to-face Kommunikation vorkommt, als auch die Überlappung von Redebeiträgen nicht möglich. Jeder Anwender wählt seinen Turn frei nach seiner Motivation, sich an einem Gespräch zu beteiligen. Murray stellt zu Recht fest:

> Thus there is an absence of turn-allocation techniques such as adjacency pairs or tag questions. This complex interaction results in layered topics, multiple speech acts and interleaved turns. The turn-taking model does not adequately account for this mode of interaction. (Murray 1989, 319)

Obwohl diese Beurteilung aufgrund der technischen Gegebenheiten einleuchtend ist, stellt sie keinen Konsens innerhalb einer Diskussion dar, in der auch das Gegenteil vertreten wird (Vgl. Wilkins (1991), Hirst (1991), Chapman (1992) und Maynor (1994)). Dieser Punkt der Dialogorganisation ist ein prägnantes Merkmal des IRC, das die Dekonstruktionshypothese wissenschaftlicher Grundannahmen für die Linguistik im Sinne Reids untermauern könnte.

Reid (1991), Rheingold (1994) und Sittek (1995) betrachten IRC als Subkultur. Nach Rheingold (1994, 219) konnte diese weltweite Subkultur aufgrund dreier Elemente hervorgebracht werden. Zum ersten durch künstliche, aber stabile Identitäten, zum zweiten durch Schlagfertigkeit der Nutzer und zum dritten durch die Verwendung von Worten, um für die Konversation einen imaginären gemeinsamen Kontext, einen virtuellen Raum zu schaffen.

Die einzige sichtbare Identität eines Nutzers hängt an dem Gebrauch seines Nicks, dessen Doppelbenutzung nicht möglich ist. Die Identitäten werden diskursiv aufgebaut, allein durch ihre kommunikative Ausgestaltung im Gespräch mit anderen. Das von mir erstellte Korpus[1] von IRC-Sitzungen belegt den Aufbau stabiler Identitäten. Bekannte IRCer werden oftmals mit der Verleihung des Channeloperatorstatus als Anerkennung begrüßt und zurückliegende Gespräche häufig aufgegriffen. Außerdem wird in Kanälen direkt nach der Anwesenheit von Nutzern gefragt. In vielen Kanälen besteht ein Stammnutzerzirkel. Die so geschaffene Gewißheit über die Identitäten der Teilnehmer ist zwar minimal, aber für den Diskurs notwendig, um eine virtuelle Gemeinschaft zu etablieren.

Als zweites konstituierendes Merkmal nennt Rheingold Schlagfertigkeit, unter der er die Fähigkeiten versteht, die ein IRCer besitzen muß, um an der per Tastatur generierten, extrem dynamischen Kommunikation teilnehmen zu können. Die Gesprächsdynamik wird durch das unmittelbare Erscheinen von abgeschickten Äußerungen in einem Kanal verursacht. Je größer die Beteiligung in einem Kanal ist, desto stärker sind die Chatter durch die höhere Bildlaufgeschwindigkeit dazu gezwungen, ihre Beiträge schneller in den Kanal zu senden. Ob ein Teilnehmer in jenem virtuellen Raum erfolgreich an Konversationen teilnimmt, hängt daher von schneller Auffassungsgabe, verbaler Schlagfertigkeit und dem technischen Vermögen ab, Gedanken schnell verschriftlichen zu können. Die Kommunikationssituation im IRC stellt in dieser Hinsicht eine bisher ungekannte Kommunikationsform dar, die sich technisch gesehen auf schriftliche Kommunikation stützt, in ihrer dialogischen Form jedoch eher der mündlichen Kommunikation entspricht, welches durch die zeitliche Abfolge von Rede und Gegenrede assoziiert wird. Die schriftlichen Dialoge sind zeitlich synchron, so daß das für die mündliche Kommunikation typische Merkmal spontaner Reaktionen zum ersten Mal einer schriftlich basierten Dialogform zugesprochen werden kann.

Nach Schütz (1995, 112) ergibt sich im IRC eine Modifikation des Textproduzenten- und Rezipientenverhaltens, die nicht viel Zeit besitzen, einen Text zu schreiben oder zu lesen. Wie in der face-to-face Kommunikation ist eine Korrektur der Äußerungen nicht möglich, dies wird durch die Häufigkeit und Vielfalt von Tippfehlern belegt. Die nach Rupp (1965, 20) ausschließlich der mündlichen Kommunikation zugesprochene Spontaneität von Äußerungen ist somit in elektronischen, schriftlich basierten Gesprächen zu finden, oder, wie Chafe (1988, 116) es nennt, *involvement* statt des vermuteten *detachment*.

„Sprachliche Elaboriertheit" als Merkmal schriftlicher Kommunikation, die zu konzeptioneller Schriftlichkeit, zu fortschreitender Trennung des Geschriebenen und Gesprochenen führe (Gauger 1986, 37), kann aufgrund der auftauchenden schriftlichen Dialogdynamik nicht mehr untermauert werden. Aus primär zeitökonomischen Gründen, d.h. zur Steigerung der Schreibeffizienz, werden die bisher eher der Schriftsprache zugeschriebenen standardsprachlichen Normen nicht mehr erfüllt. Es tauchen viele Tippfehler und grammatikalische Fehler auf. Sowohl Kommata als auch Punkte werden nur in den Fällen verwendet, in denen sie zur Verständlichkeit einer Äußerung notwendig sind. Der Sprachgebrauch tendiert zur sogenannten Umgangssprache. Dies zeigen häufige umgangssprachliche Kontraktionen, Ellipsen, Wortverschleifungen, Interjektionen, dialektale Ausdrücke und Soziolekte, sowie der Gebrauch vieler englischer Worte und Wendungen. Nach Rosenbaum (1996) kann von der Entwicklung eines *chat-slang*, einer eigenen *Internet-Sprache* gesprochen werden. Das Ökonomieprinzip steht im IRC eindeutig als Maxime der Äußerungsproduktion im Vordergrund.

4. Die Substitutionsversuche des non- und paraverbalen Verhaltens im IRC

Das von Rheingold genannte dritte Merkmal von IRC, mit dessen Hilfe eine virtuelle Gemeinschaft konstituiert wird, ist die Schaffung des sozialen Kontextes, einer virtuellen Realität ausschließlich über den Gebrauch von Wörtern.

Der komplett fehlende Bereich der non- und paraverbalen Äußerungsmöglichkeiten wird von den IRCern als extremer Nachteil empfunden, wie der Sozialpsychologe Pelz (1988) anschaulich zeigen konnte. Aus dieser Motivation wurde ein interessantes Repertoire an Symbol- und Äußerungskonventionen hervorgebracht, um die fehlende Materialisierung des virtuellen Kommunikationsraumes sprachlich zu substituieren.

Die Groß- und Kleinschreibung wird konventionell umgedeutet. Um die Intonation, die Sprechlautstärke minimal zu substituieren, besteht die Konvention, daß die Großschreibung von Wörtern das Schreien derselben bedeutet und die Kleinschreibung die normale Äußerungslautstärke bezeichnet.

5144 <RUBIO> MOIN!!!
...
5157 <Reisswolf> RUBIO: Bruellst hier ungefragt rum - was ( )[2]

Tendenziell wird aus zeitökonomischen Gründen klein geschrieben. Auch Lautdehnungen und Interjektionen werden verschriftlicht.

2249 <ZaphodB> guuuuuuuuuuuutaaaaaaaa mooooooooooooond, du gehst stihilleeeeeee.

Der Versuch, Lautproduktionen, Interjektionen realer face-to-face Kommunikation, die normalerweise nichtmorphemisierte Äußerungen sind, schriftlich darzustellen, erweckt den Eindruck der Nähe der IRC-Kommunikation zur gesprochenen Sprache. Vor allem Interjektionen werden auf vielfältige Weise zum Ausdruck von körperlichen und seelischen Empfindungen, zur Beurteilung von Äußerungen oder zur Aufforderung einer Äußerungserwiderung genutzt.

Besonders charakteristisch für IRC-Gespräche ist der Gebrauch von Emoticons, Akronymen, Actions und Actionsstrips. Akronyme können im deutschsprachigen IRC aufgrund ihres seltenen und auf wenige beschränkten Gebrauchs (s.u.) vernachlässigt werden.

Akronyme brb = be right back cu = see you (later) btw = by the way
afaik = as far as I know [3]

Chatter empfinden ihre Dialoge im IRC vielmehr als Gespräche und weniger als primär schriftliche Konversationen. Die Synchronizität der IRC-Gespräche ist für den auftauchenden Sprachgebrauch konstitutiver als die Tatsache, daß die Nutzer sich über ein graphisches Medium verständigen. Sie erzeugt das Verlangen, die im Gegensatz zur realen face-to-face Kommunikation geschlossenen kommunikativen Kanäle zu öffnen, um die dialogische Verständigung zu erleichtern. Da im IRC keine Möglichkeit zur überlegten und differenzierten schriftlichen Stellungnahme gegeben ist, zeigt der Substitutionsversuch von Mimik und Gestik, wie wichtig diese kommunikativen Mittel für die Verständigung vor allem in dynamischer Kommunikation sind.

Emoticons, meistens wird von Smilies gesprochen, deren häufiger Gebrauch ihre Wichtigkeit vermuten läßt, fungieren wie Mimik und Gestik in face-to-face Dialogen.

Emoticons	Standardemoticons	Sonderemoticons
	:-) = fröhlich	=:o) = Bill Clinton
	:-(= traurig (Frowney)	*<I:-) = Santa Claus
	;-) = augenzwinkernd (ironisch)	$-) = Yuppie
	:-o = schockiert, erstaunt	%*@;-(= verkatert

Sanderson sammelte 1995 ca. 650 verschiedene Emoticonarten im IRC. Der Gebrauch ist jedoch wesentlich beschränkter, wie die nachfolgende Auswertung zeigt.

<table>
<tr><td>Emoticonarten</td><td>:-) ;-) :) ;) :-(;-(:(;(;o) :oo) :o(O) :_) :*) .-) .o) .) :-Q :-/ :/ :? :µ) :-x .)(:-p d=) ;-= =) =| :=) (: ;-)~~</td></tr>
<tr><td>Emoticonsumme</td><td>1544</td></tr>
<tr><td>Actionsumme</td><td>796</td></tr>
<tr><td>Actionstripsumme</td><td>531</td></tr>
<tr><td>Akronymesumme</td><td>154</td></tr>
<tr><td>Äußerungssumme insgesamt</td><td>7654</td></tr>
<tr><td>Netsplits</td><td>1</td></tr>
<tr><td>Häufigkeit der Topicänderungen</td><td>14</td></tr>
<tr><td>Umbenennungen von Nicknames</td><td>38</td></tr>
<tr><td>Häufigkeit des „kick“-Befehls</td><td>16</td></tr>
<tr><td>Channeloperatorstatusverleihung</td><td>135</td></tr>
<tr><td>Servermeldungen</td><td>1203</td></tr>
<tr><td>Hereinschauende</td><td>130</td></tr>
<tr><td>Rückkehrersumme</td><td>127</td></tr>
<tr><td>Teilnehmer insgesamt</td><td>467</td></tr>
</table>

Tabelle: Empirische Auswertung des Gesamtkorpus

Mit ihnen werden Stimmungen ausgedrückt und Standardäußerungen in vielfältiger Hinsicht relativiert (Vgl. Naumann 1997). Die Mehrdeutigkeit von Äußerungen kann mit diesem komprimierten Symbolinventar eingeschränkt werden, um Mißverständnisse zu vermeiden.

6128 <Groover> rene: smilies sind sehr sinnvoll - ohne sie waere das [Verstehen] bedeutend schwieriger

Emoticons dienen zur Prävention von Mißverständnissen, zur Verstärkung von negativen, aggressiven und positiven Äußerungen. Auch wenn die Bedeutungen von Emoticons festgelegt scheinen, zeigen die aktuellen Korpusbeispiele eine Verwendung, die deutlich macht, daß ihre Bedeutung und Funktion innerhalb seines kommunikativen Kontextes erschlossen werden muß.

4561	<Gueze>	hi olav: noch immer am telekom stand?
...		
4564	<olav>	Gueze: jep, bin doch glatt nicht davon lo[s]gekommen...-)
...		
4567	<Gueze>	olav: wundert mich ;-)
...		
4573	<olav>	Gueuzte: ;-)

Elaborierter als mit Emoticons kann mit Actionzeilen und Actionstrips der non- und paraverbale Bereich simuliert werden. Obwohl Emoticons um ein Vielfaches häufiger als Actionzeilen genutzt werden, muß der Gebrauch der Actionzeilen besonders hoch eingeschätzt werden, da er mit einem Befehl generiert werden muß.

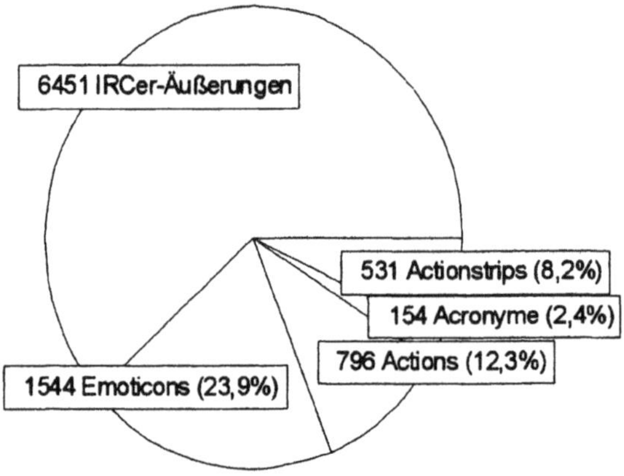

Diagramm 1: Der Anteil spezifischer Kommunikationsphänomene der CMC im IRC

Mit ihnen wird der Versuch unternommen, sowohl die fehlende materiale Welt zu simulieren, als auch das fehlende nonverbale Verhalten explizit zu ersetzen. In Actionzeilen, sie sind durch einen, Servermeldungen durch drei vorangestellte Sterne erkennbar, beschreiben IRCer oft, was sie gerade machen, machen werden oder gerne machen würden, wie sie sich fühlen oder woran sie denken u.ä.

798		* Angel geht jetzt ganz raus...Pfuerti alle
...		
801	<Sique>	Ciao, Angel
		* Frodo singt: spiel nicht mit den Schmuddelkindern, sing nicht ihre Lieder
...		
804	<devil>	bis nachher, Angel!
805.	<Sanne_>	frodo: ohhh hoer auf... du triffst ja keine ton
...		
807		* Pupser nimmt noch'ne heisse Schokolade
808		* Sique singt: Geh doch in die Oberstadt, mach's wie deine Bruehuehueder.
810		* Pupser hat den Namen popajder noch nie zuvor gehoert
		*** Angel has left channel #muenster

Das Beispiel zeigt, daß auch Actionzeilen nicht losgelöst von Standardäußerungen stehen, sondern genau wie diese initiative oder reaktive Sprechakte innerhalb von Handlungsspielen darstellen. Neben real erscheinenden Beschreibungen des Nutzerverhaltens in Actionzeilen bricht sich oft die Kreativität der Nutzer Bahn, so daß fiktive Handlungen dargestellt werden.

843		* Sanne langweilt sich
844		* CountZerO knuddelt Sanne
845		* Sique reicht Sanne ein Telespiel
846		* devil langweilt sich auch - will abba nich von Count geknuddelt werden!
847		* Sique knuddelt Devil :-)
848	<devil>	Huch....
849		* CountZerO gibt Sanne eine Telefonnummer
850		* Sanne faengt an doom zu spielen
851		* devil läeft rot an
852	<Sique>	CountZerO: Eine 0190?

So entstehen gelegentlich kreative Rollenspiele, an denen mehrere IRCer mitschreiben. In diesen Fällen sind Actionzeilen nicht als reale Handlungstranskriptionen, sondern als Gedankenspielereien im virtuellen Raum zu verstehen, in denen die Beschränkungen der realen Situation fiktiv aufgehoben werden. Actions sind jedoch nicht Selbstzweck, sondern sie werden als zusätzliche Äußerungsform genutzt, vor allem, um einem Gespräch durch ein hohes Maß an Kreativität neue Impulse zu geben. Stellen Actionzeilen eigenständige Sprechakte in komplexen Handlungsspielen dar, so findet sich die Kurzform dieser Äußerungsart in den sogenannten Actionstrips. Actionstrips werden wie Emoticons an Äußerungen angehängt und sind dadurch gekennzeichnet, daß sie zwischen zwei Sternen stehen. Sie ergänzen Äußerungen um eine Kurztranskription außersprachlichen Verhaltens. Actionstrips finden an Stelle von Emoticons Nutzung, da durch sie differenzierter Mimik und Gestik transkribiert werden kann. Sie bieten mehr Möglichkeiten, eine Gesamtäußerung zu relativieren oder Stimmungen, Gefühle und Gedanken auszudrücken.

1425	<lou>	frodo: hm, ja...eingeschrieben bin ich fuer sozpaed und studieren eigentlich nur soz, d.h. genauer, schreib ich gard meine DA *stoehn*
1655	<Peter_Pan>	moppes: also wie immer *lach* na denn, nen charmanten abend noch *evil grin*
2022	<Rince>	*such* eben war er doch noch da...
2107	<ZaphodB>	anti: ah ja *lob*
2483	<Strubi>	bl, hae? *nix blick*
2599	<ZatCat>	BL: Leipzig und Dresden ist ein Himmelweiter unterschied *belehr* Koblenz und Konstanz (oder wie das heisst:) dagegen ist nichts *mit haenden zeig*

Häufig erinnert die in Actionstrips verwendete Sprache an Comic-Strip-Sprache, aber auch an Kindersprache (Vgl. Naumann 1997 und Lenke/ Schmitz 1995, 129). Vor allem Onomatopoetika tauchen daher auf.

Die Substitutionsverfahren des nonverbalen Verhaltens, Actionzeilen, Actionstrips und Emoticons sind im IRC als ein elaboriertes Darstellungssystem vor allem von Mimik und Gestik zu beurteilen. Während Emoticons primär zur Dokumentation von Mimik genutzt werden, wird nonverbales Verhalten in Actionstrips und differenzierter in Actionzeilen transkribiert. Das Zusammenspiel der drei CMC-, bzw. IRC-eigenen Beschreibungssysteme eröffnet die Möglichkeit einer kreativen Ausgestaltung des gemeinsamen virtuellen Raumes. Es überrascht deshalb nicht, daß IRCer viele deiktische Ausdrücke benutzen, ohne Zeit-, Orts- und Personenangaben genauer zu explizieren. Daß bei der Substitution des nonverbalen Verhaltens besonders viel Energie und Kreativität aufgewendet wird, zeigt, wie wichtig Mimik, Gestik und die Zugriffsmöglichkeit auf Gegebenheiten der realen Kommunikationssituation für zeitlich synchrone Dialoge sind. Daher ist Naumann beizupflichten, der 1994 forderte:

> Ein linguistischer Dialogbegriff, der Gespräch als multifaktorielles dialogisches Handlungsspiel auffaßt, muß aber bei der Beschreibung authentischer Gespräche, die sich nicht im deskriptiven Auflisten des empirisch Gegebenen erschöpft, zumindest zwei paralinguistische Bereiche einbeziehen, 1. den suprasegmentalen Bereich des Sprechens (Intonation) und 2. den Bereich von Gestik und Mimik. (Naumann 1994, 11)

5. Gesprächsstrukturen und kommunikative Zwecke im IRC

In vielen Interneteinführungen wird der Verdacht zum Ausdruck gebracht, daß IRC mit Small Talk, mit Geschwätz, im Endeffekt mit sinnloser Unterhaltung gleichgesetzt werden kann. Dieser Vorwurf ist zu hinterfragen. Für Krol (1995, 395) ist das Modell für den multi-user-chat eine Cocktailparty, auf der die Leute über das sprechen, was sie interessiert. Nach Barron/Ooi (1996,332) steht IRC sogar im Ruf frivoler Kommunikation, doch geben sie zu bedenken, daß trotz allem auch nützliche Kommunikation im IRC zu finden ist.

In den von mir untersuchten öffentlichen IRC-Kanälen kann häufig Small Talk beobachtet werden, weil meistens Fremde aufeinandertreffen. Die Sinnhaftigkeit der Gespräche wird sogar von den Anwendern kritisch gesehen. Der Nutzer *Groover* stellt fest:

6116.	<Groover>	rene: hier wird doch eh nur mist gelabert ;)

Trotzdem können Dialoge im IRC nicht mit Small Talk, oder mit der Unterscheidung Hundsnurschers (1989) gesprochen, mit beziehungsorientierten Gesprächen gleichgesetzt und jegliche Formen resultat- oder tätigkeitsorientierter Gespräche ausgeschlossen werden. So revidiert auch Groover seine Einschätzung, indem er feststellt:

6126.	<Groover>	rene: aber ich habe schon erlebt,dass wildfremde leute mir ihre lebensgeschichte erzaehlt haben

Im Korpus sind resultatorientierte Gespräche zu finden, die sich häufig auf computertechnische Fragen beziehen. Besonders die technische Organisation von IRC in einem öffentlichen Kanal erschwert das Führen intensiver Gespräche. Die laufenden Unterhaltungen werden permanent von Servermeldungen, Begrüßungs- und Verabschiedungssequenzen unterbrochen. Die starke Fluktuation der Nutzer in einem Kanal, die viele Servermeldungen verursachen, kann mit der Tatsache erklärt werden, daß sie häufig so lange den Kanal wechseln[4], bis sie Gespräche gefunden haben, die für sie interessant sind.

Die von Hundsnurscher (1989, 238) für beziehungsorientierte Gespräche zusammengestellten Merkmale treffen auf das Gros der IRC-Unterhaltungen zu:

- offene und variable Struktur
- an beliebiger Stelle kann mit verschiedenen Techniken in sie ein-/ausgestiegen werden
- Entstehung unter besonderen situativen Voraussetzungen
- in der Regel werden mehrere Mitspieler vorausgesetzt
- sie können nicht auf ein bestimmtes Ergebnis bezogen werden
- Festlegung auf eine stringente zweckorientierte Kohärenz widerspricht ihrem spezifischen Charakter

Da Gesprächstypen und Handlungsspiele primär über ihren übergeordneten kommunikativen Zweck zu definieren sind (Vgl. Weigand 1995a, 1995b), ist dies auch für die vorfindbaren komplexen Handlungsspiele der beziehungsorientierten Gespräche zu leisten. Nach Weigand (1992, 61) kann als der grundlegende Zweck der meisten Dialoge im IRC ein deklarativer Zweck angenommen werden, da durch sie soziale Kontakte hergestellt oder aufrechterhalten werden sollen. Daneben tauchen allerdings auch direktive, explorative und repräsentative Handlungsspiele in resultatorientierten Gesprächen auf. Vor allem das explorative Handlungsspiel scheint zu dominieren. Eine weitere Untersuchung und Analyse der übergeordneten Zwecke und der Teilzwecke von Handlungsspielen müßte für den IRC geleistet werden, um deren Gesprächsstrukturen genauer fassen zu können.

IRC kann nicht mit einer bestimmten Gesprächsform gleichgesetzt werden, sondern ist ein Kommunikationsmedium mit spezifischen technischen und konventionellen Bedingungen.

Die von Sittek versuchsweise aufgestellte Benutzertypologie von Chattern, die sich an sozialen und kommunikativen Zwecken festmacht, unterstützt die Charakterisierung von IRC als Medium, dessen kommunikatives Potential seine Nutzer nach ihren Bedürfnissen ausschöpfen. Er unterscheidet stichpunktartig zusammengefaßt:

• Gelegenheits-IRCer	suchen Spaß und Zeitvertreib
• Depressive IRCer	und wollen Kontakte knüpfen, in persönlichen Gesprächen
IRC-Abhängige	eigene Probleme zu lösen versuchen
• IRC-Flirter und IRC-Paare	Kontaktscheuheit des realen Lebens kann hier überwunden werden, so daß sie andere Menschen im Netz kennenlernen können
• Informationssuchende	Suche nach gezielten Informationen und Antwort auf bestimmte Probleme – häufig technischer Natur
• Multikulturell Interessierte	versuchen sich per IRC Wissen über andere Kulturen und Sprachen anzueignen
• Computer-Beschäftigte	IRC wird nebenbei als kreative Abwechslung genutzt

Das dialogische Vorfeld und Nachfeld nehmen im IRC einen großen Platz ein. Die Begrüßungsphase gestaltet sich intensiv, indem alle Chatter zur Bekundung von Gesprächsbereitschaft und zur Identifizierung von ihnen bekannten Anwendern häufig parallel zu den von ihnen geführten Gesprächen neu hereinkommende Chatter grüßen. Zum Aufbau einer Subkultur mit stabilen Identitäten ist dies wichtig, da sich Nutzer, die beim erstmaligen Hereinkommen in einen Kanal nicht gegrüßt werden, über die Strategie des Kanalverlassens und zweitmaligen Hereinkommens neu ins Spiel zu bringen versuchen. Für die Signalisierung von Gesprächsbereitschaft ist die Begrüßungsphase von fundamentaler Bedeutung. Sie wird technisch durch eine Servermeldung initiiert, die den Eintritt eines Anwenders in einen entsprechenden Kanal verkündet. Darauf läuft eine Gruß-Gegengruß-Sequenz ab, an der sich bei kanalbekannten Chattern viele IRCer beteiligen, um dessen Bekanntheit zu dokumentieren.

1208	*** Chris has joined channel #muenster	
...		
1210	<Sanne>	hi Chris
1211	<Chris>	hi Sanne
...		
1214	<padder>	hi Chris
...		
1216	<Frodo>	Yoo chriss
...		
1219	<Chris>	hi padder

Die sofortige Verleihung des Channeloperatorstatus zeigt an, daß ein Nutzer im Kanal gut bekannt ist. Unbekannte Teilnehmer grüßen meistens zuerst zur Verdeutlichung ihrer Gesprächsbereitschaft, um dann nach einem Gegengruß in ein Gespräch einzusteigen.

Struktur einer Begrüßungsphase

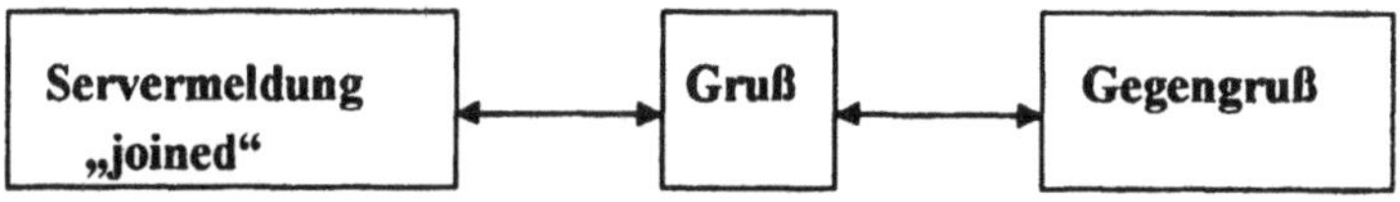

Nicht alle Anwender nehmen an den Gesprächen teil, so daß Grußsequenzen nicht selten nur halb vollzogen werden. Kanalspringer schauen nur für kurze Zeit in einem Kanal vorbei, um festzustellen, ob sie ein interessantes Gespräch finden, wie die Äußerungshäufigkeit zeigt.

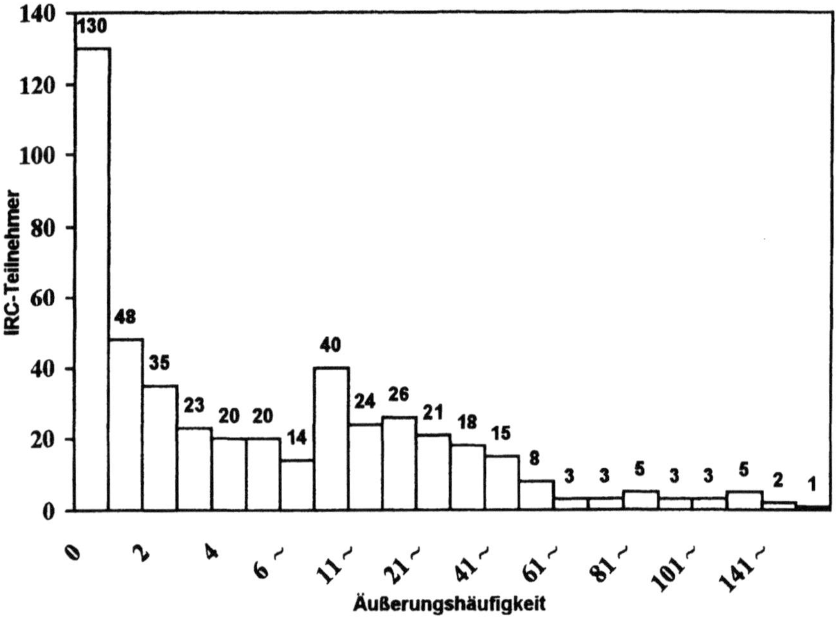

Diagramm 2: Die Äußerungshäufigkeit der 467 IRC-Teilnehmer

Auch bei den Verabschiedungssequenzen beteiligen sich die meisten Teilnehmer in einem Kanal. Ein IRCer grüßt, nachdem er explizit seine Gespräche beendet hat, um dann aber nicht sofort den Befehl zum Verlassen des Kanals einzugeben, sondern erst die Verabschiedungsgrüße der anderen Teilnehmer abzuwarten.

416	* ZaphodB macht sich dann auch mal vom acker	
...		
418	<Sique>	Ciao, ZaphodB
...		
421	<Frodo>	cu
422	*** ZaphodB has left channel #muenster	

Diese Sequenz schließt mit einer technischen Servermeldung ab.

Struktur einer Verabschiedungsphase

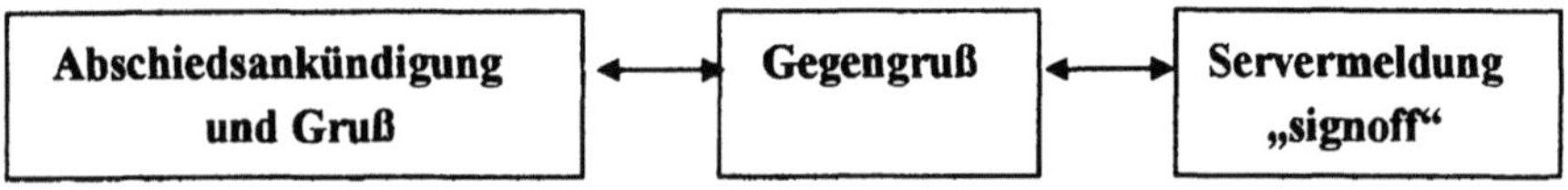

Die häufigen Servermeldungen und die mit ihnen verbundenen Begrüßungs- und Verabschiedungsphasen unterbrechen permanent den Gesprächsverlauf und nehmen einen großen Teil in der IRC-Kommunikation ein. Sie unterbrechen und beeinflußen die Gespräche zugleich, denn in ihnen ist durch die neu auftretenden Chatter immer das Potential angelegt, Gesprächskonstellationen und -themen zu ändern. Aus diesem Grunde erscheint die IRC-Kommunikation in ihrer Struktur und Kohärenz offen, variabel und oftmals nur der übergeordnete Zweck des Aufbaus und der Aufrechterhaltung von sozialen Kontakten angebbar.

Erstaunlich bleibt um so mehr der Umgang der Anwender mit ihren Gesprächen. Da sie aufgrund der Linearisierung potentiell durch das Mitlesen jeder Äußerung auf dem aktuellen Stand aller Gepräche sein können, besitzen sie die Möglichkeit, an allen Gesprächen teilzunehmen. Die bestehende Konvention expliziter Adressierung erleichtert die Herstellung von Kohärenz. Die an entsprechende Nutzer gerichteten Äußerungen können eindeutig identifiziert und alle anderen überlesen werden. Trotzdem beteiligen sich die geübten IRCer meistens an mehreren Gesprächen, Begrüßungs- und Verabschiedungssequenzen gleichzeitig. Die multiple Gesprächsbeteiligung ist ein Charakteristikum des kommunikativen Verhaltens im IRC, das in der face-to-face Kommunikation in dieser Form nicht oft zu finden ist.

Obwohl Mehrpersonengespräche mit unbegrenzter Teilnehmerzahl möglich sind, finden in aller Regel Zweiergespräche statt. Es lassen sich hauptsächlich Parallelgespräche beobachten, da die kurzzeitig geführten Gespräche mit drei oder vier Personen schnell in Zweiergespräche zerfallen. Allein die Adressierungskonvention forciert dieses Verhalten.

Durch die Instabilität der Teilnehmergruppe, die Linearisierung der Gesprächsbeiträge, die herrschende Konvention freier Adressierungsmöglichkeiten und aufgrund der großen Gesprächsdynamik ist es besonders schwer, im IRC Gespräche mit stabilen Strukturen zu führen. Auch wenn die Großzahl der Gespräche unter der Bezeichnung Small Talk subsumiert werden kann, verfälscht die Gleichsetzung der IRC-Kommunikation mit beziehungsorientierten Gesprächen den Gegenstandsbereich völlig. IRC stellt eben nicht einen einzigen, medial bestimmten Gesprächstypen dar, sondern bezeichnet ein Kommunikationsmedium, das Kommunikation auf bisher unbekannte Weise ermöglicht und beeinflußt.

6. Ausblick

Da sowohl die Nutzung von IRC als auch das Medium selbst immer noch einem starken Wandel unterworfen sind, wird weiter zu untersuchen sein, auf welche Weise es genutzt und in ihm kommuniziert wird. Der Linguistik eröffnet sich nicht nur mit dem IRC, sondern mit den verschiedenen Formen der Computer-Mediated Communication neue Forschungsfelder. Diese lassen interessante neue Analysen zu vielfältigen Aspekten erwarten und schaffen im Sinne Reids die einmalige Chance, die theoretische Reflexion im Bereich der Linguistik wesentlich voranzutreiben, indem bisher gültige Prämissen in der Auseinandersetzung mit ihrem neuen Untersuchungsgegenstand auf den Prüfstand geraten.

Anmerkungen

1) Das Korpus umfaßt verschiedene *Chatlogs* in der Länge von 24,5 h, d.h. 7654 Äußerungen. Zu verschiedenen Uhrzeiten und an verschiedenen Tagen wurden IRC-Gespräche in öffentlichen IRC-Kanälen mitgeschnitten. Die empirische Auswertung des Korpus findet sich auf S. 6.
2) Die Angabe der Äußerungsnumerierung aus dem Korpus zeigt die Linearisierung von Äußerungen allein aufgrund ihres Absendezeitpuntkes deutlich. Zwischen den beiden Äußerungen, die sich aufeinander beziehen, stehen 12 andere Beiträge.
3) Obwohl es im Englischen eine große Anzahl von Akronymen gibt, die sich aus der Hackersprache entwickelt haben, werden im deutschen IRC neben diesen vier kaum andere Akronyme genutzt.
4) Siehe obige Tabelle: „Hereinschauende" und „Rückkehrersumme".

Literatur

Baron, Naomi S. (1984): Computer-Mediated Communication as a Force in Language Change. – In: Visible Language 18 (2), 118-141.

Barron, Billy/Ooi, Lay Wah (1996): Echtzeitkonversation: Internet Relay Chat und andere Methoden. – In: Barron, B./Ellsworth, J. H./Savetz, K. M. (eds.): Internet für Insider. Übers. v. Hans Hajer u. Rainer Kolbeck. Haar.

Chafe, Wallace L. (1985): Linguistic Differences produced by Differences between Speaking and Writing. – In: Olson, David R./Torrance, Nancy/Hildgard, Angela (eds.): Literacy, Language and Learning. The Nature and Consequences of Reading and Writing. Cambridge, 105-123.

Chapman, David (1992): Computer Rules, Conversational Rules. – In: Computational Linguistics 18 (4), 531.536.

Chesebro, James W./Bonsall, Donald G. (1989): Computer-Mediated Communication. Human Relationshipss in a Computerized World. Tuscaloosa (Alabama)/London.

Fuller, Rodney (1994): Human-Computer-Human Interaction: How Computers Affect Interpersonal Communication. – In: The Arachanet Electronic Journal on Virtual Culture 2 (2). Http://www.uni-koeln.de/themen/cmc/litlist.html.

Gauger, Hans-Martin (1986): „Schreibe, wie du redest!" Zu einer stilistischen Norm. – In: Sprachnormen in der Diskussion. Beiträge vorgelegt von Sprachfreunden. Unter Mitarbeit von Helmut Henne, Hans-Martin Gauger u.a., Berlin/New York, 21-40.

Harasim, Linda M. (ed.) (1993): Global Networks. Computers and International Communication. Cambridge (Mass.)/London.

Herring, Susan (ed.) (1996): Computer-Mediated Communication. Linguistic, Social and Cross-Cultural Perspectives. Amsterdam/Philadelphia.

Hirst, Graeme (1991): Does Conversation Analysis Have a Role in Computational Linguistics? – In: Computational Linguistics 17 (2), 211-227.

Höflich, Joachim R. (1996): Technisch vermittelte interpersonale Kommunikation. Grundlagen, organisatorische Medienverwendung, Konstitution ‚elektronischer Gemeinschaften'. Opladen. (Studien zur Kommunikationswissenschaft 8).

Hundsnurscher, Franz (1989): Typologische Aspekte von Unterrichtsgesprächen. – In: Weigand, E./Hundsnurscher, F. (eds.): Dialoganalyse II. Referate der 2. Arbeitstagung, Bochum 1988, Bd. 1. Tübingen, 237-256. (Linguistische Arbeiten 229/230)

Krol, Ed (1995): Die Welt des Internet. Handbuch & Übersicht. Dt. Übers. von Holger Lübitz. Bonn.

Lenke, Nils/Schmitz, Peter (1995): Geschwätz im Globalen Dorf – Kommunikation im Internet. – In: Osnabrücker Beiträge für Sprachtheorie (OBST) 50, 117-141.

Maynor, Natalie (1994): The Language of Electronic Mail: Written Speech? – In: Little, Greta D./Montgomery, Michael (eds.): Centennial Usage Studies. Tuscaloosa/Alabama, 48-54. (Publications of the American Dialect Society 78).

Metz, Michael J. (1994): Computer-Mediated Communication: Literature Review of a New Context. – In: Interpersonal Computing and Technology 2 (2), 31-49. Http://www.uni-koeln.de/themen/cmc/litlist-html

Murray, Denise F. (1989): When the Medium Determines Turns: Turn-Taking in Computer Conversation. – In: Coleman, H. (ed.): Working with Language. A Multidisciplinary Consideration of Language Use in Work Contexts. Berlin, 317-337.

Naumann, Bernd (1994): Überlegungen zu einem Dialogbegriff als Handlungsspiel: Gestik und Mimik im Gespräch und in der Gesprächsanalyse. – In: Weigand, Edda (ed.): Concepts of Dialogue. Considered from the Perspective of Different Disciplines. Tübingen, 1-13. (Beiträge zur Dialogforschung 6)

Naumann, Bernd (1997): IRCs – schriftliche Sonderformen von Mehrpersonengesprächen. – In: Weigand, Edda (ed.): Dialogue Analysis: Units, Relations and Strategies beyond the Sentence. Contributions in Honour of Sorin Stati's 65th Birthday. In Collaboration with E. Hauenherm. Tübingen, 161-178. (Beiträge zur Dialogforschung 13).

Pelz, Jan (1988): Sozialpsychologische Aspekte eines Vergleichs zwischen direkter und Computervermittelter Kommunikation. Göttingen.

Reid, Elizabeth (1991): Electropolis: Communicaiton and Community on Internet Relay Chat. http://www.ll.mu.oz.au/papers/emr/electropolis.html.

Rheingold, Howard (1994): Virtuelle Gemeinschaft. Soziale Beziehungen im Zeitalter des Computers. Dt. Übers. v. D. Schulz u. D. Strehle. Bonn/Paris/Reading (Mass.).

Rosenbaum, Oliver (1996): Chat-Slang: Lexikon der Internet-Sprache. München/Wien.

Rupp, Heinz (1965): Gesprochenes und geschriebenes Deutsch. In: Wirkendes Wort 15, 19-29.

Sanderson, David (1995): Smileys. Dt. Übers. v. Peter Klicman. Bonn.

Schütz, Rüdiger (1995): Nachts im Cyberspace. In: Osnabrücker Beiträge zur Sprachtheorie 50, 107-115.

Sittek, Dietmar (1995): Zur zunehmenden Computerisierung der Gesellschaft – eine soziologische Analyse ausgewählter Aspekte. Arbeit zur Erlangung des Magistergrades an der soziologischen Fakultät, Münster. [Diese Arbeit liegt mir maschinenschriftlich vor.]

Weigand, Edda (1992): A Case for an Integrating Procedure of Theoretical Reflection and Empirical Analysis. – In: Stati, S./Weigand, E. (eds.): Methodologie der Dialoganalyse. Tübingen, 57-64. (Beiträge zur Dialogforschung 3)

Weigand, Edda (1995a): Looking for He Point of the Dialogic Turn. – In: Hundsnurscher, F./Weigand, E. (eds.): Future Perspectives of Dialogue Analysis. Tübingen, 75-120. (Beiträge zur Dialogforschung 8)

Weigand, Edda (1995b): Prinzipien einr Theorie des Sprachgebrauchs. – In: Hindelang, G./Rolf, E./Zillig, W. (eds.): Gebrauch der Sprache. Festschrift für Franz Hundsnurscher zum 60. Geburtstag. Münster, 388-407.

Werry, Christopher C. (1996): Linguistic and Interactional Features of Internet Relay Chat. – In: Herring (1996), 47-64.

Wilkins, Harriet (1991): Computer Talk. Long-Distance Conversations by Computer. – In: Written Communication 8 (1), 56-78.

Yvonne Grosch

Turn-Verteilung in synchroner computervermittelter Kommunikation: eine Frage der medialen Rahmenbedingungen oder der sozialen Regulierung?

1. Einleitung

Obwohl der Gegenstandsbereich computervermittelte Kommunikation (CVK) seit einiger Zeit zunehmend in den Fokus der Sprachwissenschaft rückt,[1] werden zumeist nur einige Aspekte dieses breiten Themenspektrums untersucht. Beachtung finden v.a. (tatsächlich oder vermeintlich neuartige) sprachliche Phänomene der „traditionellen", d.h. schriftbasierten synchronen (oder auch asynchronen) CVK auf der Wort- und Satzebene, die sich auf den Nenner „mediale Schriftlichkeit – konzeptionelle Mündlichkeit" (siehe Koch/ Oesterreicher 1994) bringen lassen.[2] In jedoch nur wenigen Arbeiten wird in der Beschreibung und Analyse die Grenze des einzelnen Sprecherbeitrags überschritten und die Aufmerksamkeit auf interaktive Prozesse und redebeitragsüberschreitende Strukturen innerhalb der CVK gerichtet. Eine umfassende Untersuchung eines der innerhalb der Gesprächsanalyse zentralen Gegenstände, der Organisation des Sprecherwechsels, steht dementsprechend noch aus.

In diesem Beitrag soll der Frage nachgegangen werden, ob und inwiefern sich in einem hochgradig technisierten und von der „natürlichen" Gesprächssituation, der face-to-face-Kommunikation, bzw. der Telefonkommunikation, stark abweichenden Medium wie synchroner CVK Sprecherwechselprozesse und daraus resultierende Gesprächsstrukturen noch nach dem Turn-Taking-System von Sacks/Schegloff/Jefferson (1974; hier 1978; im folgenden Sacks et al.) analysieren lassen.

2. Mediale Rahmenbedingungen im Internet Relay Chat (IRC)

Um die medialen Rahmenbedingungen, die Gespräche bzw. Sprecherwechselvorgänge in der synchronen CVK-Form IRC beeinflussen, bestimmen zu können, soll zunächst in Kürze die Funktionsweise dieses Programmsystems beschrieben werden, das 1988 von Jarkko Oikarinen entwickelt wurde und innerhalb kürzester Zeit weltweit Verbreitung fand.[3]

Das Client/Server-basierte IRC ermöglicht es, sich über einen mit dem Internet verbundenen Computer mittels eines sogenannten Client-Programmes in einen der weltweit unzähligen IRC-Server einzuloggen, auf dem üblicherweise mehrere hundert Kanäle (channels) gleichzeitig geöffnet sind. IRC-Kanäle kann man mit mehr oder minder themenbezogenen Gesprächsgruppen vergleichen, die manchmal nur aus einem oder wenigen Teilnehmern bestehen, manchmal jedoch 20 oder mehr Personen umfassen, die normalerweise räumlich getrennt voneinander sind.

Wenn man sich mittels eines bestimmten Befehls in einen der Kanäle „begibt", werden die tastaturgeschriebenen Beiträge der in diesem Kanal anwesenden Teilnehmer synchron nach der Reihenfolge ihres Eintreffens von dem Server an alle Teilnehmer übermittelt und auf deren Bildschirmen angezeigt. Mittels der Eingabe-Taste kann man eigene Nachrichten bzw. Gesprächsbeiträge nach ihrer Erstellung an den Server übermitteln und somit den anderen Teilnehmern im Normalfall innerhalb Bruchteilen einer Sekunde zugänglich machen. Ungleich zu direkten Gesprächen werden die Beiträge einzelner Teilnehmer also zwar *synchron*, aber nicht *simultan* an die Gesprächspartner übertragen, wie im folgenden anhand eines kurzen IRC-Gesprächsausschnitts dargestellt werden soll:[4]

(1)
[17:37:50] <flirt_> toemml sorry, nimmst uns nicht uebel!!
[17:37:51] <charly> nelli: nürnberg,wo in nürnberg
[17:37:58] <PankX> flirt: jaj a.. aber, ich chatte ja mit vielen :)
[17:37:58] <popl> toemml :-)
[17:38:00] <Grisu2> gump: sche*ss maus
[17:38:04] <flirt_> Grisu2 Ausch mal wieder da
[17:38:07] <PankX> Wavy: also .. alles :)
[17:38:10] <Wavy> PankX: hast schon den fuehrerschein?
[17:38:17] <nelli> charly: MAXIMUM!!!!!
[17:38:19] <Wavy> PankX: schon, ja....
[17:38:20] <gump> grisu. ja.. die maeuse... man kann nicht mit ihnen und nicht ohne sie...
[17:38:23] <toemml> flirt: naja ... mal sehen .. ich kenn euch schliesslich net, aber ich bin schon mal voreingenommen ...
[17:38:23] <PankX> Wavy: ne .. ich arbeite noch daran :)
[17:38] * popl normalisiert sich langsam aber sicher!
[17:38:32] <flirt_> PankX ist schon aber denk an uns

[17:38:37] <Wavy> PankX: hast schon ne pruefung gehabt?
[17:38:52] <PankX> Du hast die laengsten Beine, die ich je im Leben sah .. sie reichten bis zum Boden und wie unrasiert sie waren :)
[17:38:55] <PankX> Wavy: neeeeee
[17:38:56] <PankX> :)
[17:38:59] <Grisu2> gump: und nun die philosophische frage: was macht man mit maeusen?

Aufgrund der soeben geschilderten räumlichen Trennung der Teilnehmer an bi- oder multilateraler IRC-Kommunikation, der Schriftlichkeit der Gesprächsbeiträge und aufgrund der durch die Übertragungstechnik bedingten Trennung von Produktion und Rezeption[5] sind in IRC-Gesprächen grundlegend andere Kommunikationsbedingungen als in direkten oder Telefongesprächen gegeben, auf deren Basis und zu deren Beschreibung Sacks et al. (1978) das Turn-Taking-System entwickelt haben. Im Gegensatz zu direkten oder Telefongesprächen müssen Teilnehmer an IRC-Kommunikation prinzipiell nicht darüber verhandeln, wer wann mit seinem Gesprächsbeitrag „an der Reihe“ ist, denn in einem gewissermaßen stummen, nicht simultan, sondern nach dem Kriterium der zeitlichen Reihenfolge übertragenden und linearisierenden Kommunikationsmedium können sich die Beiträge rein physikalisch nicht stören. Jeder „Sprecher“ kann infolgedessen unabhängig und ungestört von seinen Gesprächspartnern darüber entscheiden, wann und wie oft er einen Gesprächsbeitrag produzieren will. Zudem hat der jeweilige „Hörer“ keinerlei Einflußmöglichkeiten auf die Gestaltung und Länge des an ihn gerichteten Beitrags, wie sie in direkten oder Telefongesprächen mittels verbalem oder nonverbalem Rückmeldeverhalten oder durch gesprächsschrittbeanspruchende Signale gegeben sind. Dadurch wird die Interaktivität zwischen Sprecher und Hörer als simultane gegenseitige Einflußnahme und Reaktion aufeinander, wie sie in direkten oder Telefongesprächen gegeben ist, in IRC-Kommunikation natürlich deutlich geschmälert (siehe Lenke/Schmitz 1995, 130).

Diese soeben geschilderten konversationellen Konsequenzen aus den medialen Rahmenbedingungen scheinen auf dem ersten Blick den dem Turn-Taking-System von Sacks et al. (1978) inhärenten Grundannahmen und Konzepten völlig entgegenzulaufen: Weder scheint die Turn-Verteilung in IRC-Kommunikation – betrachtet man IRC-Gesprächsausschnitte wie Beispiel (1) – linear zu verlaufen, wenn das Erscheinen der Beiträge im IRC letztlich von der individuellen Tippgeschwindigkeit der Teilnehmer und von dem die betreffenden Nachrichten übermittelnden Server abhängig ist; noch scheint ein lokales Management-System vonnöten zu sein, das an einem übergaberelevanten Ort (bei Sacks et al. „transition-relevance place“; im folgenden TRP), die Zuteilung eines Turns an nur einen Sprecher auf der Basis bestimmter Turn-Taking-Regeln gewährleisten soll, wenn jeder IRC-Teilnehmer ungestört von den Beiträgen anderer dann „sprechen“ kann, wann und auch wie lange er will. Letztlich scheint die Turn-Verteilung Wichter (1991, 78) zufolge nach dem „Mühlen-Prinzip“ zu verlaufen: „Wer zuerst kommt, mahlt zuerst“.

Diesen und weiteren Aspekten der Turn-Verteilung in IRC-Kommunikation im Vergleich zu direkter oder Telefonkommunikation soll im folgenden nachgegangen werden.

3. Parallelgespräche und Adressierung in IRC-Kommunikation

Wie im vorherigen Abschnitt angesprochen, scheint in IRC-Kommunikation aufgrund der medialen Rahmenbedingungen die Notwendigkeit von Organisationsprinzipien, die den Verlauf von Sprecherwechselvorgängen regulieren und gewährleisten sollen, daß zu einem Zeitpunkt nur ein Sprecher spricht („one party at a time"), nicht mehr gegeben zu sein (siehe Lenke/Schmitz 1995, 130). Diese Annahme wird bei der ersten Durchsicht von IRC-Gesprächsmitschnitten, wie im obigen Beispiel (1) bestärkt, bei denen man den Eindruck gewinnt, als würde jeder der Gesprächsteilnehmer nach Gutdünken Beiträge produzieren und an den Kanal schicken. Bei genauerer Betrachtung erkennt man jedoch, daß in Beispiel (1) mehrere Gespräche zwischen jeweils zwei Teilnehmern parallel geführt werden, die sich im nachhinein in verschiedene Gesprächsstränge unterteilen lassen:[6]

(2)
Erster Gesprächsstrang:
[17:37:50] <flirt_> toemml sorry, nimmst uns nicht uebel!!
[17:38:23] <toemml> flirt: naja ... mal sehen .. ich kenn euch schliesslich net, aber ich bin schon mal voreingenommen ...

Zweiter Gesprächsstrang:
[17:37:51] <charly> nelli: nürnberg,wo in nürnberg
[17:38:17] <nelli> charly: MAXIMUM!!!!!

Dritter Gesprächsstrang:
[17:37:58] <PankX> flirt: jaj a.. aber, ich chatte ja mitvielen :)
[17:38:32] <flirt_> PankX ist schon aber denk an uns

Vierter Gesprächsstrang:
[17:38:00] <Grisu2> gump: sche*ss maus
[17:38:20] <gump> grisu. ja.. die maeuse... man kann nicht mit ihnen und nicht ohne sie...
[17:38:59] <Grisu2> gump: und nun die philosophische frage: was macht man mit maeusen?

Fünfter Gesprächsstrang:
[17:38:07] <PankX> Wavy: also .. alles :)
[17:38:10] <Wavy> PankX: hast schon den fuehrerschein?
[17:38:19] <Wavy> PankX: schon, ja....
[17:38:23] <PankX> Wavy: ne .. ich arbeite noch daran :)

[17:38:37] <Wavy> PankX: hast schon ne pruefung gehabt?
[17:38:55] <PankX> Wavy: neeeeee

Sechster Gesprächsstrang:
[17:38:04] <flirt_> Grisu2 Ausch mal wieder da

Hier produzieren zwar mehrere Teilnehmer gleichzeitig Beiträge, jedoch innerhalb verschiedener Gesprächsgruppen, so daß keineswegs davon die Rede sein kann, daß im IRC die Regel „one party at a time" per se verletzt würde, wie Lenke/Schmitz (1995, 130) behaupten.[7] Wenn man die betreffenden sich aufeinander beziehenden Turns der in diesem Ausschnitt jeweils zwei miteinander kommunizierenden Teilnehmer „relinearisiert", d.h. sie von ihrer mehr oder weniger zufälligen Reihenfolge auf dem Bildschirm in eine gesprächslogische Reihenfolge bringt, dann erkennt man darüber hinaus, daß die Turn-Verteilung alles andere als zufällig verläuft und die daraus resultierenden Gesprächsstrukturen dementsprechend nicht immer unlinear sind. Doch darauf soll erst im folgenden Abschnitt genauer eingegangen werden.

Anhand dieses IRC-Ausschnitts wird darüber hinaus deutlich, daß die explizite Adressierung des intendierten Rezipienten eines Beitrags, die sich in direkten Gesprächen aufgrund visueller Signale wie Blickkontakt oder Körperhaltung zumeist erübrigt, in IRC-Kanälen mit mehreren Teilnehmern eine Voraussetzung dafür ist, daß der jeweilige Angesprochene erkennen kann, daß ein Beitrag für ihn bestimmt ist. Explizite Adressierung im IRC ist also in erster Linie eine Orientierungshilfe für die Teilnehmer, die es ihnen erleichtert bzw. erst ermöglicht, aus den Nachrichten, die bisweilen mit hoher Geschwindigkeit über den Bildschirm rauschen, die für sie relevanten zu filtern, weniger eine Fremdzuweisungstechnik im Sinne von Sacks et al. (1978).[8] Dementsprechend verzichten IRC-Teilnehmer im allgemeinen auch auf eine explizite Adressierung, wenn sie in einem sogannten privaten Kanal, zu dem keine dritte Person Zutritt hat, miteinander „chatten". Explizite Adressierung in öffentlichen Kanälen mit mehreren Teilnehmern erübrigt sich auch in solchen Fällen, in denen für die betreffenden Gesprächspartner aus aus dem inhaltlichen Kontext und der Sequenzierung ihrer aufeinanderfolgender Beiträge deutlich wird, wer der intendierte Rezipient ist, wie im folgenden Beispiel:

(3)
[18:24:25] <Wolfi> ute hast du nicht auch eine am diddl ?
[18:24:37] <Ute> *[ø Adressierung]* nein hab ich nicht
[18:24] *** Time2 has quit IRC (EOF From client)
[18:24] * Ute gehoert nicht zu den diddl-usern
[18:24] *** LoneWolf (xyz) has left #austria (LoneWolf)
[18:24:56] <Wolfi> *[ø Adressierung]* aber zu den diddlern ;-)
[18:25:02] <Ute> *[ø Adressierung]* ja sicher zu den schon

4. Turn-Verteilung und Nonresponsivität im IRC

In IRC-Gesprächsausschnitten wie im letztgenannten Beispiel (3) lassen sich die zugrunde liegenden Organisationsprinzipien des Sprecherwechsels wiedererkennen, die Sacks et al. (1978) auf der Basis von direkten bzw. Telefongesprächen identifizieren und in ihrem Modell systematisieren: Der Teilnehmer Wolfi beendet seinen Turn (TRP), den er durch die explizite Adressierung erkennbar an die Teilnehmerin Ute richtet, wobei er durch seine Frage, die als erster Teil einer Paarsequenz nach Sacks et al. (1978) eine der grundlegenden Fremdzuweisungstechniken darstellt, Ute den nächsten Turn zuweist („current speaker selects next"). Ute komplettiert die von Wolfi eingeleitete Paarsequenz mit ihrer Antwort, wendet dabei jedoch keine Fremdzuweisungstechnik an. Dadurch hat sie die Möglichkeit, einen weiteren Beitrag zu produzieren, wie den in Form einer Handlungsbeschreibung, der wiederum keine Fremdzuweisungstechnik enthält. Wolfi produziert nach Selbstwahl einen an den vorausfolgenden Beitrag von Ute anknüpfenden Beitrag, in dem er die Aussage von Ute ergänzt, worauf Ute schließlich mit einer Bestätigung reagiert.

Die insgesamt vier Sprecherwechsel in diesem Gesprächsausschnitt finden, wie den vorangestellten Zeitangaben zu entnehmen ist, innerhalb von nur 37 Sekunden statt, was deswegen erstaunlich ist, da der TRP eines Beitrags erst nach dessen Übermittlung und Rezeption durch den Adressaten aktuell werden kann und der zu erstellende Beitrag wiederum erst geplant, tastaturgeschrieben und an den Server übermittelt werden muß. Die hohe Geschwindigkeit, mit der die beiden Teilnehmer Wolfi und Ute ihre jeweiligen Gesprächsbeiträge produzieren, die sie dementsprechend – wie im IRC allgemein üblich – erkennbar möglichst kurz halten, um sie dem anderen somit schnell zugänglich zu machen, ist auch eine wesentliche Voraussetzung für die hier linear verlaufende Turn-Verteilung. Die vier Sprecherwechsel in diesem Beispiel erfolgen im Sinne von Sacks et al. (1978) kontinuierlich, d.h. ohne erkennbare Pause zwischen den Beiträgen.

Natürlich gibt es aufgrund der Tatsache, daß Beiträge komplett übermittelt werden und infolgedessen ein TRP für den jeweiligen Adressaten erst nach der Rezeption eines an ihn gerichteten Beitrags aktuell wird, in IRC-Kommunikation stets größere Pausen zwischen vorausgehenden und nachfolgenden Beiträgen als in mündlicher Kommunikation. Insofern räumt jeder – zumindest jeder erfahrene – IRC-Teilnehmer seinem Gesprächspartner einen angemessenen Zeitraum für die Realisierung eines diesem nach Fremdwahl zugewiesenen Turns ein. Wird dieser zeitliche „Toleranzrahmen" jedoch überschritten, empfinden dies IRC-Teilnehmer als diskontinuierliche Turn-Verteilung, also als reparaturbedürftigen „turn-taking error". Dies bringen sie ihrerseits durch bestimmte Reaktionen zum Ausdruck, wie in den folgenden Beispielen, in denen die auf die initiativen ersten

Teile einer Paarsequenz, wie Fragen, Grüße und Aufforderungen, erwartbaren reaktiven Turns ausbleiben:

(4)
[18:45:25] <TomRiker> bandi, wie wird man noMaam Mitglied?
[18:46:31] <TomRiker> bandi?

[18:17:09] <Rasta> Griaß euch!
[18:17] * Rasta says 5Hello6 to all!
[18:19:03] <Rasta> Warum grüßt mi kana?

[17:49:45] <zwottel> nelli:lass bitte meinen wavy in ruhe war nur scheiss!!schreib mal was!!
[17:51:40] <zwottel> nelli:huhu?
[17:51:55] <zwottel> nelli:ich warte

Nonresponsivität kann im IRC prinzipiell mehrere Gründe haben: Zum einen können IRC-Teilnehmer aus gesprächsstrategischen Gründen den an sie gerichteten Beitrag ignorieren und somit die mit initiativen, paarsequenzeröffenden Turns verbundene Verpflichtung zur Realisierung eines reaktiven Turns ablehnen (siehe Schegloff 1972, 77). Nur in diesem Falle kann man von eigentlicher Nonresponsivität sprechen. Des weiteren kann der jeweilige Adressat einen an ihn gerichteten Beitrag gewissermaßen überhören, weil er entweder bereits in ein oder mehrere Gespräche verwickelt und somit abgelenkt ist oder aber nur „nominell" im Kanal anwesend ist, d.h. daß er zwar in der Liste der im IRC-Kanal anwesenden Teilnehmer angeführt wird, sich tatsächlich jedoch nicht im virtuellen Gesprächsraum des Kanals „befindet". In den beiden letztgenannten Fällen steht der adressierte Teilnehmer aus gewissermaßen physikalischen Gründen nicht als Gesprächspartner zur Verfügung, Sprecherwechsel kann dementsprechend nicht stattfinden.

Üblicherweise signalisieren IRC-Teilnehmer – u.a. durch Handlungsbeschreibungen wie im folgenden Beispiel –, daß sie für eine gewisse Zeit nicht anwesend sind, also weder Beiträge rezipieren noch produzieren können:

(5)
[18:19] * Marina_ is mal eben away

Derartige Vorankündigungen muß man als „präventiven" Reparaturmechanismus betrachten, mittels dessen IRC-Teilnehmer ihre potentielle Nonresponsivität aufgrund ihrer Abwesenheit erklären und legitimieren.

5. Fehlerhafte Turn-Verteilung und Unterbrechung im IRC

Natürlich kann die übertragungstechnisch bedingte Trennung von Produktion und Rezeption, die zur Folge hat, daß der jeweilige TRP für „Sprecher“ und „Hörer“ zeitlich versetzt aktuell wird, dazu führen, daß Turns „out of sequence“ geraten, wie im folgenden Beispiel:

(6)
[17:36:50] <PankX> Wavy: was hoerst du sonst so ?
[17:37:50] <Wavy> PankX: eigentlich so ziehmlich alles, von techno bis rock, manchmal auch klassik, aber keine volksmusik, joechstens vielleicht auf festen
[17:38:07] <PankX> Wavy: also .. alles :)
[17:38:10] <Wavy> PankX: hast schon den fuehrerschein?
[17:38:19] <Wavy> PankX: schon, ja....
[17:38:23] <PankX> Wavy: ne .. ich arbeite noch daran :)
[17:38:37] <Wavy> PankX: hast schon ne pruefung gehabt?
[17:38:55] <PankX> Wavy: neeeeee

Nachdem die erste Paarsequenz durch den ersten Beitrag von Wavy ohne erkennbare Fremdzuweisungstechnik abgeschlossen ist, ergreifen beide Gesprächspartner nach dem Prinzip der Selbstwahl das Wort. Während PankX in seinem zweiten Beitrag noch die vorherige Antwort von Wavy kommentiert, leitet Wavy bereits eine neue Paarsequenz mittels einer Frage an PankX ein und reagiert erst in seinem nächsten Turn auf den betreffenden Beitrag von PankX.

Hierin besteht ein signifikanter Unterschied zwischen schriftlichen IRC-Gesprächen und direkten oder Telefongesprächen. In letzteren würde in einem Fall wie diesem – wenn zwei Sprecher an einem TRP gleichzeitig zu sprechen anfangen – einer der beiden Sprecher seinen Turn vorzeitig abbrechen und dem anderen Sprecher den „Vortritt“ zu lassen (siehe Sacks et al. 1978, 39). Im IRC sind solche in mündlichen Gesprächen reparaturbedürftigen „turn-taking errors“ aufgrund der medialen Rahmenbedingungen jedoch ausgeschlossen, da es nicht zu Simultansequenzen infolge eines gleichzeitigen Einsetzens zweier oder mehrerer Sprecher oder infolge einer Unterbrechung kommen kann. So ist es auch nicht verwunderlich, daß im IRC Verstöße gegen die Turn-Verteilung, wie sie v.a. Unterbrechungen darstellen, da durch sie bewußt das Rederecht des aktuellen Sprechers verletzt wird, nicht thematisiert, geschweige denn sanktioniert werden.

Dennoch gibt es ein mit Unterbrechungen vergleichbares Phänomen in IRC-Kommunikation, wobei jedoch nicht ein spezieller Teilnehmer, sondern alle im Kanal anwesenden aktuellen und potentiellen „Sprecher“ und „Hörer“ unterbrochen werden:

(7)
[17:49:40] <flirt_> Hallo flirt muss gehn aber ihr koennt uns anrufen 08136/1811
... (neun Beiträge und vier Servermeldungen)
[17:50:08] <flirt_> Hallo flirt muss gehn aber ihr koennt uns anrufen 08136/1811
... (drei Beiträge)
[17:50:15] <flirt_> Hallo flirt muss gehn aber ihr koennt uns anrufen 08136/1811
... (ein Beitrag)
[17:50:17] <flirt_> Hallo flirt muss gehn aber ihr koennt uns anrufen 08136/1811
[17:50:17] <flirt_> Hallo flirt muss gehn aber ihr koennt uns anrufen 08136/1811
[17:50:17] <flirt_> Hallo flirt muss gehn aber ihr koennt uns anrufen 08136/1811
[17:50:17] <flirt_> Hallo flirt muss gehn aber ihr koennt uns anrufen 08136/1811
[17:50:18] <flirt_> Hallo flirt muss gehn aber ihr koennt uns anrufen 08136/1811
[17:50:19] <flirt_> Hallo flirt muss gehn aber ihr koennt uns anrufen 08136/1811
[17:50:19] <flirt_> Hallo flirt muss gehn aber ihr koennt uns anrufen 08136/1811
[17:50:19] <flirt_> Hallo flirt muss gehn aber ihr koennt uns anrufen 08136/1811
[17:50:20] <flirt_> Hallo flirt muss gehn aber ihr koennt uns anrufen 08136/1811
[17:50:20] <flirt_> Hallo flirt muss gehn aber ihr koennt uns anrufen 08136/1811
[17:50:20] <flirt_> Hallo flirt muss gehn aber ihr koennt uns anrufen 08136/1811
[17:50:20] <flirt_> Hallo flirt muss gehn aber ihr koennt uns anrufen 08136/1811
... (ein Beitrag)
[17:50:22] <flirt_> Hallo flirt muss gehn aber ihr koennt uns anrufen 08136/1811
[17:50:22] <flirt_> Hallo flirt muss gehn aber ihr koennt uns anrufen 08136/1811
[17:50] *** flirt_ was kicked by Minstrel_ (raus_)
[17:50] *** Sylvester sets mode: +b *!*@ic1.icafe.spacenet.de
[17:50:29] <Wavy> PankX: /k flirt_
[17:50] *** Sylvester sets mode: -b *!*@ic1.icafe.spacenet.de
[17:50:35] <Freerk> pankx ok cuu viel spas
[17:50] *** gump sets mode: +b *!*cafe@*.icafe.spacenet.de

Flirt_ sendet hier – nach anfangs längeren Zeitintervallen – innerhalb kürzester Zeit immer wieder denselben Beitrag an den Kanal und blockiert dadurch vollständig den die Nachrichten übermittelnden Server; die Übermittlung der Beiträge anderer Teilnehmer wird zu diesem Zeitpunkt dadurch unmöglich. Diese massive Störung durch den Teilnehmer flirt_ wird durch zwei IRC-spezifische „Reparaturmechanismen"– mittels der Befehle /kick und /ban[9] – sanktioniert.

6. Abschließende Bemerkungen

Die in der Artikelüberschrift aufgeworfene Frage, ob Turn-Verteilung in IRC-Kommunikation letztlich eher eine Frage der medialen Rahmenbedingungen oder aber der sozialen Regulierung sei, läßt sich nach den vorherigen Ausführungen nur mit einem „Sowohl-als-auch" beantworten.

Die genannten medial bedingten gesprächsinternen und -externen Faktoren – räumliche Trennung der Teilnehmer, Schriftlichkeit der Beiträge und v.a. die übertragungstechnisch bedingte Trennung von Produktion und Rezeption – haben zur Folge, daß sich die Turn-Verteilung und die daraus resultierenden Gesprächsstrukturen in IRC-Kommunikation auf der Basis der Sacks et al. (1978) zufolge Sprecherwechselvorgängen in mündlichen Gesprächen zugrunde liegenden Organisationsprinzipien zumeist nur noch in einer im höchsten Maße abstrahierten Form analysieren lassen. Dies zeigt sich u.a. in dem oben unter dem Aspekt „out of sequence" diskutierten Beispiel (6), das zwar nach der Logik des Turn-Taking-Systems erklärt werden kann (werden im aktuellen Beitrag keine Fremdzuweisungstechniken angewandt, dann kann Sprecherwechsel nach Selbstwahl stattfinden oder der aktuelle Sprecher produziert einen weiteren Beitrag), aber insofern nicht mehr mit den Sprecherwechsel-Organisationsprinzipien von Sacks et al. (1978) vereinbar ist, als „out of sequences" in IRC-Kommunikation an derartigen Stellen geradezu vorprogrammiert zu sein scheinen und keineswegs eines wie des oben geschilderten Reparaturmechanismus bedürfen. Des weiteren sind Konzepte wie „gaps" und „overlaps", die bei der Beschreibung der Turn-Verteilung in mündlicher Kommunikation eine wichtige Rolle spielen, auf die Turn-Verteilung in IRC-Kommunikation nur noch bedingt oder überhaupt nicht mehr anzuwenden. Diese noch um einige Punkte erweiterbare Liste an Unzulänglichkeiten des Turn-Taking-Systems, die sich bei der Analyse von Sprecherwechselvorgängen unter neuartigen medialen Rahmenbedingungen wie im IRC manifestieren, deutet darauf hin, daß das Modell in wesentlichen Punkten modifiziert werden müßte. Das bedeutet aber nicht, daß die soziale Turn-Verteilung in synchroner CVK vollständig von den medialen Rahmenbedingungen bestimmt und beschränkt wird, wie Murray (1989) mit ihrer Artikelüberschrift „When the medium determines turns [...]" suggeriert. IRC-Teilnehmer entscheiden durchaus noch gemeinsam darüber, „wer wann an der Reihe ist", wie man aus der äußerst linear und sequenziert verlaufenden Turn-Verteilung in Beispiel (3) schließen kann. Im IRC werden spezielle Reparaturmechanismen angewandt, wenn sich einer der Teilnehmer nicht an die Regeln hält (siehe Beispiel 7), oder wenn man eigene potentielle Regelverletzungen präventiv erklären und legitimieren möchte (siehe Beispiel 5).

Insgesamt wird deutlich, daß es noch eingehender Forschung bedarf, um valide Aussagen über die Gemeinsamkeiten und Unterschiede zwischen IRC-Kommunikation und direkter bzw. Telefonkommunikation hinsichtlich ihrer Sprecherwechselvorgänge organisierenden Prinzipien treffen zu können.

Anmerkungen

1) Dies zeigt sich an der zunehmenden Anzahl an diesem Themenbereich gewidmeten Kongressen und Tagungen, an Seminaren und Vorlesungen, an veröffentlichten und unveröffentlichten Forschungsarbeiten und Beiträgen. In Grosch (1997) findet man eine zwar um annähernde Vollständigkeit bemühte, angesichts des „CVK-Booms" innerhalb der Sprachwissenschaft aber inzwischen aktualisierungsbedürftige Bibliographie.
2) Besonders großes Interesse finden u.a. typographische Simulationen des in einem reinen Schriftmedium nicht gegebenen nonverbalen Verhaltens (hier v.a. Emoticons oder auch „Smileys"), „phonologische", morphologische und syntaktische Besonderheiten der CVK und nicht zuletzt die Tatsache der zumeist mangelnden Orientierung der Teilnehmer an orthographischen Regeln.
3) Einleitende und ausführliche Beschreibungen zur Technik des IRC findet man zuhauf im Internet selbst, wie z.B. die von Pioch (1993).
4) Eine kurze Bemerkung zu den Zeichenkonventionen im IRC: Nachrichten, denen drei Asterisken (Sternchen) vorangestellt sind, sind automatisch erstellte Servermeldungen, die u.a. das Betreten oder Verlassen eines Kanals durch einen Teilnehmer festhalten. Davon zu unterscheiden sind Nachrichten, denen nur ein Asterisk vorangestellt ist. Hierbei handelt es sich um sogenannte „actions", d.h. Handlungsbeschreibungen einzelner Teilnehmer, die mittels eines bestimmten Befehls erzeugt werden (siehe dazu Pioch (1993) und Lenke/Schmitz (1995)). Zusammen mit den Nachrichten der Teilnehmer, bei denen immer automatisch der jeweilige Nickname vorangestellt wird, um den Absender eines Beitrags anzuzeigen, bilden die Handlungsbeschreibungen die eigentlichen Turns der Teilnehmer. Die in diesem Text verwendeten IRC-Ausschnitte unterscheiden sich von den üblichen dadurch, daß hier mittels einer bestimmten Programmeinstellung zusätzlich eine Zeitangabe der einzelnen Aktivitäten wiedergegeben wird. Diese Zeitangabe ist für die nachfolgende Analyse der Turn-Verteilung in IRC-Kommunikation von Wichtigkeit. Die hier verwendeten IRC-Mitschnitte, die einer umfangreichen Korpussammlung in Grosch (1997) entstammen, wurden am 10.2.1997 in den Kanälen #muenchen und #austria erstellt.
5) Hier sei angemerkt, daß das inzwischen veraltete Programm Talk, das synchrone computervermittelte Kommunikation zwischen nur zwei Teilnehmern ermöglicht, Nachrichten simultan anzeigt, d.h. daß der Adressat Buchstabe für Buchstabe verfolgen kann, was der Gesprächspartner schreibt. In einem für multilaterale Kommunikation angelegten Programm wie IRC ist diese Form der simultanen Übertragung aufgrund des daraus resultierenden Chaos undenkbar und auch nicht sinnvoll.
6) Beiträge ohne aus diesem kurzen Ausschnitt erkennbaren Bezug werden hier nicht wiedergegeben.
7) Das im IRC des öfteren zu beobachtende Phänomen, daß in Kanälen mit mehreren aktiven Teilnehmern üblicherweise mehrere Zweipersonengespräche parallel stattfinden, entspricht der durch das Turn-Taking-System verursachten Tendenz zum „schism of one conversation into more than one conversation" in direkten Mehrpersonengesprächen, die Sacks et al. (1978, 22f.) diskutieren. Darauf soll an dieser Stelle jedoch nicht weiter eingegangen werden.
8) Im IRC kommt es häufig vor, daß Beiträge, die nicht explizit an einen oder mehrere Teilnehmer adressiert werden, von den IRC-Teilnehmern im wahrsten Sinne des Wortes übersehen werden und somit unbeantwortet bleiben.

9) Durch den Befehl /kick verweist man einen Teilnehmer aus einem IRC-Kanal; der Befehl /ban verhindert, daß ein Teilnehmer (wieder) einen Kanal betreten kann.

Literatur

Grosch, Yvonne (1997): Schreibend sprechen? Zur Gesprächshaftigkeit in Computer-Mediated Communication (CMC), dargelegt an Internet Relay Chat (IRC). Erlangen (unveröffentlichte Magisterarbeit).

Koch, Peter/Wulf Oesterreicher (1994): Funktionale Aspekte der Schriftkultur. – In: Hartmut Günther/Otto Ludwig (Hg.): Schrift und Schriftlichkeit. Berlin/New York, 587-604.

Lenke, Nils/Peter Schmitz (1995): Geschwätz im ‚Globalen Dorf' – Kommunikation im Internet. – In: Osnabrücker Beiträge zur Sprachtheorie (OBST) 50, 117-141.

Murray, Denise E. (1989): When the medium determines turns: turn-taking in computer conversation. – In: H. Coleman (Hg.): Working with Language. A Multidisciplinary Consideration of Language Use in Work Contexts. Berlin/New York, 319-337.

Pioch, Nicolas (1993): A short IRC primer. URL: ftp://nic.funet.fi/pub/unix/irc/docs.

Sacks, Harvey/Emanuel A. Schegloff/Gail Jefferson (1978): A Simplest Systematics for the Organization of Turn Taking in Conversation. – In: Jim Schenkein (Hg.): Studies in the Organization of Conversational Interaction. New York u.a., 7-55.

Schegloff, Emanuel A. (1972): Sequencing in Conversational Openings. – In: John J. Gumperz/Dell Hymes (Hg.): Directions in Sociolinguistics. The Ethnography of Communication. New York, 346-380.

Wichter, Sigurd (1991): Zur Computerwortschatz-Ausbreitung in der Gemeinsprache. Elemente der vertikalen Sprachgeschichte einer Sache. Frankfurt am Main.

Světla Čmejrková

Czech on the Network: Written or Spoken Interaction?

According to Josef Vachek, the Prague School theoretician of spoken and written language, "the written norm of language is a system of graphically manifestable language elements whose function is to react to a given stimulus (which, as a rule, is not an urgent one) in a static way, i.e. in a preservable and easily surveyable manner, concentrating particularly on the purely communicative aspect of the approach of the reacting language user". On the other hand, "the written norm of language is a system of graphically manifestable language elements whose function is to react to a given stimulus (which, as a rule, is not an urgent one) in a static way, i.e. in a preservable and easily surveyable manner, concentrating particularly on the purely communicative aspect of the approach of the reacting language user" (1973, 16).

Does Josef Vachek's well balanced scheme of the features of orality and literacy have its permanent validity, or have the manifestations of orality and writing changed so much in the period of technologically mediated communication that it is necessary to adapt this scheme?

Computer-mediated communication such as e-mail and Internet-relay chat (IRC) can be considered an intermediate form situated between writing and orality. E-mail is sometimes closer to a traditional letter, at other times closer to a face-to-face dialogue, i.e. to a quasi-oral exchange (Violi 1998). This impression is confirmed by computer users themselves. Those for whom e-mail has become a technique of everyday communication consider their exchange rather spoken. Their messages contain **allusions to the act of speaking**:

> Zitra? Prijdu, i kdyz jses první, kdo mi o tom **rika**.
> [Tomorrow? I'll come, though you are the first to **tell** me.]
> Boze muj, tohle bude nestvurne dlouhe! Ale kdyz se mi s panem XY tak krasne **povida**. Omlouvam se, ale nestydim se.
> [Oh God, this will be tremendously long. But it is so rewarding to have **a talk** with you. I apologize, but I don't feel ashamed.]
> Velmi pekne se mi s vami **povida**. Nenapadate, diskutujete.
> [It is so nice to have **a chat** with you. You are not aggressive, you just discuss.]

However, the act of writing is referred to as well. Whereas the references to the act of speech are rather unconscious, **allusions to the act of writing** are mostly conscious and very explicit. The technology of writing is focused on, as in:

> Jak jsem uz v kteresi diskuzi poznamenal, obcas me myslenky predbihaji me **prsty na klavesnici** a pak to dopada...
> [As I have already mentioned in one of our discussions, my ideas are faster than my **fingers on the keyboard** and the result is...]
> Ja se vzdycky tak rozohnim, ze se nekoukam **pod prsty**.
> [I always get so anxious that I do not look **at my fingers**.]
> Omlouvam se kolegovi Rehackovi za misspelling v jeho jmenu. Je to tim, ze rychleji myslim nez **pisu** - nebo naopak?
> [I apologize for misspelling Mr. Rehacek's name. It is because I think more quickly than **I type** - or vice versa?]

The dual interpretation of CMC, both against the background of spoken and written interaction, is the reason why I decided to discuss the question of its orality *vs* literacy, applying the linguistic distinction between the two aspects of discourse processing: It is most important to distinguish between a purely medial as against a conceptual aspect of orality and literacy (Daneš 1989). Whilst there is a clearcut medial difference between an orally delivered and a written text, things are more intricate on the conceptual side. Medial orality can combine with conceptual writtenness and conceptual orality combines with medial writtenness (Raible 1994).

1. Conceptual orality

It is *a priori* impossible to find on the level of conceptual orality and scripturality, the same clearcut distinction we necessarily encounter on the level of medial realization. We can only state that the investigation of CMC as a specific genre of written communication resembling an oral exchange establishes several features typical of speaking:

1.1 Spontaneity: *Write the way you speak*

The interactive, often emotional use of language is responsible for the common variety of language we normally use in an oral exchange: with addressing forms, questions, requests, accompanied with particles and interjections, and other typical dialogue means (*no, jo, proste, no tak, tak co, vis?, ne?, ehm...*), that make CMC discourse so like spoken language:

> Ahoj Lucie, tento tyden, vim ze je to trapne, ale tento tyden je uplne zabity. Pristi tyden mam volny, takze... Bye, Sabina
> [Hallo Lucie, this week, it's awkward, I know, but this week is out of the question. Next week I am free, so... Ahoj, Sabina.]
> Chapes to??? Jenom me!!! To je hruza, ze jo!!!
> [Can you understand that??? Only me!!! It's awkward, isn't it?]

1.2 Contact character: *I am close to you*

Many messages are sent just to test the channel and to establish contact:

> Já to jenom zkouším, jestli už tam seš.
> [I only want to know whether you are already there.]
> > > Je tam z Vas nekdo, nebo nefunguje ten mail ?
> > Zachytil jsem Tvoji zpravu, takze mail asi funguje.
> [> > Is anybody there, or e-mail does not work?
> > I've caught your message, so e-mail seems to work.]

1.3 A high degree of interactiveness: *Don't let me wait for an answer*

E-mail exhibits a strong need for a fast reply and when the interval is longer than expected it is considered a break down of e-mail etiquette. The effects of silence in e-mail can be compared to those in spoken interaction (Violi 1997):

Neodpověděla jsi na můj poslední mail.
[You have not answered my last e-mail.]

1.4 Sharing of the topic: *Briefness. – Exactly.*

The message is contextually bound, it refers to a preceding message and usually cannot be understood without the background knowledge shared by a sender and an addressee:

Flétna? To Ti závidím.
[Flute? I envy you.]
Proste Zlocin a trest. Ja to nejak preziju.
[Just Crime and Punishment. I'll try to survive.]

1.5 Restricted code: *Got it?*

The common background knowledge of the participants in e-mail communication is responsible for the usage of a restricted code of communication with many deictic pronouns and incomplete statements.

Bude to stacit? Nebo jich chces vic?
[Will it be O.K.? Or do you need more of them?]

1.6 Fragmentariness: *Thanks – no time – later – bye*

Diky. Ted letim na prednasku, ozvu se.
[Thanks. I am going to the lecture, I'll let you know later.]

1.7 Dialogue rhythm: *I am here. – We can go on*

Cau Miro, to jsem jeste ja, sedim na Sunech a pisu program, pokud ses na koleji, mohl bys vzit s sebou tu ucebnici Excellu na ten tisk? Martin
[Ciao Miro, it is me again, I am sitting at Sun's and writing a programme, if you are in the dormitory, could you bring the Excell handbook on print? Martin]
Ahoj Martine, sedim na koleji a programuju to na dalku. Ten Excell snad nezapomenu, ale prijedu az kolem poledne. Staci? Miro
[Hallo Martin, I am sitting in the dormitory and programming it on distance. I will bring the Excell, I hope, but I will not come until noon. Will it be in time? Miro]

1.8 Sharing of the situation: *I am sorry I have to leave now*

Though the partners are not located in the same place, they are as if located in the same time. The now of the sender is assumed to be the same as the now of the addressee. The form of communication is very similar to phone conversation. When we start to write an e-mail message, we in principle presuppose its immediate reception. Whereas letters are based on the feeling of the absence of the addressee, in e-mail interaction the addressee is as if co-present. This is expressed in the form of greetings as well as in final formulas:

> Dobre rano. Hezky dobry vecer. Hezkej den preju. Preju hezky den. Zdravim Te s pondelkem a preju Ti uspesny den. Zdravim Te a zas utikam pracovat. Hola, hola, prace vola. Koncim a jdu na obed. Koncim, musim upect kolac. No, jdu jist.
> [Good morning. Very good evening. I wish you a nice Monday and a successful day. I must be going now. I am running to work. I'm hungry. I have to cook.]

The structure of e-mail interaction resembles the structure of oral exchange. If e-mail induces us to write as we speak more than we would do in a regular letter, what are the features of writtenness, then?

2. Written medium

I will trace the marks of a certain primacy or independence of script in e-mail communication and show that it cannot be considered a simple representation of spokenness. Writing is not a simple transcription system of spoken speech, but a real technology in itself. And if writing is in itself a technology, writing e-mail is a double technology, in that it adds to the act of writing some unique features. The first arguments for uniqueness of scripturality are closely tied to processing e-mail messages in Czech.

2.1 Representation of speech? Code deficiencies

E-mail uses letters of the Czech alphabet, however graphic representation of spoken utterances in e-mail differs from that in other genres of written discourse (with the exception of the telegram). The relation of script to speech is obscured as e-mail communication operates mostly without diacritic signs (some of the Czech letters have hooks and long-signs). This small peculiarity can be either neglected or focused on in linguistic analysis. It is sometimes noticed by e-mail users themselves: *Bohous nebo Bohousz? [Bohous, or Bohousz?]*

It is obvious that on the part of e-mail writers a certain degree of concentration on the code is required not to use diacritic signs. It is possible to contradict, of course, that this technique of writing soon becomes an automatic skill, and it really does. However, writing without diacritic signs may also be conceived as a marked phenomenon as it often causes homonymy in Czech, particularly on the level of vocabulary. In most cases lexical homonymy goes without notice. However, sometimes it is thematised, focused on by e-mail users. Let's have several examples of those cases which were foregrounded:

- homonymy of nouns: *krtiny: křtiny [moles: christening party], plaz: pláž [reptile: beach], pracka: pračka [paw: washer]*
- homonymy of adjectives: *horky: hořký [hot: bitter]*
- homonymy of verbs: *radit: řádit [to advise: to rage], prorvat: prořvat [to burst through: to cry], servat: seřvat [to tear down: to howl down]*
- noun - verb conversion: *jarku: jářku [vocative form of Jarek: an archaic version of I say], skoleni: školení [fell, lay low (participle): schooling]*
  voli: volí [oxen: go to polls]

The last homonymy was foregrounded in:

> Kotazce blbych volicu doporucuji prostudovat Cimrmanovu studii "Kdyz volove voli".
> [As for the question of foolish voters I recommend Cimrman's study "When the oxen go to the polls".]

Even the most frequent final formula in Czech, something like *Have a good time* that sounds in Czech *Mej se dobre, Mej se pekne, Zatim se mej* or just *Mej se*, may be accompanied by comments explaining that the writer does not mean the process of washing and that his message is not to be read as a hygienic hint (as there is a homonymy of the imperative forms of verbs *to have* and *to wash*). The technologically constrained representation of spoken utterances is thus commented on.

2.2 Written symbolization of speech style

Deficient code used in e-mail conceals an important stylistic feature of Czech. It even prevents linguists from saying, which variety of Czech is being used, written or spoken: whether it is rather standard which is typical of written genres, or non-standard, which is typical of oral genres of Czech discourse.

2.21 As the distinction between long and short vowels in verb endings is hidden (*musim, prosim, chteji, prijizdeji*), we can only guess which variety of Czech is being used. Stylistic analysis of e-mail messages is to a certain extent obstructed.

2.22 Besides the shortened pronunciation of vowels, Czech substandard has also its own endings, e.g. *-ej* instead of *-y* in adjectives. Also here the technology of computer writing constrains the free spontaneity of spoken discourse. The channel seems to exert a certain pressure on the choice of endings: shorter endings are preferred to longer ones.

The writers avoid the nonstandard usage of *-ej* instead of standard *-y*: they write *byt* (more often than *bejt*), *ktery* (more often than *kterej*), *takovy* (more often than *takovej*), *cely* (more often than *celej*), and analogously *svych*, *zajimavych*, *veselych*, *tyden* etc. At the same time they use non-standard *takovyho*, *jaky* (instead of standard *jake*) etc. The choice of morphology seems to be determined by the requirements of language economy and easiness of decoding the technologically modified text.

We can conclude that technological constraints affect the form of writing, inducing a new stylistic standard as far as the choice of word forms is concerned.

2.3 Commentaries on typing errors and orthographic norms

As Umberto Eco (1992) says, for the first time in history of literacy, it is possible to write as quickly as we think, and not to care about the mistakes. With a computer screen you are standing face-to-face with thought in its raw state. Automatic surrealist writing has finally been born. In this sense the computer is an instrument of the spirit. Eco refers here to the spontaneity of writing which is responsible for the fact that written utterances resemble an inedited speech.

In processing computer mediated discourse, a high degree of tolerance both on the part of the writer and the reader is expected. Many misspellings, and much faulty punctuation go uncorrected. Only rarely do we find a complaint about the low writing level and the claim for correctness:

> Skoda, ze i sef mensy dela gramaticke chyby. Neni sam. Prosim vas, piste bez hrubych chyb. Prestoze pravopis je vedlejsi (obsah sdeleni je hlavni), prestoze muze byt arogantni zrovna na pripade sefa Mensy upozornovat na potrebu psat co NEJJASNEJI (= obvykle podle obecne uznavane normy pravopisu). Inteligent musi zvladnout i chaos, ale spotrebovava to cas. Osobne bych nerad plytval cizim casem. Diky.
> [It is a pity, that also the chief of Mensa makes grammatical mistakes. And not only him. Please, write without mistakes. Despite the fact that orthography is subsidiary (what is important is the content) and despite the fact that it may be arrogant to remind the chief of Mensa of the necessity to write AS CLEARLY AS POSSIBLE (usually according to the generally accepted orthographic norm). A clever man has to manage chaos also, but it is time consuming and I myself do not feel like wasting other people's time. Thanks.]

This criticism is a consequence of considering CMC a form of written language with its strict orthographic norms of correct spelling and appropriate lay-out. The norms of lay-out are discussed in the following example.

P.S. Pro pana Voracka: za predlozky na konci radku se omlouvam, v tomto programu se snad nedaji odstranit.
[P.S. I apologize for the prepositions at the end of lines, in this programme they probably cannot be removed.]

2.4 Switches to English code

Focusing on the code of CMC has further consequences. Communication around computers is mostly led in English and this causes natural switches to English lexemes and formulas:

Jsem prave unesen slovem **ficura** (s carkou a s hackem). Ze neuhodnes, co to je? To je preklad anglickeho **feature**. Napr.: Zdokumentovana chyba se stava **ficurou**.
Fatal error: Nevim, co to ten pocitac hlasi, adresa je spravna.
Hlasi mi to tu jakesi **delivery problems**. Doslo Ti to?
Microsoft Exchange je pekny bumbrlicek. (pozn. aut.)
Ohledne parky, sfot **houmpejdz** na http://manes.vse.cz/X-cs...
Tak mi **mailni**! (= **Mail me**!)
Jdu **brousit** internetem. (= **browse** in internet)
Dropni mi par lajen! (= Drop me a line!)

2.5 Operations with written text: abbreviations, plays on words, acronyms

Technological peculiarities are subject to further metalinguistic considerations. The writers tend to use and comment on various specific writing procedures, such as the usage of abbreviations, so typical of written text. So, *hth* is an abbreviation for *hope this helps*, *tml* for *that's more likely*, *asap* for *as soon as possible*, *afaik* for *as far as I know*, *bfn* for *bye for now*, *bcnu* for *be seeing you*. Some abbreviations and acronyms are more usual, other are restricted to narrow discourse communities of IRC participants. Besides standard abbreviations we can find various plays on words based on condensed communication:

Djkg - Drahy Jardo kup gin [Dear John buy gin],

or analogously,

(10^9 !, Cu) – (= cipher Miliardo!, Cuprum) – to be read: Mily Jardo, kup rum [Dear John, buy rum]

which can be decoded only using a graphic medium. Further kinds of cipher codes and text-compression are applied:

> Sifrovy klic bohuzel neznam, a tak timto onoho dotycneho, ci dotycnou zadam, aby mi ten klic
> poskytla, abych se konecne dozvedel, co jsem sem vlastne napsal. Dekuji.
My ten klíč bohužel také nemáme, ale alespoň jsme prohnali vaši zprávu čtyřtaktním kombajnem s automatickým oddělovačem plev a píšete v podstatě tohle:
[> Sorry I have not got the deciphering key, that's why please let me in so that I finally learn what I > have written. Thanks
We do not have the key either, however, we have sent your message through a four-stroke combine with an automatic separator of the grain from the chaff and you have principally written this:]
"hapihbn j io iorhfaOuhukha:fh fi:h jhdk: gkuaggfuhfg: fgauifgyaufg hfgh hvubbvilu rgaljgfhjgfjgh..."
Jsou totiz nejen zasifrovane, ale take stlacene (compressed). Abychom vsak ctenare neochudili a zasadni informace, tady je vycet stezejnich bodu z rozbaleneho (decompressed) prispevku:
[Your message is not only cipher-coded, but compressed as well. However, not to deceive the reader, we are providing him with the principal pieces of information. Here is the list of main issues of your unpacked (decompressed) contribution:]
-na str. 25: deti vyrazeji ze skoly a na ceste potkavaji sedlaka Matejku, ktery si vyndava strep z chodidla. Nervozni sedlak po nich vrhne hul, ktere se deti v posledni chvili vyhnou. Ve mlyne je vsechno v poradku, pouze celedin Ondra se nemuze smirit s opakovane odmitavym postojem devecky Klary.

Metalinguistic operations with the written code are conceived as something that has its validity in itself, as a specific semiotic performance. In the following example all the words start with the letter P. Whereas in spontaneous speech this feature cannot be achieved, the written medium is an appropriate environment for various plays with word arrangements:

Predseda povzbuzuje pritomne: pratele pristupte, podiskutujte, pokritizujte, pochvalte, proneste prognozy, promluvte par poznamek. Postupne povstavaji predem pripraveni pracovnici povereni pronest prispevky. Povetsinou pochlebuji predsedovi, prskajice pres pysky. Predseda polichocene prikyvuje. Pritomni podrimuji pripadne promysleji pracovni problemy. Po pohnutem podekovani prednasejicim pak povadle pracovniky postupne pohlcuje pozdni pondelni podvecer.

Admiration of metalinguistic writing operations reminds us of the medieval belief that the outer arrangement or pattern of written texts bears an additional sense.

2.6 Simulation of intonation and emphasis marking devices

Written representation of spoken utterances generally registers words without accompanying intonation and gestures. CM writing attempts to get over this constraint. First, the standard means such as exclamation marks and question marks are utilized. However, punctuation marks are often combined and multiplied: ...., *?????, !!!!!!!*

Besides that, the writer of e-mail often attempts to depict iconically further characteristics of a situation. The foregrounding devices are capitalization, italics, bold letters:

> Kazda ruka se hodi. FINISUJEME!
> Hi Svetla, (BIG sigh)...our semester is over!

Particularly popular is a doubling of letters used to emphasize exclamations, modality expressions, interjections, greetings, requests, compliments, evaluations, etc. Emphasis marks depict the author's emotions, mood, and state of mind:

> (ahooooj, aaaaahoj, horiiiiii!!!!!!, SSSSOOOSSS, soooooorry, Bafff!!!!, juuuuu, aaaaach jooooo, HURAAAAA, pomoooooooc, heeeeeelp, pozooooor, paaaaaani!, diiiiiiiky, no jooooo, AAAAAAAAAACH??????, ufffff!!!!!!, Caaaaaaaago!!!, byyyyyye!).
> Subject: HURAAAAA!!!!!!
> Zkompiloval jsem to!!!! Jedu za Tebou a budu ladit. Nevim, co bude s obedem, je mi nejak spatne.
> Subject. Horiiiiiiiii!!!!!!!!!
> Sice primo nehori, ale mam se s Tebou co nejdrive spojit kvuli zprave o expedici (konferenci) mladych lingvistu. Potrebuji pomoooooooc s tou zpravou do aktualit.

The subjective character of messages is expressed with emphasized evaluative adjectives: *velikaaanský, paraaaaadniiii* - and mainly with interjections: *Nikdo mi nepise beeeeeeeeee. [Nobody writes me beeeeeeee]*

It takes no pains to use double signs in computer writing, it is much easier than in handwritten language and that is why e-mail users do not feel constrained in doing so. They create thus a slightly modified version of written language.

2.7 Emoticons and other iconic signs

E-mail gives a graphic transmission to a number of emotional and physical actions, accompanying the act of speech, simulating them in a graphic code. It does so either using a mediation of the spoken word, as in the case of rendering intonation and emphasis, or without the mediation of the spoken word, as in other modes of transmission of bodily phenomenology. Particularly the latter case shows that the possibilities of script are newly tested and challenged to express the speaker's state of mind, body behaviour and actions. The tendency to take advantage of the ideographic elements of script develops in CMC more quickly than in a regular letter. Among the characteristic devices are emoticons (= emotional icons) and other iconic signs.

> Most popular are smileys: :), :)), :))), :-), :-)), :-))), ☺, ☺☺,
> or, on the contrary, frownies: :(, :((, :-(, :-((, :-C, ☹, ☹☹.
> Besides a *small grin* :-) there is also a *big grin*, which has an abbreviation *bg* and a symbol :->.

The emoticon :-| is a sign for a dull person, as well as :-] and (:<.), :=O, :-v are emoticons for a talkative person, called also a *chatterbox*.

The emoticon <|-) is a symbol for *to be a local Chinaman*, i.e. for a participant who does not understand what the others talk about.

Emoticons for accompanying gestures increase in number. Their appearance is mostly regulated by the keyboard set-up, some of them are more usual, the others are rather individual, or occasional. Naumann (1998) quotes e.g. a message containing the symbol for smoking:

> ich geh jetzt mal in ruhe eine ===~~~.

Though the participants do not have access to their bodily phenomenology, they wish to simulate it. This is a significant feature of **face-to-face scripturality**.

2.8 Transactional iconicity procedures

The writer of e-mail may not only aim at depicting his own emotional state and his own speech situation, but he tries to hit, or capture that of his addressee, as well. When writing a letter we sometimes also wish to send an addressee along with a verbal message some physical traces so to speak of the situation – a drawing, a flower, a fingerprint, or a kiss. E-mail expands the possibilities using its own graphic mode.

****
It is the first snowball fight of the season. Consider yourself hit.
Toto je prva gulovacka v tejto sezone. Povazuj sa za trafeneho myslim tym zasiahnuteho.

>>> snowballsnowball
>>> snowballsnowballsnowball
>>> snowballsnowballsnowballsnowballs
>>> snowballsnowballsnowballsnowballsnowball
>>> snowballsnowballsnowballsnowballsnowballsno
>>> snowballsnowballsnowballsnowballsnowballsnow
>>> snowballsnowballsnowballsnowballsnowballsnowba
>>> snowballsnowballsnowballsnowballsnowballsnowba
>>> snowballsnowballsnowballsnowballsnowballsnowba
>>> snowballsnowballsnowballsnowballsnowballsnowba
>>> snowballsnowballsnowballsnowballsnowballsnow
>>> snowballsnowballsnowballsnowballsnowballsno
>>> snowballsnowballsnowballsnowballsnowball
>>> snowballsnowballsnowballsnowballs
>>> snowballsnowballsnowball
>>> snowballsnowball

You are now involved in an e-mail snowball fight. Send this to all your friends and relatives. Have fun with it. Remember in an online snowball fight no one gets hurt and no one gets cold and soaking wet. So nail your friends before they nail you.
Prave si sa zapojil do e-mailovej gulovacky. Posli tento e-mail vsetkym svojim priatelom a pribuznym. Dobre sa zabavaj a pamataj, ze v online = gulovacke sa nikomu neublizi a nikto neprechladne. Takze smelo do toho, zloz svojich priatelov skor ako oni Teba.

The exchange is accompanied with the following commentaries.

At mas taky petardu!! A do tebe!!! Dost bolo gulovačky!!!!
Diky za osvezeni. Taje mi to tu.
[Thank you for a refresher. It is thawing here.]

3. Conclusion

My conclusion on Czech in the network is similar to that of Naumann's (1998) article on IRC in German. CM discourse is characterised by the configuration of features of both the spoken and written speech, with prevailing features bound to the medium (cf. DuBartell 1998). In this respect, CM discourse is a kind of creative language use, which supports the observation of the well-known semiotician of written language, Roy Harris:

"It is possible to formulate written messages (exploiting contrasts of position, direction, size, colour, font etc.) which cannot be rendered in the more restricted channel of oral-aural communication. But it is difficult to imagine examples of spoken messages which could not, in principle, be rendered by a graphic system." (Harris 1994,45).

The self-representation of a writer is highly peculiar to the medium and so are the social relations in discourse communities created by CMC users. In contrast to face-to-face oral exchange in which the speakers find themselves in social contact, in "face-to face scripturality" the participants of CMC feel they are very close to each other on the computer network, however, they are in social isolation. They are not exposed to any pressure of a social situation, they are, in fact, alone with their computers and this, at the same time, multiplies their inventive potentialities. The participants learn to be nice and friendly, familiar and joking. It is because only those who really wish to communicate use the channel. It often seems that there is more kindness in CM discourse than in our normal social life. Despite the fact that CM discourse is highly individualistic, as Violi (1998) puts it, it creates an impression of sociability and even love. In English there exists an obvious verbal parallel of *mail* to *smile* which is manifested in numerous smileys.

I do not know, whether in German or in English there exists any verbal connection between mail and love. But in Czech we have an assonance, or rhyme of the words *milovat (to love)* and *mailovat (to mail)*. That's why the discourse on e-mail is often opened by the slogan: *Miluj and mailuj? [Love and mail]*, or regretful or lamenting *Nikdo mi nemailuje* [Nobody mails me] referring to *Nikdo mi nemiluje [Nobody loves me]* .

As in German there are various paraphrases of the final greeting formulas *Auf (baldes) wiedersehen, Auf wiederschauen, Auf wiederhören,* which sound in Czech *Na (brzkou) shledanou, Na viděnou, Na slyšenou,* there is also a final formula in Czech *Na brzkou mailovanou.*

References

Anglicko/český slovník Internetu. Chat-slang (1997): Praha: Ivo Železný (transl. from Chat-Slang. Lexikon der Internet-Sprache, München: Carl Hanser Verlag 1996).

Daneš, František (1989): Existenzmodi des Textes. – In: Jan Kořenský/Wolfgang Hartung (eds.): Gesprochene und geschriebene Kommunikation, Linguistica XVIII, Prag: ÚJČ ČSAV, 49-56.

DuBartell, Deborah (1994): Language and Technological Media: Devising Parameters for the Relationships Between Speech and Writing. – In: Světla Čmejrková/František Daneš/Eva Havlová (eds.): Writing vs Speaking. Language, Text, Discourse, Communication, Tübingen, Gunter Narr, 167-174.

DuBartell, Deborah (1998): Methodological Issues in Computer-mediated Discourse. – In: Světla Čmejrková/Jana Hoffmannová/Olga Müllerová/Jindra Světlá (eds.): Dialoganalyse VI, Tübingen: Niemeyer, 241-248.

Eco, Umberto (1992): Computer is an Instrument of the Spirit. – In: Literární noviny, 12.

Harris, Roy (1994): Semiotic Aspects of Writing. – In: Writing and Its Use. Berlin/New York: De Gruyter 1994, 41-47.

Naumann, Bernd (1998): Stirbt die deutsche Sprache? Überlegungen zum Sprachwandel durch IRC (Internet Relay Chat). – In: Světla Čmejrková/Jana Hoffmannová/Olga Müllerová/Jindra Světlá (eds.): Dialoganalyse VI, Tübingen: Niemeyer, 249-262.

Raible, Wolfgang (1994): General Aspects of Writing. – In: Writing and Its Use. Berlin/New York: De Gruyter, 1-17.

Uhlířová, Ludmila (1994): E-mail as a New Subvariety of Medium and Its Effects Upon the Message. – In: Světla Čmejrková/František Štícha (eds.): The Syntax of Sentence and Text, Amsterdam/Philadelphia: John Benjamins, 273-282.

Vachek, Josef (1973): Written Language: General Problems and Problems of English. The Hague: Mouton.

Vachek, Josef (1979): Written Language Revisited. Amsterdam/Philadelphia: John Benjamins.

Violi, Patrizia: Electronic dialogue between orality and literacy. A Semiotic Approach. – In: Světla Čmejrková/Jana Hoffmannová/Olga Müllerová/Jindra Světlá (eds.): Dialoganalyse VI, Tübingen: Niemeyer, 263-270.

Annely Rothkegel

Interaktion und Interaktivität in Hypermedia

1. Information und Kommunikation

Die neuen Informationstechnologien kreieren einen neuen Umgang mit Information und Informationsflüssen. Hypermedia als Medium für den interaktiven Umgang mit Information in verschiedenen, häufig gemischten Zeichensystemen ist ein Mittel der computervermittelten Kommunikation (CMC, computer mediated communication), das Eigenschaften eines Massenkommunikationsmittels und Tendenzen der Individualisierung in sich vereinigt (Herring 1996). Welche Auswirkungen Hypermedia gerade wegen seiner Massen-Nutzung haben kann, ist noch nicht vorherzusehen. Fragen kann man allerdings, welche Prinzipien eine Rolle spielen und inwieweit solche Prinzipien durch linguistische Methoden erfaßt werden können (vgl. Lutz 1995). In diesem Sinne werden die Aktivitäten der Nutzer beim Gebrauch von Hypermediasystemen, die üblicherweise mit dem Begriff der Navigation etikettiert werden, differenziert nach Gesichtspunkten, die durch die medienabhängige Organisationsstruktur der vermittelten Information (Inhalte) bestimmt sind und solche, die durch Ziele und Gewohnheiten der Nutzer bestimmt sind. Ersteres fassen wir unter den Begriff der Interaktivität. Er bezeichnet die Eigenschaft des Mediums bzw. der Software im Hinblick auf ihre Funktionalität. Für den Umgang der Nutzer mit Hypermedia zu selbst bestimmten Zwecken verwenden wir den Begriff Interaktion. Gemeint ist hier, daß – wie für Texte und/oder Dialoge – eine kommunikative Situation vorliegt, die durch Informationsgeber und Informationsnehmer (also nicht primär durch das Medium) bestimmt ist.

Ähnliche Versuche, jeweils eine der beiden Perspektiven zu fokussieren, beziehen sich zum einen darauf, die Eigenschaften von Hypermedia im Sinne einer Hypertextstruktur und diese im Sinne von Texteigenschaften zu thematisieren (u.a. als rhetorische Relationen (links) in Thüring et al. 1991); zum anderen wird die dem Hypermediasystem zugrundeliegende Datenbankstruktur aufgefaßt als Basis eines Expertensystems (bzw. als Frage-Antwort-System), dessen Schnittstelle – wie für solche Art von Systemen bereits eingeführt – für den Gebrauch als Dialog modelliert wird (Jonassen 1992, Thiel 1995). In der Regel wird, auch bei der nicht-technischen, sondern eher didaktisch orientierten Diskussion eine solche Unterscheidung nicht vorgenommen (Oliveira 1992, Issing/Klimsa 1997). Die Aktivitäten werden vielmehr generell unter dem Punkt „Navigation" zusammengefaßt. Z.B. führt Haack (1997, 156) in Anlehnung an Gall/Hannafin (1994) verschiedene „Interaktionsformen" innerhalb der Navigation an: „searching" als gezielte Informationsanfrage, „browsing" als Durchwandern ohne ein klar umrissenes Informationsziel, „connecting" als das Herstellen neuer Verknüpfungen zwischen Informationen und „collecting" als Erzeugung neuer Ensembles von Informationen.

Die Differenzierung von zwei Ebenen des Geschehens, Interaktivität und Interaktion bzw. Funktionalität und Anwendung eines Systems, bedeutet linguistisch Folgendes: Interaktivität ist organisiert in erster Linie nach Gesichtspunkten inhaltlicher Art, z.B. wie Kohärenz über verschiedene Vernetzungen hinweg erhalten bzw. aufgebaut wird. Interaktion ist dagegen organisiert nach Sequenzmustern der Kommunikation, in denen eine bestimmte Aktion eine bestimmte Reihe von Antwort-Optionen festlegt, von denen jede wiederum eine Aktion mit weiteren Optionen darstellt. Eine Möglichkeit für eine linguistische Betrachtungsweise wird im Folgenden anhand eines Beispiels aus einer Online-Hilfe demonstriert. Wir gehen in der Weise vor, daß wir zuerst näher anschauen, wie „Interaktivität" unter Inhaltsgesichtspunkten zu verstehen ist, bevor die Einbindung des Inhalts in die Interaktion betrachtet wird.

2. Inhaltsorientierung der Interaktivität

Bezug wird genommen auf Organisationsprinzipien, die generell dem Hypermedium zugrundeliegen, so z.B. der Organisationsstruktur des Internets oder derjenigen auf CD-ROMs, wo ganz unterschiedliche Wissensinhalte für variable Nutzungen präsentiert werden. Die verwendete Basisstruktur bezeichnet man allgemein als „Hypertext", dies mit dem Hypertext-Erfinder Bush, der mit seinem System MEMEX und dem begleitenden Artikel mit dem Titel „As we may think" 1945 eine neue Ära in der Informatik einleitete, die offensichtlich große Folgen für die Massenkommunikationsmedien hat. Gemeint ist die Vernetzung von Informationseinheiten unterschiedlicher Art in einer Datenbankorganisation, die den Anwendern das Verfolgen der Pfade in dieser Netzstruktur gestattet. Mit Interaktivität beim Gebrauch von Software ist generell gemeint, daß Information portionsweise und dementsprechend geordnet präsentiert als Output verfügbar gemacht wird, wobei das System für die jeweilige Selektion der Information einen mehr oder weniger festgelegten Input der NutzerInnen verarbeitet. Es ist die „Eigenschaft von Software, dem Benutzer eine Reihe von Eingriffs- und Steuermöglichkeiten zu eröffnen" (Haack 1997, 153).

2.1 Arten der Linearität

Ein solches Verfahren setzt eine darauf angepaßte Organisation der Informationen bzw. der diese vermittelnden Texteinheiten voraus. Textlinguistisch interessant sind dabei drei Organisationsprinzipien: Fragmentierung, Fortsetzung und Fokussierung. Es handelt sich um Prinzipien, die als solche im Hinblick auf den linearen Text Geltung haben. Hier werden sie nun auf die Hypertextorganisation angewendet. Damit wird – anders als sonst, wenn auf die Unterschiede von Text und Hypertext abgehoben wird (Überblick in Storrer 1998) –, die Ähnlichkeit beider Strukturen hervorgehoben. In diesem Sinne unterscheiden wir nicht zwischen linearem Printtext und nicht-linearem Hypertext (Kuhlen 1991), sondern zwischen monolinearem Printtext und multilinearem Hypertext (Jaynes 1989; vgl. Diskussion in Rothkegel 1998). Dem liegt eine texttheoretische Auffassung zugrunde derart, daß ein Text gleichermaßen wie ein Hypertext auf mehreren Ebenen strukturiert ist (vgl. Textebenen in Rothkegel 1993, Motsch 1996). Als Textebenen können u.a. unterschieden werden eine semantisch-thematische Textebene und eine intentional-funktionale Textebene, deren Einheiten auf einer textsyntaktischen Ebene der Textorganisation angeordnet sind. Diese Ebene der Textorganisation umfaßt sowohl hierarchische als auch sequentielle Ordnungen. Hier zeigt sich der Unterschied von Text und Hypertext in der Weise, daß die hierarchische Ordnung im Hypertext deutlicher sichtbar ist, so in der immerhin ebenfalls impliziten Hypertextbasis, die als hierarchische Struktur definiert ist (vgl. Abb. 1).

HILFE		=>	THEMEN				
		=>	drucken	=>	Probleme		
				=>	Schritte		
				=>	Definition	=>	Spezifikation
						=>	Anleitung
	=>	INDEX					
	=>	STICHWÖRTER					
		=>	drucken	=>	Probleme		
				=>	Schritte		
				=>	Definition	=>	Spezifikation
						=>	Information

Abb. 1 Beispiel für Hypertextbasis (Online-Hilfe für „drucken" in Textverarbeitung)

Im traditionellen Text dagegen steht die sequentielle Ordnung im Vordergrund, d.h. die Festlegung auf eine der möglichen Alternativen, wie sie im Hypertext als gleichzeitige Optionen angeboten werden und wo erst in der Nutzung eine bestimmte Reihenfolge selektiert wird (zu Online-Hypertexten vgl. Rubens/Krull 1988, Price 1988).

Die hierarchische Ordnung in diesem Beispiel sieht zwei verschiedene Teilbäume vor, die zu Angaben über den Vorgang „drucken" führen, einmal über THEMEN, das andere Mal über STICHWÖRTER. Der Pfad unter THEMEN endet mit einer „Anleitung zum Drucken", während der Pfad unter STICHWÖRTER eine spezifische „Information" gibt. Im Printtext würde eine solche Aufteilung zwei getrennten Teilthemen (Textsegmenten) entsprechen, die nacheinander aufgeführt würden. Abb. 2 skizziert eine mögliche Konvertierung des Hypertextes in eine hierarchische und sequentielle Printform.

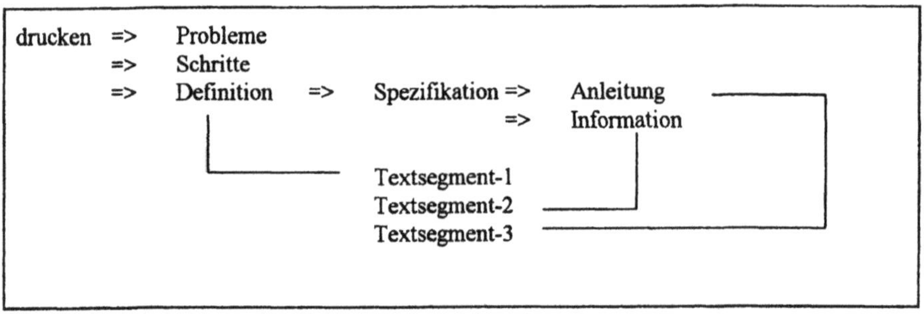

Abb. 2 Hierarchie und Sequenz im Printtext (konvertiert aus Hypertext Online-Hilfe)

2.2 Fragmentierung (groß, klein)

Verzweigung bzw. Vernetzung setzt voraus, daß die zu vermittelnden Informationen in separaten bzw. separierbaren Teiltexten organisiert sind. Dies bedeutet Fragmentierung in kleine Textpäckchen, die insgesamt kohärent sein sollten. Es ist einleuchtend, daß die Kohärenzbildung im Printtext relativ einfacher ist, da hier die Einheitenbildung einen besseren Überblick ermöglicht. Sind die Einheiten dagegen relativ klein, ist die thematische Blockbildung unter Beibehaltung einer übergreifenden kohärenten Struktur erschwert. Linguistisch ausgedrückt: de Hypertext setzt eine stärkere Planung (beim Konzipieren) bzw. deutlichere Erkennbarkeit (zum Rezipieren) der Makrostruktur voraus (Shneiderman 1989, Anwendung auf ein Modell der Textproduktion in Rothkegel 1997). Dies widerspricht der ursprünglichen Hypertext-Idee, nämlich der Möglichkeit des freien Assoziierens von Inhalten.

2.3 Fortsetzung (stabil, instabil)

Prinzip des Hypermediums ist es im weiteren, daß solche Teiltexte in mehrfacher Weise miteinander verknüpft werden können. Um das Ganze im textlinguistischen Sinne kohärent zu halten, ist es also notwendig, jede potentielle Anknüpfungsstelle im Hinblick auf die erwünschten Fortsetzungen anzulegen. Nun kann man davon ausgehen, daß die Organisation der Fortsetzung im Printtext in zwei Richtungen verläuft (Details in Rothkegel 1993). In der Richtung links => rechts (oder oben => unten) zielt der Text vorwärts auf Komplettierung des Textthemas, d.h. die Fortsetzungsoption betrifft die neue Information, die an die bereits eingeführte angeknüpft wird (Thema-Rhema-Progression). Die dabei aufkommende Instabilität wird aufgefangen in der zweiten Art der Gerichtetheit, nämlich rechts => links (oder unten => oben), d.h. die Anknüpfung erfolgt rückwärts an das Vorhergehende durch Wiederholung bzw. Wiederaufgreifen des bereits Eingeführten (Anaphorik). Eine ähnliche Zuordnung findet sich bereits bei Roman Jakobson (1954 (1996)) in der Herausarbeitung zweier Prinzipien des Sprachgebrauchs, die die Fortsetzung der Rede organisieren: die paradigmatische Fortsetzung (dasselbe noch einmal sagen, Anaphorik bzw. Wiederholung) und die syntagmatische Fortsetzung (etwas anderes sagen, Progression).

Im Hypertext ist nun die stabilisierende Fortsetzung weniger realisierbar – man kann nicht unbedingt im voraus wissen, welcher Knoten der Vorgänger wessen anderen Knotens ist. Infolgedessen besteht hier das Risiko einer höheren Instabilität. Diese läßt sich kompensieren durch zusätzliche Überblicksdarstellungen, die allerdings permanent verfügbar sind.

2.4 Fokussierung (Vordergrund, Hintergrund)

Der mögliche Wechsel der Richtung im Hypertext verlangt ein Konzept, das einer solchen Dynamik Rechnung tragen kann. Ein Rahmen für eine derartige dynamische Informationsorganisation bietet eine Dreiteilung, die unterschiedliche Grade der jeweiligen Aufmerksamkeit seitens des Rezipienten erfaßt: Fokus, Vordergrund und Hintergrund. Danach stünde im Fokus die aktuell bearbeitete Information, den Vordergrund bezeichnete die Informationen, die zugleich mit dem Fokus präsent sein können, aber schwächer beachtet sind, und Hintergrund wäre das, was aktuell nicht zur Verfügung steht, aber verfügbar gemacht werden kann. Mit Bezug auf die Präsentation im System entspricht der Fokus dem, was jeweils selektiert wird, der Vordergrund enthält das damit gleichzeitig auf dem Bildschirm sichtbare Tableau, d.h. das zusammen aufgeführte Ensemble von Informationen in den Textpäckchen. Der Hintergrund schließlich ist gegeben durch die darin enthaltenen Optionen, die aus dem Tableau herausführen und Zugänge zu anderen Tableaus offerieren.

In der Verbindung von Fortsetzung und Fokussierung ergibt sich Folgendes: übersetzt in thematisch-semantische Kategorien enthält der Vordergrund neben direkten Repetitionen Paraphrasen, Spezifikationen, Detaillierungen, Generalisierungen, Kontrastierungen, der Hintergrund dagegen neue Themen. Themeneinführung, Themenwechsel, Themenabschluß sind hier die Kategorien, die zum Tragen kommen. Der Fokus bildet den beweglichen Teil, der je nach Anwenderinteresse ausgewählt wird. Ihm zugeordnet sind Vordergrund und Hintergrund. Dies bedeutet, daß in Abhängigkeit des jeweils gewählten Fokus unterschiedliche Vordergründe und Hintergründe zu organisieren sind. Dies ist der zentrale Punkt der Multilinearität, der eine Interaktivität von Inhaltlichen her gesehen sinnvoll macht.

3. Information und Ziele in der Interaktion

Unter dem Etikett Hypermedia-Design geht es u.a. darum, die Möglichkeiten zur Übernahme der Dialoginitiative durch die Anwender zu organisieren und dabei einen potentiellen „cognitive overload“ (Conclin 1987) zu vermeiden, der dadurch entsteht, daß Anwender sowohl ihre eigene Fragestellung im Kopf behalten möchten und gleichzeitig die implizite Struktur des Hypertexts rekonstruieren müssen, um nicht die Orientierung zu verlieren. Dies spricht dafür – wie in unserem Ansatz ausgeführt – beide Ebenen zu trennen. In diesem Sinne ist also ein zusätzliches Konzept erforderlich, das den Zielen der AnwenderInnen Rechnung trägt. Hierzu schauen wir uns ebenfalls nach linguistischen Konzepten um, die hilfreich sein könnten, wobei wir voraussetzen, daß die sogenannte

Mensch-Maschine-Interaktionen durch Interaktionsmuster begünstigt wird, wie sie aus Dialog- und Konversationsanalyse bekannt sind. So zeigen sich hier parallele Entwicklungen zu denen, die die Forschung in bezug auf automatische Textgenerierungsverfahren oder Dialogverfahren für Expertensysteme bestimmt haben: Versuche, das was wir bereits aus Untersuchungen zu Text und Dialog aus der Mensch-Mensch-Kommunikation kennen, in die Modellierung programmierbarer Systeme einzubringen. Winograd/Flores, bereits 1986, sprechen von einem neuen Design, das nach Maßstäben einer „social cognition" die Mensch-Maschine-Interaktion prägen könnte.

Die diesbezügliche Diskussion reicht von der Konstruktion eigener Interface-Sprachen über Gestaltungsfragen von Bildschirmseiten bis zur „task-action-grammar", einem Versuch, die Interaktion in Form von Handlungsplänen darzustellen (Howes/Young 1996). Ein Ziel ist, „to bridge the gap between social and technological dimensions in computer design and use" (so Mantovani 1996). Hier scheint wiederum das Winograd-Modell durch. Winograd, ein Altmeister der KI, hat für die in der Dialogforschung bekannten Interaktionssequenzen eine Repräsentation in Form einer Übergangsgrammatik (Übergangsnetzwerk) vorgeschlagen.

Der Kern einer solchen Grammatik ist folgender: ausgehend von einem Zustand-1, der durch eine initiierende Aktion bestimmt ist, gibt es eine ganz bestimmte Reihe alternativer Reaktionen, die als Fortsetzungsoptionen zu einem Zustand-2 übergehen. Für den nächsten Zug erhält dieser Zustand-2 wiederum den Status als Zustand-1 mit ebenfalls festgelegten Optionen, die ihrerseits zum Zustand-n führen. Indem einige der Reaktionen wiederum zum Ausgangszustand zurückführen, entstehen Zyklen (Rothkegel 1994).

Winograd/Flores (1986) haben die Interaktionsgrammatik am Beispiel „eine Anfrage/Anforderung stellen" („requesting") demonstriert. Die Angabe der Alternativen sieht im Ausschnitt und informell wie folgt aus (Abb. 3):

(1) A stellt eine Anforderung =>		
(2a) B macht ein Versprechen	=> (3a) A akzeptiert	=> (4) B bestätigt
(2b) B lehnt ab	=> (3b) A zieht zurück	

Abb. 3 Alternativen im Interaktionszyklus (Winograd/Flores 1986)

Im Rahmen der Dialoggrammatik sind ähnliche Sequenzmuster erstellt worden, z.B. zum INSISTIEREN (Franke 1983), desgleichen für die Modellierung von Dialogen in Expertensystemen (Sitter/Stein 1992). Nun geht es beim Gebrauch von Hypermedia in erster Linie um ein INFORMIEREN, das sich weniger im Hinblick auf die sozialen Rollen als durch die Art der betreffenden Informationen differenzieren läßt (auf die Handlung UNTERHALTEN wird an dieser Stelle nicht eingegangen). Bringen wir eine solche Differenzierung mit den inhaltlichen Gesichtspunkten wie Fragmentierung, Fortsetzung und Fokussierung zusammen, dann ergibt sich Folgendes:

Die einzelnen Fragmente bestimmen jeweils eine Fragehandlung (FRAGEN), auf die vom System mit einer Antwort reagiert wird (ANTWORTEN). In der Anwendung entspricht dem FRAGEN die Selektion dessen, was angeklickt wird, weil zu dem betreffenden Punkt weitere Information erwünscht ist. Eine mögliche Fortsetzung bestimmt sich danach, ob weiterhin Information vom Vordergrund benötigt wird, also mehr Information zum gleichen Sachverhalt in der näheren Umgebung des gewählten Fokus, oder ob ein Themenwechsel vorgenommen werden soll. Dies bedeutet dann, daß ein anderer Teilbaum im Gesamtnetz aufgesucht wird. Ersteres ordnen wir der Handlung NACHFRAGEN zu, letzteres der Handlung WEITERFRAGEN. Auf dieser Grundlage läßt sich ein grobes Schema für die Interaktion in der Perspektive der Anwendung festlegen (Abb. 4):

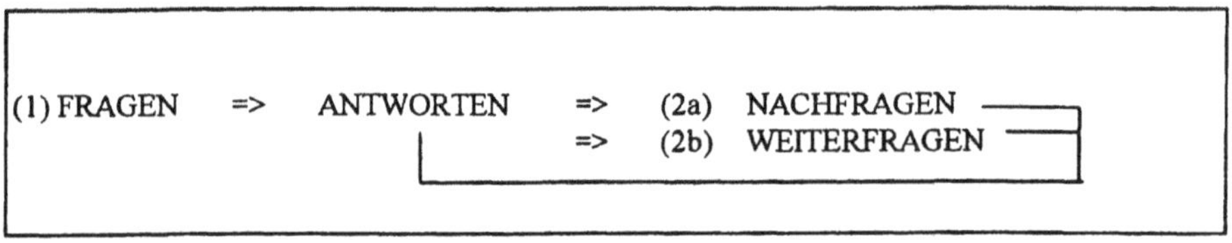

Abb. 4 Interaktionszyklus mit unterschiedlicher Fokussierung

Bei NACHFRAGEN wird eine Antwort erwartet, die als Zuordnung zum Vordergrund eine Paraphrase sein kann, eine Detaillierung oder Spezifizierung. Bei WEITERFRAGEN wird eine Antwort erwartet, die das Thema komplettiert bzw. die ein neues Thema einführt.

Gehen wir nun zurück zu unserem Beispiel „drucken" aus der Online-Hilfe, so ergibt sich folgende Zuordnung: Direkt bei der ersten Selektion für HILFE muß eine Festlegung auf je eines der Themen erfolgen (das ist einsichtig, da weitere Erklärungen zu dem, was HILFE bedeutet, an dieser Stelle nicht sinnvoll sind), d.h. nach

(1) FRAGEN (anklicken von HILFE) und ANTWORTEN (Anzeige des Systems mit den Optionen THEMEN, INDEX, STICHWÖRTER) ist die Alternative

(2b) WEITERFRAGEN bereits durch die Hypertextstruktur vorgegeben. Hier muß zunächst das gewuenschte Teilthema festgelegt werden. Erst dann kann das Subthema „drucken" mit

(2a) NACHFRAGEN ausführlicher durch weitere Spezifikationen behandelt werden (vgl. PROBLEME, SCHRITTE, DEFINITION).

Diese grobe Einteilung bildet einen Rahmen für weitere Elaborationen auf der Grundlage empirischer Untersuchungen (Beispiele auch in Rothkegel 1998).

4. Schlußfolgerung und Perspektiven

Insofern als ein Hypertext ein Text ist, können linguistische Text- und Dialogmodelle genutzt werden, nach denen Informationsauswahl und Informationsfluß in Abhängigkeit der anvisierten Interaktionsziele analysiert bzw. gestaltet werden können. Aus dieser Perspektive heraus wäre dann im weiteren die Interaktivität des hypermedialen Produkts zu analysieren bzw. im Rahmen einer Produktion zu organisieren. In einem weiteren Horizont ergibt sich mit den neuen Medien – vor allem mit Hyper- und Multimedia – eine neue Perspektive für die Integration von Geisteswissenschaften und Informationstechnologie. Diese Medien erweitern das bisherige Spektrum, in dem Sprache und Kommunikation den Anwendungsbereich für Softwareentwicklung bildet (Information Retrieval, Expertensysteme und Maschinelle Übersetzung). Der neue vierte Bereich betrifft den von Hyper- und Multimedia, der bislang vorwiegend unter hard- und software-technischen Aspekten weiterentwickelt wird. Hier ergibt sich eine Möglichkeit, linguistisches Expertenwissen für Analyse und Konstruktion, aber auch für neue Fragestellungen in der Forschung einzubringen.

Literatur

Barrett, Edward (ed.) (1988): Text, ConText, and HyperText. Writing with and for the Computer. Cambridge (Ma): MIT Press.

Barrett, Edward (ed.) (1989): The Society of Text. Hypertext, Hypermedia, and the Social Construction of Information. Cambridge (Ma): MIT Press.

Bush, Vannevar (1945): As we may think. In: Atlantic Monthly 7, 101-108.

Conclin, J. (1987): Hypertext: An introduction and survey. – In: Computer, 20 (9), 17-41.

Franke, Wilhelm (1983): Insistieren. Eine linguistische Analyse. Göppingen: Kümmerle.

Gall, J. E./Hannafin, M. J.(1994): A framework for the study of hypertext. – In: Instructional Science, 22, 207-232.

Haack, Johannes (1997): Interaktivität als Kennzeichen von Multimedia und Hypermedia. – In: Issing/Klimsa (Hrsg.): Information und Lernen mit Multimedia, 151-166. Weinheim: Beltz.

Herring, Susan C. (ed.) (1996): Computer-Mediated Communication. Linguistic, Social and Cross-Cultural Perspectives. Amsterdam: Benjamins.

Howes, A./Young, R. (1996): Learning consistent, interactive, and meaningful task-action mapping: a computational model. – In: Cognitive Science 20, 301-356.

Issing, Ludwig J./Klimsa, Paul (Hrsg.): Information und Lernen mit Multimedia. Weinheim: Beltz.

Jakobson, Roman (1956/1996): Der Doppelcharakter der Sprache und die Polarität zwischen Metaphorik und Metonymie. – In: Haverkamp, Andreas (Hrsg.): Theorie der Metapher. Darmstadt: Wiss. Buchgesellschaft, 163-174.

Jaynes, Joseph T. (1989): Limited freedom: linear reflections on nonlinear texts. – In: Barrett (ed.), 148-161.

Jonassen, David H. (1992): Adding intelligence to hypertext with expert systems and adding usability to expert systems with hypertext. – In: Oliveira (ed.), 188-197.

Kuhlen, Rainer (1991): Hypertext. Ein nicht-lineares Medium zwischen Buch und Wissensbasis. Berlin: Springer.

Lutz, Benedikt (1995): Hypertextlinguistik: Erfahrungen aus der Praxis – Anregungen für die linguistische Forschung. – In: Schmitz, Ulrich (Hrsg.): Neue Medien. Osnabrücker Beiträge zur Sprachtheorie, 50, 155-163.

Mantovani, Giovanni (1996): Social Context in HCI (Human Computer Interaction). – In: Cognitive Science 20, 237-269.

Motsch, Wolfgang (Hrsg.) (1996): Ebenen der Textstruktur. Sprachliche und kommunikative Prinzipien. Tübingen: Niemeyer.

Oliveira, Armando (ed.) (1992): Hypermedia Courseware: Structures of Communication and Intelligent Help. Berlin: Springer.

Price, Jonathan (1988): Creating a Style for Online Help. – In: Barrett (ed.), 329-341.

Rothkegel, Annely (1993): Textualisieren. Theorie und Computermodell der Textproduktion. Frankfurt/Main: Lang.

Rothkegel, Annely (1994): Interactional cycles. – In: Schön, Jackie (ed.): Le Dialogue en Question. Actes du Colloque, Lagrasse 1993. Cahiers du Centre Interdisciplinaire des Sciences du Langage, no. 10, Toulouse, 273-281.

Rothkegel, Annely (1997): Wie entsteht ein Text? Skizze zu einer Hypermedia-Anwendung. – In: Sprache und Datenverarbeitung-1(21), 53-62.

Rothkegel, Annely (1998): Präsentation und/oder Repräsentation in Hypermedia. – In: Hielscher, Martina/Sichelschmidt, Lorenz/Strohner, Hans (Hrsg.): Medium Sprache. Tübingen: Narr.

Rubens, Philip/Krull, Robert (1988): Designing Online Information. – In: Barrett (ed.), 291-308.

Schuler, Wolfgang/Hannemann, Jörg/Streitz, Norbert (eds.) (1995): Designing User Interfaces for Hypermedia. Berlin: Springer.

Shneiderman, Ben (1989): Reflections on Authoring, Editing, and Managing Hypertext. – In: Barret, Edward (ed.): The Society of Text. Cambridge (MA): MIT Press, 115-131.

Sitter, Stefan/Stein, Angelika (1992): Modeling the Illocutionary Aspects of Information-Seeking Dialogues. – In: Information Processing and Management, Vol. 28 (2), 165-190.

Storrer, Angelika (1998): Hypermedia als Kommunikations- und Publikationsmedium in den Geisteswissenschaften. – In: Sprache und Datenverarbeitung, 1/98, 5-9.

Thiel, Ulrich (1995): Interaction in hypermedia systems: from browsing to conversation. – In: Schuler et al., 43-54.

Thüring, M./Haake, J./Hannemann, J. (1991): What's Eliza doing in the Chinese room? – Incoherent Hyperdocuments – and how to avoid them. – In: Proceedings of the 3rd ACM (Association for Computing Machines) Conf. on Hypertext '91. New York: ACM Press, 161-177.

Winograd, T./Flores, F. (1986): Understanding Computers and Cognition. A new foundation for design. Reading: Addison-Wesley.

Henning Westheide

Interactivity in Language Learning: The Multimedia Classroom

Die Annahme einer fremden Technik ist ein Unterwerfungsakt, dessen Folgen um so gefährlicher sind, als er sich zunächst im Geiste vollzieht. (Ernst Jünger: Der Arbeiter 1932)

1. From language laboratory to the multimedia classroom

"Investment in the future" is the slogan of the hardware for the multimedia classroom I am working with. The multimedia classroom is supposed to enable the students to learn actively and independently, appropriate to their abilities and pace. The learning situation is described as stimulating and motivating. It should remove the teacher from the front of the classroom and give him the position of a tutor instead. And fore all, it is called interactive. As computer assisted language learning (CALL) is supposed to replace classroom teaching to some extent, I want to discuss the question what kind of interactivity we can expect in this framework. To me this aspect is part of a far wider change, which is taking place in the field of education just now.

In the past education is thought of as a field where more than in any other domain of our life communication takes place between partners from different families, different social, and more and more even different cultural backgrounds. The effect of the introduction of multimedia learning on the communicative process in the classroom will be, that the classroom is going to loose this character to some extend. Are we sure that the benefits of multimedia learning will compensate this loss? I will discuss this question using my CALL-program LEXIGRAM.DUITS as an example.

If we are thinking of innovations and their benefits in modern language learning we are reminded of the language laboratory and its failure. The language laboratory in the first place was planned to acquire pronunciation and language rules by imitation and drills. But apparently this was not enough to gain communicative competence. We all know the high investment into this new technology did not pay. The failure of the language laboratory was traced back to its inability to an interactive learning process. The isolation of the learner was experienced as demotivating, and the result was the availability of language forms and rules without the ability to use them appropriate in concrete situations.

Foreign language learning aims at communicative competence. The communicative method therefore claimed that the learning itself also had to be communicative. As I argued elsewhere (Westheide 1995) this means that the learning process should be dialogic in concept. The learners have to be trained to act and react in purpose oriented communicative processes. Communicative language learning therefore means that the aim of the language acquisition process at the same time also is its prerequisite: acting in a dialogue means acting as an individual responsible person with a free availability of the language. Thus you actually should already have to your disposal what you are supposed to learn in the future. On the other hand, the discourse world of the classroom is different from those in the outside world (Ellis 1990, 85), which leads to what Edmondson (1985, 162) once has called the teacher's paradox: "Wee seek in the classroom to teach people how to talk when they are not being taught". Classroom process research has shown the need of linguistic models for foreign language learning (Westheide 1994, 110f.). There is only one situation where language can be learned by merely communicating: the first language acquisition where linguistic and communicative competence grow simultaneously. It is far from astonishing that the communicative approach was supported by the theoretical model that second language mirrored first language learning. The results of the firm application of the communicative method do not prove this hypothesis and have correctly been described as "irremediably inaccurate fluency" (Garrett 1986, 133); we all know this.

As a result of this the increasing dissatisfaction with the outcomes of the communicative approach grammar becomes once again a contemporary issue (Goodfellow/Metcalfe 1997) and this especially in connection with CALL; or is it just the case that it is CALL itself that causes the new interest in grammar? Again even more expensive investments into the multimedia classroom are made, but are we sure that they will pay better this time than the language laboratory did?

2. The benefits of learning a foreign language in the multimedia classroom

In the first place computer based learning is suitable to independent study. If the software allows it, you even can work at home at your PC. It is in combination with hypertexts that grammar plays a dominant role in most of the CALL-programs.

While book-based grammars are linear in their exposition of material and therefore thought of as being of little use for individual language learning, the non-linear structure of hypertextsystems should be the ideal vehicle for an independent study resource. It is said that the resource is structured in such a way that it can respond to the learner's needs. McBridge and Seago (1997, 21) are convinced that "the interactive nature of a hypertext-based grammar bridges the gap between communicatively embedded grammar teaching and the linear exposition of grammar books." They believe that "the multi-layered structure of hypertexts can mimic the didactic spiral of language instruction". Interactive questions and linked exercises at every step of the process should allow immediate transfer from the theoretical level to practical application. The multi-layered design gives the possibility to hide information beneath the surface. "Thus the top level provides the linear expository development, while the deeper levels can be opened up to provide further explanation, exceptions, examples and increasingly sophisticated knowledge." (McBridge and Seago 1997, 21f.) The interactive potential is at its best in problem solving: "... interactive questions involve learners in a process of induction and deduction by inviting them to formulate hypotheses and draw their own conclusions from the material presented so far; opening up hidden text guides their exploration or gives the 'answer' thus providing feedback whether their deductions were correct or not." (McBridge and Seago 1997, 24)

Some scholars even claim as the ultimate justification of the use of this new technology "a total synergy between the medium and the message" (Goodfellow/Metcalfe 1997, 6). Following artificial intelligence research some of them believe in the congruence of the resource of their programs and the structures of the language to be learned.

3. Working with LEXIGRAM.DUITS

My work in the multimedia classroom depends on an installation which consists of three components:

(1.) the hardware equipment of DIDACNET
(2.) the software schedule of HOLOGRAM, and
(3.) my language learning program LEXIGRAM.DUITS.

3.1. The hardware equipment of DIDACNET

DIDACNET provides a teacher and a student panel. The teacher panel enables the observation of the students at work, but also different ways of teacher-student communication.

teacher panel

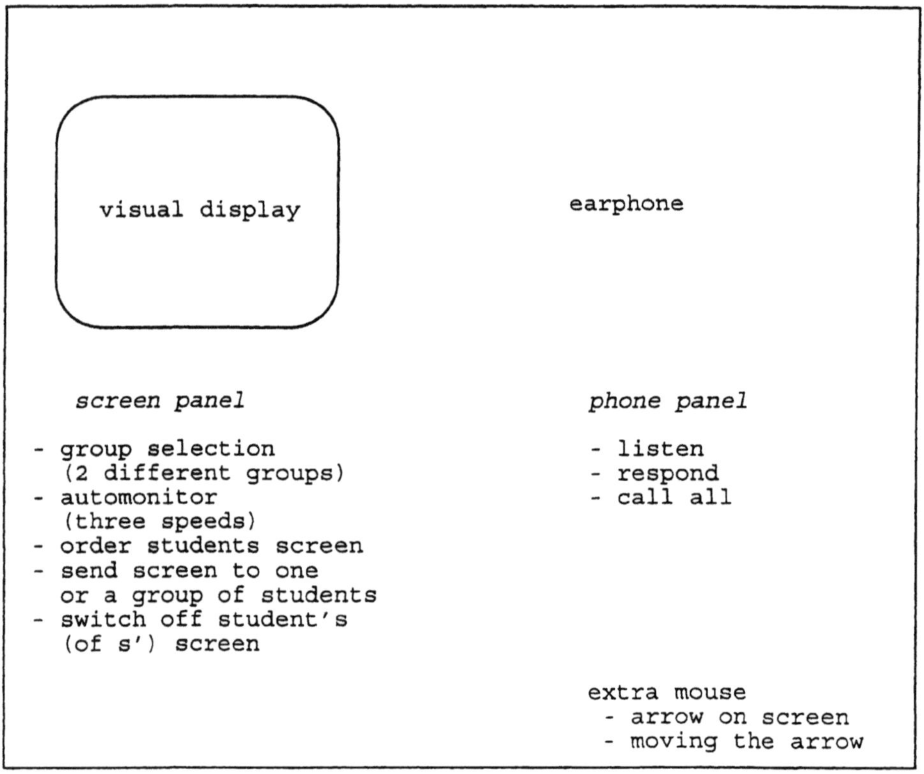

On the screen panel there is the possibility to select two different groups. An automonitor switches in three different speeds you can choose from student screen to student screen of the group selected. The teacher can order a special student screen and take over the mouse to demonstrate an action to the individual student. An additional mouse enables him to support his demonstration through an arrow which he can move on the screen. This screen again can be sent to groups of students in order to let them take part in the demonstration. This visual communication can be completed by oral communication via an earphone.

student panel

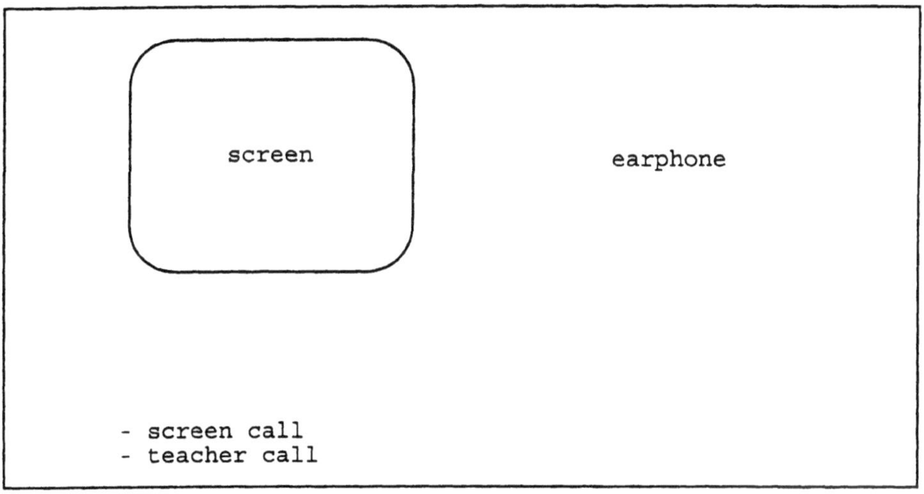

3.2. The software schedule HOLOGRAM

The software schedule HOLOGRAM is designed by the university of Groningen in order to teach grammar in addition to classroom teaching. It consists of a teacher and a student module.

The teacher module enables the individual teacher to make her own programs in the form of exercises, feedback and extended grammatical information. The program supplies the user with three kinds of exercises: 'multiple choice', 'drag and drop', and 'fill in'. In multiple choice exercises the student has to choose between several answers, in drag and drop exercises he drags with the mouse the appropriate word into a gap, and in fill in exercises he has to fill in one or several gaps with language material which he can make up out of the context or through additional information. The exercises cannot be linked directly to parts of the hypertext-theory, this has to be done from the feedback which belongs to every single exercise, linked to the answers, right or wrong ones.

It is the rapport module that makes working with HOLOGRAM so attractive. Not only that it enables the teacher to inform on the scores of individual students or on average results but, what is most interesting, it shows the wrong answers of the single exercises, so that it facilitates error analysis. The error analysis enables the designer of the program to anticipate the learner's action through formulating the feedback and linking it with information out of the hypertext.

The student module makes up individual exercise sets and it enables the student to ask whether his answer to a single exercise is right or wrong. If it is wrong, he can ask for feedback or for the right answer. The feedback can be formulated in a way (for instance through an additional question) that the student is stimulated to make use of his own knowledge to correct his wrong answer. He also can be asked to make use of the hypertext. Terminological expressions which could be unknown to the student are combined with pop-up screens which give short definitions. The hypertexts are combined via marked text fragments which can open screens with further hypertexts of the theory module. So the student should be able to look up all the information he needs. At any moment the student is informed about the ratio of right and wrong answers, and at the end of a sample of exercises the program tells him if he succeeded or if he has to do it over again.

3.3. My language learning program LEXIGRAM.DUITS

My language learning program LEXIGRAM.DUITS is based on my learners' lexicon "Contrastief idioomboek Duits" (Westheide 1997). The grammatical properties of the German language are presented in connection with lexical material of language use. The data are organized according to onomasiological principles on the macro- and meso-level, further down contrastivity is the organizing principle. The design of the exercises is orientated to the learner's difficulties as a result of the differences between the German and the Dutch language. The theory module as the actual hypertext is hierarchically structured starting with general syntactic and semantic rules and becoming more specific to end with a special usage with its formal aspects. The exercises are as open as possible (mostly 'fill-in' exercises) so that there are many good answers which all have to be foreseen. According to the results of our study of the language use of Dutch students of German (Westheide 1979), we took the major German verbs in their most frequent ways of use as a starting point.

If we compare the organization of our hypertext with a building according to Rothkegel (this volume), the basement is formed by feedback information which is bound up with the single exercise. The information provided by the feedback texts in the first instance is purely paradigmatic[1], that means that the task of the exercise is reformulated so that the student can have another try with a better chance of success. It would be desirable that the student even than would be provided with such an additional information if he did not understand the task which is to be done and therefore did not answer it at all. The problem is that this could be inconsistent with the organization of HOLOGRAM which is based on right and wrong answers.

If the students answer is wrong the feedback text should make explicit that part of the task that caused the trouble. This of course presupposes careful error analysis, and even then, as in the case of German case morphology, you sometimes cannot know if an error is caused by a wrong case or by a wrong grammatical gender of the noun in question. If the student even then is not able to find the right answer, he could be guided into other stages of the hypertext building where he is confronted with information which Jacobson calls 'syntagmatic', because it leads a step further.

On the first floor he finds information bound up with the lexical unit which forms the nucleus of the exercise. All other information in respect to grammatical, lexical, pragmatic or cultural properties that could cause trouble could be stored in separate apartments of an annex of the building. So grammatical gender, the inflection of the nominal group or inflectional rules of verbs, though not subject of this learning program, can be introduced in cases where they cause trouble. The lexical information of the first floor in the first instance consists of rules of the use of the lexical items. But there could be a need of information that is only of importance in connection with wrong answers. For example, if through interference with the Dutch language a German lexical unit is used which is wrong only in the context given by the exercise, we inform the student how it could be used appropriately.

HOLOGRAM has three hierarchically organized hypertext ranges which form the theory module. So, there are two floors left which can provide further information. While the second floor represents the meso-structure of our learners' lexicon, the third floor is reserved for general rules which form the basis of our learners' lexicon. Thus we have four large apartments on the third floor with the following inhabitants:

(i) General syntactic rules of the German sentence as the organization of case-marked roles according to the frames given by the usage of a verb in a group of contexts ('Satzbaupläne').

(ii) General semantic rules as those of semantic roles represented by the case-marked arguments or general restrictions to this rules through collocation or use as conversational routines etc.

(iii) General pragmatic rules of verb usage in types of situations bound up with, for example, rules of use in respect to status or politeness.
(iv) General cultural information concerning language use in standardized situations, so as for example the acceptance of openly opposing in a discussion or in respect to explicitness in DIRECTIVES.

Besides building up our hypertext building we have a second task which is not less complicated: the organization of the connecting paths inside the building. The entrance normally takes place via feedback texts, but of course the building above ground level could be used as well as a sort of grammar where you should be able to inform on all aspects of a lexical case-grammar of German. A contents page and an index of grammatical items should give an optimal access to all parts of the building, beside the paths starting with wrong answers. As is said before, the most important improvement of hypertexts is the possibility to create connection throughout the whole building. So you can reach each apartment on your floor but also from floor to floor up and down. It is of most importance that the connections are according to the needs of the students. Thus, even here we have to observe the way the student makes use of the resource.

The following page gives an example of how the student could be guided through the building. He starts with the exercise where the student intuitively would choose the accusative because the person in question is affected by the action. In the feedback question the task has been made explicit. On the first floor he finds the rule how to choose the case in different usages of the verb. Alternatively he could find information of the contrast with another verb with the same meaning, but different case structure. A further text about the conditions under which a third verb could be used, would be of no use in this case.

On the second floor our student would find information about the form of arguments of all verbs of social action concerning other people and the groups of verbs with the same case-structure. If the rule of the use of the verb in question could not be interpreted by the student because of a lack in the understanding of the terms 'Ziel-Rolle' and 'Thema-Rolle', he would find an explanation in the text of the first floor. Thus, the leading principle is to anticipate on possible questions of the student.

Theory module third floor: Diese themantischen Rollen sind bei bestimmten Gebrauchsweisen an Kasus gebunden. ...	Bei der Ziel-Rolle ist die Handlung auf eine Person oder Instanz gerichtet. ...	Die Form eines nominalen Arguments nennen wir Kasus. ...
Theory module second floor: Bei den Verben auf Menschen bezogener sozialer Tätigkeiten müssen je nachdem, ob die Handlung primär auf die Ziel-Rolle oder auf die Thema-Rolle gerichtet ist, verschiedene Satzbaupläne gewählt werden. ...	Die Verben verteilen sich auf folgende Satzbaupläne. 1. mit Thema-Rolle im Akkusativ und Ziel-Rolle im Dativ: *liefern, leihen*, ...	
Theory module first floor: 'Kündigen' kann entweder mit Akkusativ als Thema-Rolle oder mit Dativ als Ziel-Rolle verwendet werden: *Der Betrieb hat ihm gekündigt* oder *Der Geschäftspartner kündigt den Vertrag*.	Ohne Lokal-Rolle ist *entlassen* mit direktem Objekt synonym *kündigen* mit Dativ: *Der Betrieb entläßt den Mitarbeiter*.	Neben *kündigen* und *entlassen* wird bei politischen Funktionen auch *entheben* mit Genitiv gebraucht: Wegen der Affaire wurde der Richter seines Amtes enthoben.
Feedback text: Handelt es sich um eine Thema- oder eine Ziel-Rolle?		
Wrong answer: Wegen seines Fehlverhaltens hatte *ihn der Chef gekündigt.		
Exercise: Setzen Sie das Personalpronomen mit dem richtigen Kasus ein: Wegen seines Fehlverhaltens hatte ... der Chef gekündigt.		

4. My experiences working with this installation

According to Hubbard (1996, 21f.) the following points should be part of a "humanistic, communicative approach" of CALL:

(1) The courseware provides meaningful communicative interaction between the student and the computer.

(2) The courseware provides comprehensible input at a level just beyond that already acquired by the learner.

(3) The courseware promotes a positive self-image in the learner.
(4) The courseware provides a challenge but does not produce frustration or anxiety.
(5) The courseware acts affectively as a catalyst to promote learner-learner interaction in the target language.

To Ashworth (1996, 82) interactivity "refers to the degree to which a user of a program is involved in, or has control over, that program".

To assess the degree of interactivity you should consider the following questions:

a) How often can you interact? (frequency)
b) How many choices are available? (rage)
c) How much the choice really effected matters? (significance)
d) The feeling or not that one is participating in the ongoing action of the representation. (participatoriness)

Most of the criteria effect the quality of the feedback. Only if the student makes use of feedback and profits from it in one way or another, we reach a dimension which is more than merely using the book of exercises.

One can think of four different types of feedback:

(1) an indication of the correctness or incorrectness of the answer;
(2) a comment on the reasons for an answer being correct or incorrect;
(3) a score, grade. or other cumulative evaluation;
(4) tutorial information, such as a suggestion to review information internal or external to the program. (Hubbard 1996, 25)

As we have seen, even (1) can be a problem and then (3) is one as well. (2) asks, that you already know what the answer will be, anticipating thus is one of the major tasks of the designer. The rapport module is a great help of course, but only as the corpus of wrong answers is big enough, you can anticipate meaningful errors; but how does the student know that his answer is a mere mistake? If the student repeatedly experiences that the feedback is insignificant, he won't use it any more. (4) leads to the problem of the hypertext, which more or less is nothing but a grammar. For me, it is the problem of language, that counts. If the language of the hypertexts differs to much from that of the exercises, it will not work. In my program all examples unfortunately were spoiled, because they were written in italics. As a result of this, the students did not use the hypertexts. The abstract formulation of rules did not come up to their expectations, or do they expect nothing but an algorithm?

Until now I am far away from the situation described by Pinnington (1996, 12f.) in her book "The Power of CALL", and I am not sure if I ever wish to come there. "The more the computer and the user work as a team, the more the computer can be said to be partnering the user's cognitive processing, "shadowing" and enabling the user's processing of information."

5. Conclusion

I am not yet convinced that the multimedia classroom is the solution to all our problems, but it has had one positive effect anyway: Grammar is back in the classroom and with it the discussion what kind of information could support foreign language acquisition of learners which are older than seven years. Error analysis and contrastive analysis which plaid such an important role in the sixties and the seventies have not been in vain and CALL could be an impulse to improve (applied) linguist research.

Besides programs for vocabulary and grammar learning there are corpus-based ones making use of multilingual corpora (McEnery and Wilson 1997, 6). Like text production programs (Schulze 1997) these make possible the application of even more pragmatic linguistic knowledge. But even then, working with media cannot replace classroom interaction, but perhaps it can bring about a better basis on which real dialogic processes can take place.

Note

1) For the use of the terms 'paradigmatic' and 'syntagmatic' to distinguish paraphrasing from extending information, see Rothkegel (this volume)

References

Ashworth, D. (1996): Hypermedia and CALL. – In: Pennington (ed.): 79-96.

Edmonson, W. (1985): Discourse Worlds in the Classroom and in Foreign Language Learning. – In: Studies in Second Language Acquisition 7, 159-168.

Ellis, R. (1990): Instructed Second Language Acquisition. Oxford.

Garrett, N. (1986): The problem with grammar: what kind can the language learner use? – In: Modern language Journal 70, 133-148.

Goodfellow, R./Metcalfe, P. (1997): The challenge – back to basis or brave new world? – In: ReCALL 9:2, 4-7.

Hubbard, Philip L. (1996): Elements of CALL Methodology: Development, Evaluation, and Implementation. – In: Pennington (ed.), 15-32.

McBridge, Nicole/Seago, Karen (1997): Bridging the gap: grammar as hypertext. In: – ReCALL 9:2, 17-25.

McEnery, Tony/Wilson (1997): Teaching and language corpora (TALC). – In: ReCALL 9:1, 5-14.

Pennington, Martha C. (ed.) (1996): The Power of CALL. Houston: Athelstan.

Pennington, Martha C. (1996): The Power of the Computer in Language Education. – In: Pennington (ed.), 1-14.

Schulze, Mathias (1997): Textania – text production in a hypertext environment. – In: Computer Assisted Language Learning 10:1, 71-82.

Westheide, Henning (1979): Grenzen des Zweitsprachenerwerbs? Eine linguistische Analyse des Deutsch niederländischer Germanistikstudenten. Leiden. Now: Bern etc.: Peter Lang 1981.

Westheide, Henning (1994): Dialogue Analysis and the Lexical Syllabus in Foreign language Teaching. – In: Weigand, E. (ed.): Concepts of Dialogue. Considered from the Perspective of Different Disciplines. Tübingen: Niemeyer, 107-122.

Westheide, Henning (1995): Fremdsprachenvermittlung auf der Basis dialogischer Texte. Heutige Praxis und Zukunftsperspektiven. – In: Weigand, E. (ed.): Perspectives of Dialogue Analysis. Tübingen: Niemeyer, 185-199.

Westheide, Henning (1997): Contrastief idoomboek Duits – Handleiding voor doelmatig taalgebruik. Bussum: Coutinho.

Maria Freddi

Dialogue Analysis and Multimedia Translation

1. Introduction

Multimedia translation was dealt with only marginally by researchers until the early nineties when theorists and professionals started discussing both theoretical and practical issues. An increasingly large number of television programmes coming from the United States, i.e. serials, sitcoms, soap operas, and the like,[1] have increased the business of dubbing in countries such as Italy, which have always traditionally dubbed rather than subtitled. Commercial reasons like this together with the need for highly trained translators have aroused new interest on the part of academics in the theoretical issues involved in dubbing. The questions I would like to pose here are, firstly, at which point does translating cease and dubbing take over? In other words, what exactly is the difference between translation proper and adapting a script for the TV screen? And, secondly, can Dialogue Analysis provide the dubbing scriptwriter with useful criteria for a critical reading?

2. Multimedia Translation: Maximum Constraint or Maximum Freedom?

To answer the first question on the level of theory, I have drawn from two traditional definitions of multimedia translation, namely Cary's *traduction totale* (cf. Cary 1960), which is adopted by Mounin (1965), and Pavesi's *traduzione vincolata* – constrained translation (cf. Pavesi 1994). What constraints and how they affect the translator's task and strategies is precisely what recent stances from within the Translation Studies are interested in investigating (cf. Delabastita 1990; Snell-Hornby 1996). Similarly, professionals advocate the need for an interdisciplinary approach required by the complexity of this kind of translation (cf. Galassi 1994 and Cipolloni 1996). Semioticians tell us that filmic signification proceeds along two channels: visual (made of light waves) and acoustic (air vibrations). Therefore, dubbing inevitably interferes with image-sound synchronicity. It is constrained by images, often referred to by professionals as *iconic constraint*, and by sound, i.e. the soundtrack, music and effects, as well as the linguistic and paralinguistic features of the original verbal code.

I suggest that dubbing be described using a musical metaphor, the *minus one* performance. Here a missing melody mingles with an existing harmonic texture, a voice fills an empty slot with the given duration, rhythm and interpretation. The missing part/voice combines with the other parts/voices to make up the signifying whole. Similarly, dubbing is constrained, wrapped, as it were, in the non-verbal codes which constitute that complex sign that we call film. Indeed, in adjusting to the original script, dubbing scriptwriters, unlike minus one performers, abandon one language code (SL) to embrace another (TL). In other words they leave part of a culture – the source language – to adopt a new one – the target language. So far the task of the dubbing scriptwriter does not differ much from that of any other translator, yet the former employs a target language which ought to match with other expressive codes belonging to the source culture. Should a coming-apart of the dubbed text and the co-existing non-verbal codes be perceived, the original script would emerge abruptly, and instigate the viewer's disappointment and criticism. The discrepancy is all the more evident when it occurs between what is heard and what is seen or perceived through the other codes of the film sign, rather than between what is heard and what is latent, i.e. the dubbed and the original script.

This is best illustrated by an extreme though not uncommon example: the gestural jargon of the wild teenagers in *Clueless*, a modern version of Jane Austen's *Emma*. Here the teens' jargon is not only spoken but also visible on the screen because of the gestural code indicated by the initial letters of the words intended, for example, a *W* standing for an unspoken *Whatever!* expressing boredom and carelessness towards life. Or *L* standing for *Loser* with which they dismiss their male peers. Here the parallelism image-sound is not homogeneous. It is, in fact, a critical point where the proximity between what is said and what is seen is extremely strict, so much so that the dubbing scriptwriter has to think of an equivalent in accordance with the image/grapheme. To go back to the musical metaphor, if a dissonance between verbal and visual code is created in the dubbed version, it will awaken the viewer's memory of the submerged original text, thus ending the illusion of harmony.

On the other hand, a dubbed script is also considered autonomous. Many professionals point out that it is a work of art in itself and not merely a technical device or release stratagem. Since the adaptation becomes the film itself in the country where it is released, it is not, they argue, a *prosthesis*[2] but rather an original creation. The internal coherence and autonomy of any adaptation is reflected by its linguistic status. Scholars, and above all linguists (cf. Herbst 1994 and 1996; Pavesi 1994), have observed how the language of dubbing is neither of the source nor of the target language – it avoids both norms and creates a third which assures consistency in dubbed films. This third language, being highly influenced by SL and intuitively influencing TL, has been labelled *dubbese*[3]. According to Pavesi (1994) dubbese is unmarked phonologically and rather hypermarked morphologically, in that diatopic and diastratic variations are lost at the level of phonology and usually retrieved by exasperation of morpho-syntactic features. This compensates for the sociolinguistic variety like, for example, the use or even misuse of the *ci* to render the colloquial register[4]. Also, dubbing scriptwriters tend to draw from fixed equivalents, which are the result of the artificial nature of the fictional dialogue of SL and which contribute to the internal consistency of the film-dubbing system. This is also stressed by Delabastita (1990) who recommends the use of *genre markers*, that is "stereotyped elements that further conform the target film to the target audience's expectations" (Delabastita 1990: 102). Indeed, these elements are often fixed expressions which are typical of dubbese.

The point I would like to make is that if we considered a continuum of freedom-constraint, dubbing would fall in between a minus one performance, with which it shares similar constraints, and creative rewriting, which allows for almost total freedom. This is the theoretical stance from which I see this special type of translation practice.

3. Dialogue Analysis and TV Dialogue Adaptation

On the level of practice, one should consider the questions that the translator, be it consciously or unconsciously, asks himself/herself when adapting a film dialogue. According to Galassi (1994), scriptwriter and director of dubbing who has recently been working on the theory of film adaptation, these questions have three stages: *denotation*, *connotation*, and *synchronisation*. During the preparatory stage of denotation, a literal translation is carried out, and so can be undertaken by a third party. In the second stage – connotation – an attempt is made to extract subtexts by deconstructing and segmenting the original script and reconstructing it according to the *compensation principle*, which consists in making meaning shifts from one chunk of the text to another with a view to the global economy of meaning. Later, the dubbed text will take up new meaning elements in the recording studios with the intervention of the director of dubbing and the actors themselves, and finally in the mixing stage – synchronisation. In Bussi's words the whole process is ruled by the idea of finding an *energetic equivalent*, that is to say of recreating the original expressive and communicative force (cf. Bussi 1997).

I will now consider an example of a teleplay and analyse some excerpts lasting only a few minutes of the entire footage. *Tell Me No Secrets* is a standard television product, thus something with which the dubbing scriptwriter is faced most of the time. It belongs to the subgenre of lawyer movies, those with the trial as the centre of the plot. The dialogue is simple, ordinary, rather fast and sober. While adapting it into Italian, I was first faced with the difficulty of maintaining the pace of the original script, the tempo which characterises the exchanges of short and sharp utterances, and avoiding long-winded sentences. The reason why I chose the following extracts is that they raise some of the questions that according to Delabastita (1990: 102-3) help the translator describe the rapport between original and dubbed films.

First of all, one should consider how to render the diatopic and diastratic variations of SL, together with the registers and idiolects of the various characters, without misinterpreting the stylistic choices of the original script. *Tell Me No Secrets* is rather simple as regards the sociolinguistic connotation of the dialogue, so the standardisation to which any dubbed version is usually subjected is not of great importance in this case. What is important is that slang and colloquial expressions (*having a squeeze*, *smacks of, you've been there; done that*, etc.), and sometimes even swear words, alternate with the technical terminology from the law semantic field – for example, Jess's lines (my italics) "Mr. Ferguson, if you come within fifty yards of Ms. Ching (...) I'll have your *bail revoked* and your *ass in jail*, you understand?" Analysis of the whole script has shown that Don's language is more consistent. As for the variation of accent, again, it is not a significant element of this teleplay.

There are other features which are peculiar to dubbing, such as the rendering of taboo elements like swear words. I suggest an overall toning-down of the vulgar language, for example, the above mentioned "I'll have your bail revoked and your *ass in jail*" becomes "Le faccio revocare la cauzione e la *sbatto al fresco*". The same polish applies below in "You know I can't stand watching you eat this *crap*" According to the definitions in three current monolingual dictionaries, namely COBUILD, CIDE and OED, "crap" is "offensive", "slightly taboo slang" and "shocking and indecent", respectively. What I opted for in Italian is less marked as vulgar and aggressive (see *schifo* rather than *merda*), yet the loss can be compensated for elsewhere in the script, or by transferring the colloquial tone from the lexical level onto the level of syntax in the same turn. This is why I chose to use the more direct subjunctive rather than the more literal objective clause ("Lo sai che non sopporto *che mangi* questo *schifo*" rather than "Lo sai che non sopporto *vederti mangiare* questa *merda*"). Very often this procedure must follow the polishing policy of the release companies.

In the following excerpt, Jess meets Don, fellow lawyer and ex-husband. Jess finds out that Don is the defender of the man she is prosecuting for rape. Only later will she learn the truth, that Don is in fact a psychotic who, out of jealousy, killed her mother and has hired the defendant to harass her. The exchange opens with Don's voice over. His tone is slightly threatening, the stress being on the second half of the utterance *Those things'll* *kill you*. As the dialogue develops, there is a tug-of-war between Don and Jess that later degenerates into a full-blown argument. In order to maintain the defiant tone of Don's lines, I opted for a semantic sliding from *injure somebody's hand* to *kill* in Jess's "Touch this one you lose your hand", and translated "Prova a toccarlo e sei morto", which also refers back to Don's opening turn, and thus adds internal cohesion to the dialogue. Similarly, Don's "Not wearing panties to a bar smacks of consent to me" becomes "*Sotto il vestito niente* in un bar sa di provocazione" which hints at the title of a popular movie belonging to the same genre. Whilst allowing the dubbing scriptwriter to synthesise otherwise long-winded sentences, this reference gives the Italian viewer further insight into the plot in the possibly unconscious association with the genre, and thus improves general cohesion.

EXT. FARMER'S MARKET - DAY (11) 01.15.25.17.3
Jess is at a vendor's stand, receiving a giant hot dog with all the fixings from the vendor.
She pays him, then takes a big bite.

MAN'S VOICE (O.S.) Those things'll kill you.	VOCE MASCHILE (F.C.) Questa roba ti ucciderà.

Jess takes in the sound of the voice, and a smile comes to her lips despite herself.
She turns to Don Shaw, about eight years her senior. Impeccably dressed. Touches of grey in his hair.

DON You know I can't stand watching you eat this crap.	DON Lo sai che non sopporto che mangi questo schifo.

He grabs the hot dog out of her hand and throws it into a nearby garbage can.

JESS I can't believe you did that!	JESS Ehi! Non ci posso credere!

She gestures for another hot dog, then looks at Don.

JESS Touch this one you lose your hand	JESS Prova a toccarlo e sei morto.
DON I heard your closing arguments from the doorway.	DON Ho sentito la tua arringa oggi dal corridoio.
JESS What did you think?	JESS Beh, cosa ne pensi?
DON You were convincing, dramatic, sincere. Committed. (shaking his head) Don't know if you'll get a conviction, though. Not wearing panties to a bar smacks of consent to me.	DON Sei stata convincente, drammatica, sincera. Impegnata. (scuotendo la testa) Non so se gli daranno la condanna, però. "Sotto il vestito niente" in un bar sa di provocazione.
JESS Yeah, and the knife to her throat was foreplay.	JESS Già, e il coltello alla gola erano i preliminari.

She takes the hot dog and bites into it. Don grimaces in disgust.

DON Can I just buy you something that is not gonna stop your heart?	DON Ti dispiace se ti compro qualcosa che non ti rovina lo stomaco?
EXT. FRUIT STAND-DAY (12)	ESTERNO GIORNO (12)
JESS So, what's this I hear about you having a new squeeze?	JESS Allora, signor rubacuori, c'è davvero una nuova fiamma?
DON Where'd you hear that?	DON Come l'hai saputo?
JESS Word gets around, Counselor... I'll bet she's very bright, very pretty, with very blond hair, and a wicked laugh.	JESS La gente mormora, avvocato... Scommetto che è un tipo brillante, bellissima, biondissima e ha una risata irresistibile.
DON (laughing) Ash blonde. Is she a fellow lawyer?	DON (ridendo) Biondo cenere. Ed è una collega?
JESS No, you've been there. Done that. Probably an interior decorator named Terry or Tawny.	JESS No, ci hai già provato una volta. Sarà un'arredatrice d' interni, Terry, o magari Tawny.
DON Trish. Clothing designer. How irritating! And you? Seeing anyone special?	DON Trisha. E fa la stilista. Oh, smettila! E tu? Eh? Esci con qualcuno?

Also, the question is raised of the rendering of the pragmatic components of SL such as discourse markers, exclamations, deictics and forms of address. The problem is strictly connected to the broader issue of *lip synchronisation*, since these elements are the tiny parts of the script that are more likely to be either added or omitted to reach the length needed or to stick to the prosodic patterns of SL. Whether a line is too long or too short, the discourse marker, form of direct address, etc. will be either added in TL or omitted if present in SL. This is why I added *ehi*, *beh* as fillers in the exchange above. In the excerpt that follows, Jess's turn "Please don't tell me a joke! He's an animal. He's a sick, low-life..." becomes "Stai scherzando, *Don*! Quello è un animale, un maniaco, un..." (my italics). I decided to avoid translating the last element of the reiterative chain *low-life,* and replaced it with the direct form of address which compensates for the firm, rather disgusted tone of Jess's utterance.

Delabastita also poses the problem of the dubbing scriptwriter's attitude towards loans and linguistic interference in general, which leads to inappropriate or at least artificial forms in TL. Again, dubbese can serve as a norm to which one should refer, without it becoming a constraint, though. As mentioned above, excessive transfer of foreign idioms from SL to TL can lead to a highly artificial dialogue. So, the standardised expressions that I have in a sense unconsciously chosen, such as *qualcosa non va?*, or *smettila*, or *aspetta un momento, fammi capire* are no doubt stereotyped and function as markers of dubbese, yet, if not misused, also serve the purpose of conforming the teleplay to certain expectations of the audience.

Jess moves away.

DON	DON
What's going on?	Qualcosa non va?
JESS	JESS
I'm having an exceptionally weird day.	E' stata una giornata molto strana oggi.
DON	DON
Well, what happened?	Cosa ti è successo?
JESS	JESS
A man started following me.	Qualcuno che mi ha seguita.
DON	DON
What man?	Chi è?
JESS	JESS
Sean ferguson, a guy who I'm...	Sean Ferguson, è il caso di cui...
DON	DON
(interrupting)	(interrompendola)
...prosecuting for rape next month. Did you see his face?	...il caso di stupro di cui ti occupi. L'hai visto in faccia?
JESS	JESS
No, I didn't see his face...	No, non l'ho visto in faccia...

DON
Recognized his voice?
JESS
No, but... I know it was him.
DON
You didn't see him, you didn't
hear him, and yet, you...
JESS
Wait, wait a minute. You sound
like you're defending him in court.
DON
That's why I'm here. He's
hired me to represent him.
JESS
Please don't tell me a joke!
He's an animal. He's a sick, low-life...
DON
The man might be innocent.
JESS
The "man", as you generally refer
to him, has been identified by the
woman he attacked.
DON
And she couldn't be mistaken?

DON
Hai riconosciuto la voce?
JESS
No, ma... so che era lui
DON
Non l'hai visto, né sentito e ti
tostini a dire che...
JESS
Aspetta un momento, fammi capire,
parli come fossi tu a difenderlo.
DON
Quell'uomo mi ha assunto per
difenderlo. Per questo sono qui.
JESS
Stai scherzando, Don! Quello è
un animale. Un maniaco, un...
DON
Potrebbe essere innocente.
JESS
"Quell'uomo", come lo chiami tu,
è stato identificato dalla donna che
ha aggredito.
DON
E se fosse lei a sbagliarsi?

Finally, dubbing raises the issue of the rendering of puns and wordplays which convey the communicative *vis* and the humour of the script. Here, two opposing tendencies clash: the dubbing scriptwriter's and that of the director of dubbing. Indeed, the former may be too literal, while the latter ignore literariness in order to insert a bad joke at all costs. The closing lines of the teleplay offer a good example of this. See:

EXT. ART'S HOUSE-AFTERNOON
(89)
JESS
Hi. Thanks for coming.
ADAM
You sure you want me here? Your family
doesn't know me...
JESS
....from Adam? Come on.
FADE OUT

ESTERNO CASA DEGLI
ART-POMERIGGIO (89)
JESS
Grazie di essere venuto.
ADAM
Sei sicura di volermi qui? I tuoi non
mi conoscono...
JESS
...non ancora! / ...adorano gli avvocati!
DISSOLVENZA

The English expression *not know someone from Adam* meaning "not knowing the difference between one thing or person and another" is a wordplay on the name of the second male character, Adam, also a lawyer. Given that there is no equivalent idiom in Italian, the translator has two choices: he/she either omits the joke, as I suggest in my first version, *...non ancora* or he/she thinks of something else such as my second solution which contains an element of irony if not an actual joke by making reference to Jess's mad ex-husband who is also a lawyer, see *...adorano gli avvocati.*

4. Conclusions

The excerpts analysed, though short, lead to the following conclusions. First, what characterises TV dialogue adaptation is its multimedial nature. The various problems I considered during the adaptation of *Tell Me No Secrets*, i.e. the rendering of register, slang, wordplays, pragmatic elements, etc., are identical to other types of translation practices. All these obstacles become specific to multimedia translation because of the constraints imposed by images (the script serves the images and vice versa) and sound (synchronisation with length, speech rhythm and lip movement of the original script). In other words, the answer to my initial question "at which point does dubbing take over translation proper?" is to be found in the semiotic complexity of filmic and television fiction. It follows that criteria of congruence with images and adherence to the original sound – to which the problem of speakability is linked – should be dominant in the process of adaptation. Besides, reference to the norm of dubbese should be welcomed by the dubbing scriptwriter though never seen as constraint.

Second, I suggest that Dialogue Analysis can provide the dubbing scriptwriter with a useful tool for global reading of the script in that it is a way of identifying all the important meaning elements that should not be lost in the adaptation process. These meaning elements emerge from the linguistic characterisation of the various characters and from the dialogue as a whole, and cannot be grasped by the dubbing scriptwriter if he/she proceeds turn by turn rather than adopting a more global approach to the script. This latter approach should help the dubbing scriptwriter to instil a general feature into the dubbed version in order to recreate the original balance.

Notes

1) Cf. Heiss (1996) quoting Paolinelli (1993) according to whom 90% of television fiction in Italy is imported.
2) Cf. Murri (1996); also Raffaelli (1995) suggests that film adaptation be considered a co-authoring process.
3) For a systematic account of the linguistic aspects of TV dialogue adaptations in German, see Herbst (1994).
4) It is Pavesi (1994) who quotes the exchange “Lo vuoi anche tu un panino, Nat? Sottaceti?” – “Certo che *ci* voglio i sottaceti” and other examples of the use of *ci* as a marker of colloquial register.

References

Bussi, G. Elisa (1997): Unpublished paper. Lecture given during the Postgraduate Course in Multimedia Translation held at the Forlì centre of the University of Bologna.

Cary, Edmond (1960): La traduction totale. – In: Babel 6, 3:110-115.

Cipolloni, Marco (1996): La traduzione per il cinema come campo di studio e di ricerca. – In: Traduzione multimediale per il cinema, la televisione e la scena. Bologna: Clueb, 401-408.

Delabastita, Dirk (1990): Translation and the Mass Media. – In: Translation, History and Culture. London: Pinter, 97-109.

Galassi, Gianni G. (1994): La norma traviata. – In: Il doppiaggio. Trasposizioni linguistiche e culturali. Bologna: Clueb, 61-70.

Herbst, Thomas (1994): Linguistische Aspekte der Syncronisation von Fernseherien. Phonetik, Textlinguistik, Übersetzungstheorie. Tübingen: Niemeyer.

Herbst, Thomas (1996): Why dubbing is impossible. – In: Traduzione multimediale per il cinema, la televisione e la scena. Bologna: Clueb, 97-115.

Mounin, Georges (1965): La traduzione per il cinema. – In: Teoria e storia della traduzione. Torino: Einaudi, 159-65.

Murri, Serafino (1996): Un italiano per tutte le stagioni. – In: La questione doppiaggio. Roma: Aidac, 81-5.

Pavesi, Maria (1994): Osservazioni sulla (socio)linguistica del doppiaggio. – In: Il doppiaggio. Trasposizioni linguistiche e culturali. Bologna: Clueb, 129-42.

Raffaelli, Sergio (1995): E fu subito autore. – In: Produzione e Cultura 9, 45-46.

Snell-Hornby, Mary (1996): ‘All the world’s a stage’: Multimedial Translation – constraint or potential? – In: Traduzione multimediale per il cinema, la televisione e la scena. Bologna: Clueb, 29-46.

Carla Bazzanella

"Address Inversion" and "Teknonymy" as Involvement Markers in an Italian Talk Show

1. Person and Social Deixis

1.1. General Issues

Fillmore (1975,76) defines social deixis[1] as "the study of that aspect of sentences which reflect or establish or are determined by certain realities of the social situation in which the speech act occurs." Levinson (1983,89) restricts it "to those aspects of language structure that encode the social identities of participants (properly, incumbents of participant-roles), or the social relationship between them, or between one of them and persons and entities referred to."

Many aspects of language usage depend on these relations (see for example the wide topic of *Politeness,* cf. Brown and Levinson (1987)), but only the grammaticalized ones (for example 'polite' pronouns and titles of address) are relevant to social deixis[2]. Roger

Brown and Alfred Gilman in their seminal paper (*The pronouns of power and solidarity*) studied the formal (V) and informal (T) second person pronouns, and the symmetric or asymmetric uses of them in social interactions in several languages[3]. But, as Fillmore (1975, 79) rightly states: "[...] knowing merely that a language has a distinction between two second person pronouns called formal and informal is not at all the same as knowing what the social and emotional significance of the use of these forms might be."

More interestingly, the same social relations can be re-coded on the basis of some given circumstances: a case in point could be the so-called "insincere usage": "In English, the assumptions associated with the use of a possessive pronoun with a kinship term allow the possessive to be used insincerely in some cases, cases where the relationship is perfectly clear but the speaker, probably as a joke, wishes to act as if one or other of the partners does not have the mentioned relationship to the individual referred to. I have in mind conversations between husband and wife about their young daughter Peggy. When Peggy does something particularly praiseworthy, the father says to the mother, *Look at what my daughter did.* When Peggy does something offensive, however, the command becomes: *Look at what your daughter did.*" Fillmore (1975, 81).

Linguistic phenomena such as these are clues to a better understanding of what is going on at a social/interactional level (cf., e. g., Goffman (1961), Renzi (1993)).

1.2. Allocution

The second general issue, which I will only touch on briefly before entering the specific topic, is the significance of allocution in dialogue. Benveniste (1966,252) already stressed the role of allocution and its correspondence with the second person pronoun: "[...] *je* est 'l'individu qui énonce la présente instance de discours contenant l'instance linguistique *je*'. Par conséquent, en introduisant la situation d''allocution', on obtient une définition symmétrique pou *tu*, comme l'individu allocuté dans la présente instance de discours contenant l'instance linguisitique *tu*".

More recently, Stati (1982,42), in a chapter of his book on dialogue (*Il dialogo*) dedicated to "La dimensione allocutiva", points out that: "In quanto parte costitutiva di un dialogo, qualsiasi enunciato è orientato verso un partner, potenzialmente attivo. Analizzando il contenuto delle battute al livello pragmatico, il ricercatore non potrà fare a meno di prendere in considerazione la relazione interlocutiva (locutore-allocutore)".

In this paper I will deal with two specific and unusual forms of social deixis in a specific setting; the kind of social deixis which is selected seems to be constrained by, and, in a sense, to characterize the kind of interaction.

2. Specific problems

2.1. "Address Inversion"

2.1.1. Definition

Two non-standard forms of social deixis will be analyzed in the present contribution: "Address Inversion" and "Teknonymy".

"Address inversion" is a special pattern of nominal address, where the message corresponds to the sender[4]. The expression was coined by Renzi (1968) as "Allocuzione inversa" with regard to Rumanian. By it we mean "the use of a term, usually a KT [= kinship][5] term, which does not (as would be usual) express the addressee's, but the speaker's role in the dyad; e.g. a mother addressing a child as *mama*. This phenomenon may also occur with fictive kinship. In Arabic a senior male unknown to the speaker can be addressed as '*ammi* 'my uncle'. By means of inversion the same term can now be reciprocated to the junior." Braun (1988,12).

Spitzer (1928, quoted in Renzi 1968) spoke of an inversion of roles: "[...] the mother says *mama*, the father *tata*, to the same child, both playing the game of inverting the roles of parent and child", but, as Renzi (1968,6) rightly states, there is no inversion of roles; there is one-way imitation, from the superior role to the inferior one (as in figure 1). From turn to turn an echo occurs: CHILD: *tata...*,FATHER: *tata...*, etc.; but it is only the adult who is playing, and inverting the roles by making herself/himself a child.

It should be stressed that in "address inversion" there is, besides the intimacy/affection feature, a difference in authority which allows this use: "The authoritative aspects of inversion – sometimes mere undertones, sometimes overt demonstrations of superiority – were found in Arabic, Georgian, Italian, Mingralian, Norwegian, and Rumanian." Braun (1988, 292).

Another essential feature of "address inversion" was pointed out by Renzi (1968,3): whereas in a dialogue different allocutions are used, in address inversion a single message is produced: "In un dialogo tra due si usano normalmente allocuzioni distinte (Tipo I: allocuzioni dirette); [...in alcuni] casi [...si realizza] un messaggio unico (Tipo II: allocuzione diretta+allocuzione inversa)."

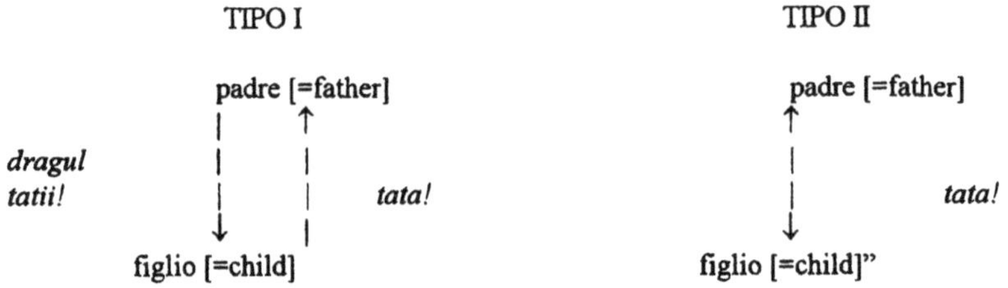

Figure 1 “Allocuzione diretta” and “Allocuzione inversa” (cf. Renzi (1968,3))

The ambiguity of this form results from the neutralization of the usual oppositions (feminine vs. masculine, singular vs. plural), which is solved by the linguistic and extra-linguistic contexts.

2.1.2. Usages

“Address inversion” is found in various languages and cultures: “Albanian, *Arabic*, Armenian, Avar, Bengali, Berber, Bulgarian, Dari, French[6], Georgian, German, Gimi, Greek, Hungarian, *Italian*, Mingrelian, Norwegian, Persian, Rumanian, Russian, Serbo-Croatian, Svan, Turkish, Yansi”[7], as Braun (1988,266) lists, but cf. also Sorrento (1950), Renzi (1968) for the Rumanian and some other languages in general, and Sgroi (1990,214), who studied the Sicilian dialect in particular.

What is unusual from a typological point of view is the complete unrelatedness of the languages where “address inversion” is used; as Braun (1988,266) points out: “It is not restricted to a stock of related languages, neither to languages in geographical vicinity, nor to languages in culturally related communities.” The only common features seem to be the conservativeness of the zones where it is used, and the familial register which characterizes it.

2.2. “Teknonymy”

2.2.1. Definition

“Teknonymy” is related to baby talk; following Malsch (1987,417) we can define it as “the use of a kin term appropriate to a different kin relationship”. More precisely, in a family, when one speaks to a child, one refers to the members of the family with the name which the child would use. E.g. the mother says to the child: “Gigino, look and see if dad’s come", where 'dad' is the name by which the child would call the father (cf. Renzi (1993,367)).

In other words, another member of the family adopts the child's point of view, and the child constitutes a stable deictic center, which is not subject to the conversational deictic shift:

Child: How are you *daddy*?
Father: *Daddy* is fine.

With regard to person pronouns, instead of the first person pronoun, the third person pronoun is used, when the reference is not lexicalized (as in *Daddy is fine*, instead of *I'm fine*).

As in the case of "address inversion", in "teknonymy" there is a mirroring of the dyadic relationship, which is reflected in a sort of linguistic echoing: *daddy/daddy*[8].

2.2.2. Usages

"Teknonymy", as a feature of baby talk, is quite common in many languages, especially in western ones where the child has a central role in the family[9].

As an extension, "Si può avere tecnonimia quando i genitori si chiamano tra di loro 'papà' e 'mamma', uso piuttosto limitato (ma che ho potuto osservare direttamente in parti diverse d'Italia. Nell'ambito familiare quest'uso è generale quando tra gli appartenenti alla famiglia ci si riferisce a un terzo pure membro della famiglia" Renzi (1993,375-376).

2.2.3. Common Features

We can either distinguish the two above-mentioned forms of social deixis or assimilate them.

Actually, what interests us more here is the common features of the two phenomena, that is:

1) the prevalence of the addressee's point of view.

Both in "address inversion" and in "teknonymy" the speaker takes the addressee's point of view. As Fillmore (1975,82) says: "There are many ways of referring to people which can best be thought in terms of the speaker's taking the addressee's point of view."

Another example of this use is given in Levinson (1983, 104) "[...] it is common in many languages (e.g. German; Hymes 1974,56) for mother to say to father, in the presence of little Billie, something like:

"Can Billie have an ice-cream, Daddy?"

taking the point of view, for the purpose of vocative selection, of the audience.

2) the intimate feature.

Both in "address inversion" and in "teknonymy" the intimate feature is an essential constraint for these uses which create involvement.[10]

Furthermore, both "address inversion" and "teknonymy" refer to a small group, typically the family. As Renzi (1968,6) states, with regard to "address inversion, it is not peculiar to Rumanian, but is common to many societies, especially rural, closed, and patriarchal ones."

3. Some Data Taken from an Italian Talk Show

3.1. The corpus

Both "address inversion" and "teknonymy" were found to be used in an Italian talk show (*Amici di sera*)[11], which used to be broadcast[12] once a week, on Wednesdays, on Channel 5, from 8.50 p. m. to 11 p.m., that is, at peak viewing time[13]. Parents were invited to discuss with their children the problems between them which had already been presented to the audience by the talk show host (cf. (1)). The studio audience participated directly by making suggestions, and proposing analyses of the family situations.

(1)
Host. allora Samantha↑ (--) dove sei↑ (--) sedici anni↑ figlia di genitori separati (--) rapporto però con tuo padre eh vivi con la mamma (-) tu hai telefonato a questa trasmissione perché ti senti (--) non sai se tuo papà ti vuole bene davvero (-) papà te lo dice sempre però di volerti bene↓
Samantha. Sì
[...]
Host. tu vuoi fare una serie di domande a tuo padre per capire se lui realmente ti vuole bene o no↓

Host. well Samantha↑ (--) where are you↑ (--) sixteen years old↑ daughter of separated parents (--) you are in touch with your father eh you live with your mother (-) you called this program because you feel (--) you don't know if your father really loves you (-) but dad always tells you that he loves you↓
Samantha. Ya
[...]
Host. you want to ask your father some questions to find out whether he really loves you or not↓

Incidentally, I would like to express my criticism of this kind of program where real (or supposedly real) problems are 'exposed' by someone who writes to propose herself/himself and her/his family, not so much in order to solve the conflict, but in order to appear in public and to play the central character (cf., in Weigand's contribution in this volume, the parallel between being on the stage and being seen/being known). In order to be listened to, the audience has to be amplified! The TV appears to be the theater where emotions and relationships of everyday life have to be represented in order to be 'real', and the audience, instead of the people involved, appear to be the ones entitled to find the right solution.

3.2. "Address inversion"

We found examples of "Address inversion" in three father-daughter dyads out of 12 where the daughters reproved fathers for not taking care of themselves.

In fragments (2), (3), and (4) the father uses the address form which expresses his role (that is, *father*) in the dyad. Even more surprisingly, in (4) the address form referring to himself is a tender one (*dear daddy*).

(2)
Alessandra. no↓ io gli volevo dire se TU vuoi bene a tua moglie e ai tuoi figli↓ me lo devi dire (-) perché non lo so↓
Father. e allora ti posso dire papà (–) eh (-) te lo posso dire↓

Alessandra. no↓ I wanted to ask him whether YOU love your wife and your children↓ you must tell me (-) because I don't know it↓
Father. then I can tell you dad (–) eh (-) I can tell you↓

(3)
Alessandra. e mi fai paura che vuol dire↑
Father. ma non è vero papà non è vero↓

Alessandra. you scare me what does it mean↑
Father. it's not true dad it's not true↓

(4)
Father. Io se c'ho un problema caro papà (-) se c'ho un problema mio (-) lo vado a sfogare a una persona di famiglia (-) a un caro amico

Father. If I have a problem dear daddy (-) if I have a problem (-) I go and talk it over with a member of the family (-) with a dear friend

These examples confirm the regional component: as I said before (v. 2.1.2), "address inversion" is used only in some central and southern regions of Italy, and the taped fathers whose uses have been quoted above speak with a strong southern accent. As Braun

(1988,306) rightly observes, in emphasizing the role of variation in address behavior: "Investigation of address in various languages showed that the selection and the availability of forms of address is correlated with certain characteristics of the speakers. Important factors are: regional origin, age, social status/education/occupation, sex, group membership, political/religious views, and personality."

3.3. "Teknonymy"

Instances of "teknonymy" have been found in our corpus.

In (5) we found *papà* instead of a first person pronoun (see 2.2.1).

A sort of balance between the urgency of subjectivity and the quest for objectivity seems at stake in the program. Note the same oscillation in (2) quoted above where the daughter uses her father's (and not her) perspective: *tua moglie*, *i tuoi figli*, in order to 'distance' her role and to make her question more 'objective', while at another moment she uses "mammina" (= mummy, i.e. a diminutive[14]), which stresses her emotional involvement and induces the audience's participation (compare the procedure used by the host (3.2)).

(5)
Father. ha diritto di dormire un po' papà

Father. daddy needs to sleep a bit

In (6) the identification process is pushed so far that the father speaks of his daughter's mother as "your wife", though he auto-corrects himself after a short pause. In a pretend-play where passions are not expected to be bridled, but given free rein, real involvement finds its mode of expression and bursts out in an unusual form[15].

(6)
Father. parlo con tua moglie (-) tua mamma

Father. I'm speaking to your wife (-) your mummy

What is particularly interesting in the next example is that "teknonymy" is resorted to not by a relative (that is an "authorized speaker" Levinson (1983,91)), but by the host (Maria De Filippi) of the talk show, who, in so doing, pretends in a sense to be part of the family, and induces the same attitude in the audience (cf. (7)). In this case one might speak of "absolute" rather than "relational"(ib.) deixis[16]: surprisingly, absolute deixis appears to be used in a domain where the relationship is essential, that is, in the family.

(7)
Host. a sei anni mamma se ne va (-) perché si innamora di al- di un altro uomo (-) e voi non andate con lei (-) ma rimanete a vivere con la nonna

Host. when you are six mummy goes away (-) because she falls in love with another man (-) and you don't go with her (-) but stay and live with granny

3.4. Forms of address and emotional settings

Both the above-mentioned forms of social deixis are motivated on a pragmatic level by the particular kind of setting, where involvement is not only forcefully induced but has to be 'externalized', in order to capture the audience. As Penz (1996,175) claims: "[...] talk show hosts and producers create constellations and use strategies which encourage the expression of emotion. High affective levels of the interaction in talk shows are valued because they create audience involvement, which in turn is reflected in high ratings."

Furthermore, conflict and confrontation are chosen by the talk show hosts "to enhance the liveliness of the shows, and thus to attract viewers." Penz (1996,170).

Our limited data show that the choice of an emotional setting (the topic of the talk show has been chosen in order to trigger conflicts, confrontations, and displays of feelings in general) is enhanced by the attitude and the linguistic strategies used by the host, who, by using "teknonymy", pretends that she herself, the guest, the studio audience, and the viewers at home share the same family, and that the guest's problems are everybody's problems.

The strong link which is created *via* the "address inversion" is thus expanded *via* "teknonymy" to embrace the whole audience: from the microcosms of parental relations to the 'virtual' family.

Notes

1) It has to be said that the distinction between person deixis and social deixis is not a clear-cut one, and several authors (cf., e.g., Conte (1988,15)) do not accept it, but refer only to person deixis.
2) A boundary between deictic and sociolinguistic uses can be drawn): "Social deixis is thus concerned with the meaning and grammar (e.g. the problems of honorific concord) of certain linguistic expressions, while sociolinguistics is concerned, *inter alia*, with how these items are actually used in concrete social contexts classified with reference to the parameters of the relevant social system." Levinson (1983,93)

3) It is noteworthy that "[...] even in language communities which are as much in contact with each other as the French, German and Italian, the social conditions calling for one or another of the pronoun usage patterns differ a great deal." Fillmore (1975,78).
4) "Nell'allocuzione inversa il messaggio corrisponde al mittente, secondo un movimento inverso rispetto a quello dell'allocuzione diretta, dove i vari messaggi denotano, com'è normale il destinatario che è lo stesso referente." Renzi (1968,4)
5) "Address inversion is not restricted to KTs, one may speak of inversion whenever a form of address contains semantic features applicable to the speaker rather than the addressee." Braun (1988,12).
6) "*French* (colloquial) is mentioned by Sorrento (1950:261) as possessing constructions similar to Italian address inversion. Unfortunately, no further information is supplied." Braun (1988,270). It can be hypothesized that Sorrento was referring to Maghrebin French where the Arabic influence is strong.
7) Italics indicate that material is comprehensive and does not discriminate between the various sub-languages or dialects: e.g. "address inversion" is found in the following Italian regions: Abruzzo, Basilicata, Calabria, Campania, Lazio, Molise, Puglia, Sicilia.
8) With regard to dialogic repetition, and the several functions it can perform, cf. Bazzanella 1996.
9) "Baby Talk is part of a more pervasive cultural orientation to children among mainstream Americans [...]mainstream American society is highly child-centered and [...] there is a very strong expectation that those in the presence of young children will accomodate tochildren's perceived wants and needs." Ochs (1991,349)
10) "[...] è chiaro che il mittente, dicendo *mama*, non fa riferimento al destinatario, né invoca la mamma - ma fa sempre in un certo modo riferimento a se stesso. Egli si attribuisce una sorta d'identità materna metaforica rispetto al destinatario, identità che esprime sentimenti caldi, di partecipazione. Quest'uso si può quindi chiamare: allocuzione inversa metaforica." Renzi (1968,8)
11) The data was collected by Cristina Musella for her thesis in Philosophy of Language, Università degli Studi di Torino 1996-1997: *La deissi personale, la deissi sociale e i termini di parentela. Tematiche teoriche ed usi parlati e scritti.* I wish to thank Davide Ricca for his collaboration.
12) Before 1995, the same host was conducting *Amici* on Saturday, from 13 p.m. to 15 p.m.; given its success, the new program *Amici di sera* started.
13) Twelve episodes of the program were videotaped, i.e. in alltwenty four hours of recording in all.
14) As Dressler/Merlini Barbaresi 1994 point out, the main communicative situation favoring the use of diminutives is the "child-centered speech situation."
15) Other expressions of emotions (e.g. weeping) will not be taken into account, even if they are significant clues to what is going on, particularly when the 'players' get carried away by emotion in an unexpected and uncontrolled manner. Aggiungere il pezzo da Penz del controlo dell'host, e mettere l'esempio del far andare inonda la pubblicità per abbassare la tensione durante Alessandra.
16) With regard to "address inversion", Renzi (1968,6) claims that "[addiungere la citaz intera] in certi casi il grado fittizio di parentela diventa una sorta di epiteto fisso."

References

Braun, Friederike (1988): Terms of address. Problems of patterns and usage in various language and cultures. Berlin/New York: Mouton de Gruyter.

Brown, Roger and Alfred Gilman (1960): The pronouns of power and solidarity. – In: Thomas A. Sebeok (ed.): Style in language MIT Press, 253-276.

Brown, Penelope and Levinson, Stephen C. (1987): Politeness, Cambridge: CUP.

Conte, Maria-Elisabeth (1988): Condizioni di coerenza. Ricerche di linguistica testuale, Firenze: La Nuova Italia.

Dressler, Wolfang U. and Merlini Barbaresi, Lavinia (1994): Morphopragmatics: Diminutives and intensifiers in Italian, German and other languages. Berlin: Mouton de Gruyter.

Fillmore, Charles J. (1975): Santa Cruz lectures on deixis, Bloomington, Indiana: Indiana University Linguistic Club.

Levinson, Stephen (1979): Pragmatics and social deixis in proceedings of the Fifth Annual Meeting of the Berkeley Linguistic Society, 260-233.

Levinson, Stephen (1983): Pragmatics, Cambridge: Cambridge University Press.

Lyons, John (1977): Semantics, vol. 2. Cambridge: Cambridge University Press.

Malsch, Derry L. (1987): The grammaticalization of social relationship: the origin of number to encode deference. – In papers from the 7th International conference on Historical Linguistics, ed. by A. Giacalaone Ramat, O. Carruba, G. Bernini, Amsterdam: Benjamins, 407-418.

Ochs, Elinor (1991): Indexing gender. – In: Duranti, Alessando and Goodwin, Charles (ed.): Rethinking context, Cambridge: CUP, 335-357.

Penz, von Hermine (1996): Language and Control in American TV Talk Shows. An Analysis of Linguistic Strategies. Tübingen: Gunter Narr.

Renzi, Lorenzo (1968): Mama, tata, nene, ecc.: il sistema delle allocuzioni inverse in rumeno. – In: Cultura neolatina 1, XXVIII, 1-11.

Renzi, Lorenzo (1993): La deissi personale e il suo uso sociale. Studi di grammatica italiana. XV, 347-390.

Renzi, Lorenzo (1995): La deissi, in Renzi L. et al. Grande Grammatica Italiana di consultazione, vol. III, Bologna: Il Mulino, 350-375.

Sgroi, Salvatore C. (1990): Per una linguistica siciliana. Tra storia e struttura. Messina: Sicania.

Sorrento, Luciano (1950): Un caratteristico fenomeno sintattico di linguaggio affettivo. – In: Sintassi romanza, 239-269.

Stati, Sorin (1982): Il dialogo. Considerazioni di linguistica pragmatica, Napoli: Liguori.

Weigand, Edda: Dialogue in the grip of the media, this volume.

Willibrord de Graaf/Geeske Hoogenboezem

Dialogues and Drama
The Dutch Homeless Theatre Project as a Case

1. Introduction

Since the early seventies the empowering effects of theatre and acting are generally known. In this respect, an exciting and unique experiment took place in the Netherlands last year. The play 'Homeless' had its première; homeless persons were the actors, and the play was based on their experiences and lifeworld. Afterwards the play was performed thirty times all over the country, in schools, psychiatric institutions, community centers, theatres and the like. The television transmitted a documentary on the development of the project and newspapers paid much attention to the players and their background.

To give you an impression of the play we will present a very short summary of its story. The play takes 55 minutes. In the first 25 minutes almost nothing happens at the relief center where a group of homeless people are assembled. There are hardly any dialogues, and the interaction there is, considers daily needs as money and coffee. Then Willem's bag is introduced. Willem is a homeless man known to the people present, but they have not seen him for quite some time. The bag is plundered, the wine it contains is shared, the cigars are smoked jointly, and the drawings by Willems children are looked at sentimentally. When the wine is finished and one of the groupmembers finds a lot of money in the bag, the companionship appears to be short-lived and fragile. The youngest boy in the group disappears with the money, some go after him and the last visitor takes all things of value with him and leaves.

In this paper we will look into the impact of dialogues on the process of making the play. In this context we define dialogue as any form of direct face-to-face interaction, as in interviews or rehearsing the play, but also as the developing of textual dialogues in the play itself. In this latter respect we will also discuss the meaning of 'reality' which was attributed by the actors to the play. It will be impossible to discuss here all these forms in detail. We especially want to bring to the fore the conditions in which dialogues are made possible. This has to do with the peculiar situation of homeless people who seldom talk to each other or to outsiders about their predicament. In the theatre-project many efforts have been invested in the engagement of the players and the forming of a group. To start with we will describe the development of the project, and at the end we will discuss the asymmetries and symmetries in the dialogue-positions of the different participants in the project.

2. The start of the project

As just said, homeless persons have learned to be on their guard on the street, and not to disclose too much about their past. Interaction between homeless persons is mostly instrumental for survival on the streets, and is superficial and characterized by a fundamental distrust of each other. Against this background participation in a play is hardly obvious. In order to recruit homeless persons for the play the director and the play-writer undertook a diversity of activities. They visited all kinds of centers for the homeless, tried to get known, and after a while they organized meetings for those who were interested in the possibility of participation. These actions led to a group of 11 persons who agreed to participate. The director had individual interviews with each of them. In these interviews he focused on their life history, or important parts of it, in connection with their actual situation of homelessness and he asked them why they wanted to be an actor in this play.

In most interviews the homeless indicated that the play should show that homeless persons are alike others, and that homelessness could happen to everyone under conditions of misfortune. Participation in the play was also motivated by the wish 'to come out', to face the existence as homeless person and to come to terms with their experiences.

> Director: "Why do you think it important that there should be a play? Why is it needed?"
> Player: "It is good to show that those people are the same as the others. All people are the same. Maybe some have different feelings, but... My family thinks that you stay away from homeless people, because everything arises from their attitude. But this is not true. That kind of things should be made clear."

> Player: "For me it was a challenge to play the role of the alcoholic [because he had been an alcoholic himself, WdG/GH]. To become stronger, to put it more aside. At the start I found it difficult sometimes. But when it was finished, I said to myself: 'Look, so it has been, but it will never be like that anymore.'"

Director: "Is it good to act it out?"
Player: "Yes. That was, I think, the main reason to participate in the play."

In indicating their motives, some already refer to the different position of the director and themselves: they expect that the play will be his responsibility.

Director: "...The other variant is to show that things like these happen, that people can show how they surmounted their difficulties. An example of how it can be."
Player: "If you and your play can show to people, in spite of their prejudices, that the homeless are people like everyone else, than you have succeeded."

Director: "What should the play be about? What must be in it anyhow?"
Player: "That is up to you to decide!"

The asymmetry which is expressed in these lines, is characteristic for the role of the director in the project, as seen by the players and by himself. We will return to this point, but will continue now with the description of how the project got started.

After the initial interviews with homeless, group-meetings were organized. Here participants could get acquainted with each other and could talk about their experiences on being homeless, on how outsiders treated them etc.. These meetings were open for outsiders like the makers of the television-documentary, researchers, trainees, and interested homeless persons. Because of their lifestyle, it proved difficult for many of the homeless participants to attend these meetings regularly. The director and writer had to call them, write notes, visit them and so on in order to engage them to be present. Some of the originally interested persons dropped out, and after some months a core of seven persons remained. But also this core did loose some members and some extra recruitment activities were necessary.

The meetings took place once a week, on a fixed evening and place, and created thus a spatio-temporal continuity. Besides, the meetings developed into a typical pattern: at the beginning everybody got assembled around the table, get a cup of coffee, and then everybody introduced her/himself (which was often necessary because of the new people who were present). Then the director announced what to do, or what had happened. After that, the rehearsal started, even if there were only one or two players to do the job. This determination on the part of the director has been very important to create a climate of faith in a happy ending of the project. Again we see here the asymmetry in the relationship between actors and director: he decided what was done and when it was done. However, the rehearsals consisted also of a reworking of the proposed text fragments, in which the homeless actors were very active in pointing out what was 'realistic' to present to the public. So despite the asymmetry, the homeless actors played an important part in establishing the content of the play. We will discuss the issue of symmetry and asymmetry later on in this paper.

Summarizing, we conclude that the setting of a fixed evening and a recognizable routine in the possible interactions formed the condition for communication and cooperation between the players, the director and writer, and all the other 'outsiders'.

3. Forming a group

In the course of developing the play, the character of the interaction in the meetings changed. For a long time the players mostly communicated with the 'outsiders' attending the rehearsal, and hardly amongst themselves. Even during the rehearsals the communication between the homeless actors was most of the time mediated by the director. However, during a weekend of intensive rehearsing, some 8 weeks before the première, a turning point was established. At the end of this weekend the play was performed in full length and before an audience for the first time. The players felt that they had to take responsibility towards each other for the success of the project. This became also clear to them because one member dropped out during this weekend, and left the group with the task of completing the play. Ever since this weekend, the meetings got more lively, the players discussed about their roles and about the play and they expressed their new status as a group to the outsiders (like the interested press).

The increasing involvement with the group is demonstrated in the following dialogues.

> Director: "How do you feel about the contact with the other players in the group? For example, when someone drops out or is in trouble, or if someone cannot deal with it. Do you think they are losers?"
> Player: "No, you should accept people as they are. Respect each other under whatever conditions. I noticed that in the first half of the year the group stuck together like grains of sand. Only later did I feel that a certain solidarity developed. ...But it has been a process of growth."
>
> Director: "Isn't the making of the play as satisfying as playing the final result?"
> Player: "The result, that has to be shown, but the making of the play has brought me a lot of pleasure. To be in touch with other people, that I did not know for years."

The increasing involvement as a group appeared also in activities as attending a birthday, visiting a festive evening, or attending the funeral of one member of the group together. It also showed in criticisms of each other (for instance, too much drinking before a performance was not allowed) or in collective clearing away of the equipment after the performance.

4. The constitution of the text

At the start of the project there was no plot, no text. Based on the visits to the homeless-centers, the interviews and the group-meetings, the first text-fragments were written. These fragments were read together and discussed with the players. When they proved to be 'realistic' in the eyes of the players, they constituted the first parts for playing. After that the director and the writer proposed a story line in which the fragments could be fitted. This initial story line was accepted by the players, but has seen considerable change during the rehearsals. This was due to the procedure in which the players were asked to judge the staging of the fragments and the credibility of the configuration of the parts and the transitions in the play. For example, the initial story was enacted at the funeral of a homeless man. Later on, this story line proved inconsistent with the proposed fragments, and therefore the entourage of the play was changed to a relief center for homeless.

Some players were very active in indicating the ambiguities of the homeless existence: the claim of being one's pals does mostly not correspond to the practice of cheating one another, and hierarchical relations are important in the daily negotiations about getting what from whom. All this was important because the players attached much value to the realistic character of the play: it should represent how it feels to be homeless. They were looking for the recognition of their own experiences through the play. In this sense the play represented for them more a personal dramatization of their reality than a theatrical piece.

In theatre there is always a tension between the reality of the play and the playing with reality, between fiction and reality, or better, in theatre the reality is always an interpretation needing to be interpreted. It was obvious that the director was very well aware of this difference between theatre as a vehicle for playing with reality and drama as the expression of real personal experiences. To the players, their participation in the group had more to do with drama then with theatre. They valued the opportunity to experience again and in this way deal with their experiences as homeless, as the dialogue between the director and the former alcoholic shows [one]. Furthermore, the players liked the fact that they could get in touch with "outsiders", sometimes for the first time in years, as was indicated in several other dialogues we presented earlier [three]. However, the aim of the director was to make theatre not drama. This could be one of the causes of the asymmetric relation between the director and the players.

Because to the players their involvement in the group was about drama, about their own experiences, it was very important to them that the scenes they played were real to them. At first this aspect of reality has been written down in explicit dialogues in the text-fragments. However, lots of these verbal expressions disappeared gradually and have been replaced by gestures, by nonverbal interactions. There was a pragmatic reason behind this: most players found it difficult to remember large quantities of text. But it also had to do with the feeling that the nonverbal representation corresponded better to 'how it actually went'. Here we will present two examples: an example of nonverbal interaction and an example of an explicit dialogue.

> Victor is out of cigarettes and wants to get some from David. Victor is in the position that he does not have to ask or to beg cigarettes from David, he simply walks up to him, shows David his empty package and David offers him his pack of cigarettes. David does not pay much attention and therefore Victor can change the packs and returns the empty pack to David and keeps the full pack to himself.
>
> A little later, Victor tries to borrow money from Johan.
> Victor: "Hey, Johan! Johan!"
> (Johan does not react; he is reading his paper)
> (Victor takes a seat next to Johan and leans towards him)
> (Johan does not react and continues smoking his cigarette)
> Victor: "Hey Johan, give me some money so that I can get a beer. I am as sick as a dog. I am shivering man, look at me!"
> (No reaction)
> Victor: "Hey man, come on man!"
> (No reaction still)
> Victor: "Hey, come on now. Give me some money, I am shivering so much that I can hardly smoke a cigarette!"
> (Johan does not react)
> Victor: "Hey, come on now!"
> (Now Johan reaches for his pocket without saying a word. He arrogantly shakes his head and hands some money to Victor. Victor snatches the money out of Johans hand and leaves the room in a hurry.)

5. Conditions for dialogue

The main point we want to make is that the making and performing of the play took place in asymmetric conditions for dialogue. We distinguish four dimensions in this asymmetry between the parties involved in the project: the director and the homeless players. The first dimension concerns the making of a play, the second dimension involves the aims for participating in the project, the third dimension has to do with the extent to which both parties had knowledge of the world of the homeless and the last dimension concerns the ability to trust. This is not to say that asymmetry prevents dialogue. On the contrary, it can be argued that this was just the starting point for a development of an eventual successful communication. Furthermore, in distinguishing these four dimensions we do not want to present a static image of the relationships between both parties. Let us try to present the developments regarding these four dimensions.

With respect to the making of the play, we emphasize once again that two parties can be discerned: the director (and writer) and the homeless players. From the start it was clear that the director had the initiative: he had the ideas about making a play, he interviewed the participants, he gave form to the meetings and the like. The director was dominant in respect to the quantity of speech, the interactive moves, and strategic interventions in the dialogues. Of course this had to do with his position as the instigator and professional of the theatre project, a position which was acknowledged by the players. However, since the director determined largely by himself the story line and the message the play was to convey, the players had difficulties creating an image of the play for themselves. Thus, along this dimension of asymmetry, the inequalities between the two parties remained during the course of the project.

The second dimension involves the aims for participating in the project. Somehow the homeless players felt dependent on the director for the realization of their wish to get public recognition for their homelessness, a wish for a play which could correct prejudices about homeless people. However, the aim of the director was a different one. He considered his play as a means that could help the homeless participant in finding their way back to society. Although the players had thus motives of their own for participating in the project, they did not for a long time feel on equal footing with the director regarding the fulfillment of the project. This dimension of asymmetry changed, as we will show below.

The third dimension has to do with the extent to which both parties had knowledge of the world of the homeless. Obviously, with respect to this dimension the asymmetry works the other way around. The players knew all about this world, whereas the director had to learn from them in order for him to be able to present a credible representation of the lifeworld of the homeless. The director had a self-confident competence to deal with this asymmetry, in order to elicit reactions from the players. This happened especially in the continuous remaking and rehearsing of the play. Precisely at this point he needed the players. According to the players, in the lifeworld of the homeless, hierarchical relations between several categories of homeless people are very important. These hierarchies determine who can get what from whom and the effort it will take to get things like money or cigarettes from somebody. To the players it was very important that these hierarchies were represented truthfully. In handout four we showed two of the dialogues in which such unequal relations can be traced. Experiences of homelessness were the privilege of the players, and they were invited by him to take the floor and bring in all they had.

The last dimension concerns the ability to trust. Although the players responded to the request of the director to share information on homelessness with him and were active in the staging of the play, they remained rather passive in relation to each other personally and as a group for a long episode. We emphasized before that this lack of trust is related to the necessity to be on your guard on the streets. When this passiveness changed and they began to perceive themselves as a team, as the owners of a project (which could not have succeeded without them as they started to realize), they also started to intervene more daringly in the general course of things. They developed a kind of self-confidence – enhanced by the public interest for their undertaking – which created more competence in engaging dialogues with the director and other 'outsiders'. It follows that the players moved forward along the dimension of trust. This development also influenced the dimension concerning the aims for participating in the project. We stated above that for a long time the players did not feel on equal footing with the director. Along with the development of trust between both parties, these feelings of inferiority decreased as well.

Overlooking the material we presented to you this afternoon, we want to conclude the following. From the beginning there were many asymmetries between the two parties involved in the homeless theatre project. However, it may have been exactly these asymmetries which have enabled the dialogues described to take place. If the director would not have had the initiative, if he would not have had very outspoken ideas about making a play, in other words: if he would not have been dominant, the dialogues described in this paper would not have been possible. Sometimes, asymmetric relationships can give rise to very interesting dialogues and may develop into more equal relations.

References

Chase, S. E. (1995): Taking narrative seriously. Consequences for method and theory in interview studies. – In: Josselson, R. and Lieblich, A.: Interpreting experience. The narrative study of lives, London, Sage.

Hasselt, Peter van (1985): Doen alsof...?: Dramatisch spel in het basisonderwijs, Tilburg.

Linell, P. and Luckman, T. (1991): Assymetries in dialogue. Some conceptual preliminaries. – In: Markova, I. and Foppa, K. (1991): The dynamics of dialogue, New York, Harrester/Wheatsheaf.

Markova, I. and Foppa, K. (1991): The dynamics of dialogue, New York, Harrester/Wheatsheaf.

Toneelgroep Utrecht (1997): Dakloos, thuisloos: Verslag van een toneelproject met dak- en thuislozen, Utrecht.

Wessels, Charlyn (1987): Drama, Oxford.

Way, Brian (1967): Vorming door drama, Groningen.

František Daneš

Intonation and Related Vocal Phenomena in Mass-Media Debates

1. The situation and structure of round table debates

In my paper I focus on a type of round table political debates in Czech television programmes. To begin with, I will analyze in some detail the situation and structure of group debates of the round table type without audience in the studio. Their public character implies a large audience of TV lookers on, who represent the invisible addressees of the debate. Nevertheless, their existence is reminded by the presence of cameras in the studio. In spite of this fact, the participants behave as if not noticing them, they do not face them, do not try to get into contact with the assumed audience of lookers on. But we may be sure that the debaters bear in mind the presence of them, they are fully aware of the fact that it is the audience that is the very objective of their action, and, consequently, they behave during the debate *sub specie* of this objective. They mostly do not, in fact, try to persuade their co-debaters, but through the course of the debate and particularly through their personal contribution to influence or to persuade the lookers on or to win their sympathy at, least. With other words, a political debate appears rather as a sort of theatre performance (as S. Èmejrková recently remarked), in some cases even with individual parts distributed in advance.

It is clear that the operation of cameramen and of their director play a rather important role in the development of the debate. Cameras scan not only the behaviour of the just debating participant, but now and then they focus on another one. The camera shows the momentaneous facial expression and gestures of him, thus revealing in one case, say, that he is not following the debate, in another that he is expressing a positive stance to the argument, or, in turn, that he is disapproving it, or he may express an unfriendly attitude to the speaker, show his alleged superiority, an ironic approach, etc. Thus the operations of cameras actively enter into the course of the debate and can have a not negligible impact on the reception of the debate by the audience.

The said facts reveal also that what appears relevant is not only the current speaker at his turn, but that all participants and active parties of debates are essential. It was truly said that "all the time belongs to all interlocutors" and that "each contribution to dialogue appears to be something that originated from the interaction of different subjects and cannot be standardized according to a parameter such as turn, owing to its fragmented nature" (Contento and Stame, 1977, 59).

2. The nature and position of the vocal component of dialogue. Its catalytic function

The underlying idea of my talk is that understanding of the communicative interaction is possible only if the integration between verbal, vocal, and gestural behaviours is recognized, analysed and interpreted (as I postulated in 1985). The three behaviours represent a functional whole and are physically as well as functionally intertwined, so that in the case when we try, for methodical reasons, to divide the particular components of this whole, we should bear in mind that, in fact, we are committing a kind of violence on the reality and, consequently, should look for the interrelatedness of the components and subcomponents, all the time.

Generally speaking, the vocal component belongs more with the gestural than with the verbal one (at least certain classes of it – cf. the notion of "vocal gestures"). The vocal component itself represents a broad diapason of different features (linguistic ones on one pole, extralinguistic on the other, and paralinguistic in between).

Concerning the notion of intonation, it has a protean character and is conceived of by individual scholars in a narrower or a broader sense, thus stretching from the domain of systemic linguistic (phonological) phenomena to that of paralanguage. In my paper I will deal, however, mostly with the complex, heterogeneous (partly amalgamated) configurations or clusters of phonological, paralinguistic, and extralinguistic phonic features. It appears that all phonic discourse features having a communicative or at least informative effect (or are able to have it), i.e. any voice (vocal) phenomenon which can "tell something" to the hearer in a regular manner (e.g. even yawning, coughing, a shaky voice) should be taken into account (at the stage of a first approximation, at least). The following idea of Jakobson appears relevant here: He maintains that besides distinctive features the sound shape of language contains other kinds of likewise semiotically pertinent features.

Sounds of speech are tools of verbal communication and their entire make up is an ensemble of diverse types of features, all of which fulfil an interplay of tasks essential for communication. In the process of it, none of these features remains insignificant or immaterial (28).

There is a number of phonic parameters relevant to discourse. First, there are variations along the parameters of pitch (voice height) and intensity (especially in the complex of intonation), tempo, duration, voice and sound colour, rhythmicity, distribution of pauses. These qualities are of a graded character and variable, e.g.: fortissimo – pianissimo, crescendo – decrescendo (diminuendo), lento – presto, accelerando – ritardando. From the large set of "musical" terms several others may be named, e.g. various "manners of speech", such as staccato, legato, detache, tenuto, portamento, rubato, tranquillo, ... (some manners are of a complex character, e.g. drawl, clipping, jabbering). Several scholars mention further items: voice qualities or speaker's tone of voice and their control (spread – narrowed pitch range, harshness – openness, sharp – smooth transitions, forceful – relaxed speech, smooth – jerky rhythm, resonant – thin voice), and "vocalisations" or "vocal characters" (e.g. laughing, crying, yelling, whispering, sobbing, moaning, etc.). Last but not least, the basic set of idiosyncratic (i.e. individual or personal) set of voice characteristics (timbre, natural pitch height, volume of the voice) need to be mentioned.

Admittedly, the above list of voice features or qualities is far from being complete and represents rather a list of names than of clear-cut notions or exact terms: they are mostly impressionistic and partly overlapping.

As for the possible functions or meanings of this set of features, it is evidently highly multiplex and in no case there is a simple one-to-one relation between particular features and their possible meanings. The concrete meaning function of a speech unit or a stretch of speech is a rather complex and heterogeneous whole and in the process of decoding it, the hearer has to employ several principles.

The first of them is that of context-dependent functional complementarity of vocal features (i.e., the speaker can achieve the same effect trough a variety of means), the second one is that of functional specification, bearing on the fact that to one and the same vocal feature different meanings will be assigned in different contexts. (By context I mean here not only the vocal one, but also the verbal one comprising its meaning side.) A telling example: Very roughly speaking, falling intonation correlates with assertiveness, new information, and finality, as the case may be, and rising one with the lack of them. (Cf. Hollensteins concept of plurifunctionality.) As the third principle, Bühler's psychological concept of abstractive relevance is to be mentioned. It assumes – from the hearer's side – a simultaneous projection of a comprehended concrete phonic shape of a speech stretch on a presupposed set of functional levels (parameters), that means, a functional decomposition of the whole shape.

Underlying these principles, several psychological aspects are at work: First, the assumption that mental processes occur parallel on different levels and in interaction. Second, the so called dichotic theory of hearing. Third, our brains process information in part digitally (yes – no) and in part in an analogue manner (more – less, especially in the domain of emotions, music, etc.).

Practically, e.g., in the global sound shape of an actually uttered question "Have you arranged for it?", the hearer comprehends not only its propositional meaning and that he is asked, but also further pragmatic meanings, at least that the utterance was pronounced as an energetic inquiry in haughty tone, with a (potential) rebuke and with a degree of mistrust.

It appears to me that it is just such clusters of phonic and functional/meaning features (partly amalgamated) that are primarily relevant in discourse interaction and that they also appear as proper units of our description and transcripts. (I will return to this point later.)

The vocal component of discourse undoubtedly has a large set of various functions. But I will point here to one of them only which I would call *catalytic* one. What I mean are cases in which certain vocal behaviour of participants, parallel with their gestural behaviour, influences the course and development of the debate without bringing in new factual semantic information, i.e. without changing its propositional meaning contents and structure. I conceive catalysis here in a broad sense: As a catalyst, vocal behaviour can effect acceleration or retardation of the course of the debate, it can contribute to changes in the direction of its development, it can bring forth some alternations of mutual relations between the participants, etc.

Thus, for instance, a speaking participant, seeing and hearing that several of his co-debaters are giving consent to his argument by nodding in agreement and expressing an agreeing paralinguistic sound, he decides to further develop his argument, commenting his decision with such words as "Since I recognize your assent to my point, so I will go on".

Vocal component is typically a bearer of emotions. From the fact that emotions tend to evoke this or that emotion in the partner or partners, and that they promote or, in turn, hinder cognitive and verbal activities, it follows that this component often has a conspicuous impact on the ongoing of the debate.

3. The gesture-like nature of intonation and further vocal features

In his famous book "Language", Bloomfield made a revealing suggestion that besides intonation with phonological relevance ("distinctive patterns of speech") we use intonation in a manner of *gestures*, when we speak, e.g. sharply, derisively, angrily, kindly, and the like. The idea of the gesture-like nature of intonation was taken up by the late Professor Dwight Bolinger (as early as in 1946 and later in 1983). At least two points deserve our attention in this context: the semiotic relatedness of the two domains and the parallel employment of intonation and the like, and gestures in discourse. Moreover, this relatedness was recognized also by some theoreticians of gestures, who speak about "speech related gestures" and "vocal gestures".

Concerning the semiotic aspect of intonation etc., let us consider the instance of the move of voice height at the end of yes-or-no questions: the intonation is, roughly speaking, rising, nevertheless, the concrete phonological form of it (the intonation contour) is language specific, conventional and consequently, representing a symbol. But at the same time its symbolizing power appears to be based on a primitive mechanism that rises pitch as tension rises and lowers it as tension falls, so that its symptomatic (indexical) nature is attested. And it is not difficult to find cases where the semiotic character of intonation can be interpreted as predominantly iconic. But on the whole, the predominantly symptomatic and iconic characters are typical for vocal phenomena.

An analogous situation holds with gestures: There are conventional gestures (called emblems), pointing gestures with indexical character as well as representing gestures of iconic nature. Let us mention in this connection the theory of the gestural origin of language, seeing vocal gestures as a possible connecting link in phylogenetic, and perhaps also ontogenetic, evolution from gestures to language.

For the parallel use of intonation and gestures (or for their synergetic cooperation), Bolinger (1983) adduced a revealing example: Let us imagine the phonic shape of the utterance "Absolutely!" uttered by a speaker who wishes to emphatically express his agreement with what his interlocutor has said. Now, to underscore his agreement, he may use a gesture of the type called "batton" (aptly discussed by Contento and Stame, 1997), i.e. to wag his index finger forward and back at about the level of the chin (having a meaning like "note well"). At the same time he may nod his head, or shake it. The nod is a further intensification of the affirmation, and the shake is aimed at all opponents of the view expressed: "Let no one say the contrary!"

In certain situations, a gestural configuration accompanying an utterance can be used separately, independently, out of concert with the corresponding linguistic utterance, simply as its substitute. Once more an example: A gestural utterance for "do not know" goes like this:

Lips pursed: "No comment"

Eyebrows arched and/or shoulders raised: "I am wondering, too"

Head tilted sidewise: "Evasion"

Hands held slightly forward, palms up: "Empty, no information"

This gestural performance could surely be accompanied by a hummed intonational tune corresponding to the respective underlying verbal utterance.

We could say that in this way the meaning content of the expression "not know" has been decomposed into such subcomponents for which the language of gestures affords means of expression.

4. How to transcribe spoken dialogues?

Any discourse has two basic existential dimensions: that of *linearity* and that of *simultaneity*. The simultaneity (vertical) dimension was underlined especially by R. Jakobson, who used the terms "Achse des Beisammen" and "Achse des Nacheinander". Simultaneity holds both on the level of linguistic form and linguistic meaning, and with it, the above mentioned principle of abstractive relevance, as well as the existence of feature clusters go together. The phenomenon of the simultaneous co-existence of various features in speech – be they vocal or gestural – has serious consequences for the **transcription** of dialogical texts. Since the current transcriptions have, on the whole, the form of a written text, they are to a high degree linear in character (in spite of the use of various "suprasegmental" signs or marks).

It seems to me that an ideal format of transcription could have the form of an "orchestra parts" (German "Partitur"). Somewhat similar idea was proposed by Ehlich (HIAT). Nevertheless, frankly speaking, there are many practical obstacles which make theoretically ideal transcription not feasible. (For example, it would be highly difficult for the analyst to identify and graphically note all the various nuances of voice qualities with their pragmatic meanings and functions in a given case.)

I mean that a reasonable and realistic approach to the solution of this complicated task might start by answering the following three questions: How?, What?, and Why? and by abandoning the unrealistic idea of a universal and allencompassing system of transcription.

The answer to the last of the three question will specify the actual aim or purpose of the transcription of the particular piece of dialogue. Knowing this, we have to decide which phenomena or classes of them in that discourse deserve to be actually identified and transcribed (more precisely, noted). And now, on the basis of these two decisions, we have to find out or devise an adequate system of transcription (notation).

I conclude with a comment and a suggestion. First, the vocal and gestural components have been somewhat neglected so far, in spite of the fact that videorecording affords an excellent basis. Second, I think that it is not necessary in all cases to undertake the extremely laborious detailed analysis and transcription of the said phenomena: Very often a global verbal characterization along with noting the most relevant vocal and gestural features could suffice. Thus in the case of a particular speech turn "Yeah" it would suffice to state that it was pronounced with a falling intonation, in a laconic and expressionless way, with a tone of superiority, and that the speaker finally concedes to his opponent, though unwillingly and with annoyance. May be that such an impressionistic specification could be objected to by those who are prone to strict objectivity and exactness. Nevertheless, I find this way realistic, practical, and acceptable, for certain purposes, at least.

References

Bolinger, Dwight L. (1946): Thoughts on 'yep' and 'nope'. – In: American Speech 21, 90-95.

Bolinger, Dwight L. (1983): Intonation and gesture. – In: American Speech 58, 156-174.

Contento, Silvana/Stame, Stefania (1997): Scripts and Transcriptions in Dialogue Analysis. – In: Weigand, E. (ed.): Dialogue Analysis: Units, Relations and Strategies Beyond the Sentence (Beiträge zur Dialogforschung 13), Tübingen, 3-12.

Daneš, František (1985): Intonace v textu (Intonation in text). – In: Slovo a slovesnost XLVI, 83-100.

Gabriele Diewald

Die dialogische Bedeutungskomponente von Modalpartikeln

1. Einleitung

Die Modal- bzw. Abtönungspartikeln treten bevorzugt in mündlich-dialogischen Formen sprachlicher Kommunikation auf. Dies wird meist mit der Feststellung in Zusammenhang gebracht, daß Modalpartikeln keine referentielle Bedeutung aufweisen, sondern schwer erfaßbare „subjektive" bzw. „situative" Aspekte des kommunikativen Austausches zum Ausdruck bringen. Aufgrund dieser schwer faßbaren Bedeutung wurden die Partikeln zunächst, d.h. vor dem Einsetzen einer intensiven Partikelforschung vor etwa 30 Jahren, als „Füllsel", „Würzwörter" und ähnliches bewertet. Sie galten als beliebig eingestreute, im Grunde überflüssige Zutaten zu einem Typus von sprachlicher Kommunikation, der sich ebenfalls durch relative Regellosigkeit und sprachliche Unachtsamkeit auszuzeichnen schien.

Durch die geradezu stürmische Entwicklung der Partikelforschung, die z.B. in den Kongreßbänden von Weydt (1979), (1983), (1989) dokumentiert ist, ist die Auffassung von der relativen Bedeutungslosigkeit bzw. Bedeutungsvagheit der Modalpartikeln heute überwunden und hat einer Vielfalt von Bedeutungs- und Funktionszuschreibungen Platz gemacht. Diese reichen vom Ausdruck „subjektiver" Einstellungen des Sprechers bezüglich emotiver, wertender und kommentierender Aspekte über Hörersteuerung bis zum Ausdruck und zur Modifikation illokutiver Funktionen. Eine in Zifonun [u.a.] (1997) angeführte Liste veranschaulicht das Spektrum der Vorschläge, die in der Forschung bisher unterbreitet wurden. Die Bedeutung bzw. Funktion der Partikeln wird u.a. beschrieben als: „sprechaktangebotmachend", „situationsdefinierend", „Ausdruck für Sprecheremotion", „konversationssteuernd", „gesprächsgliedernd", „gesprächsphorisch", „kontaktschaffend", „beziehungsindizierend", „illokutionstransformierend", „konsens/dissenskonstituierend", „themeneinordnend", „propositionsabschwächend/-verstärkend", „interaktionsstrategisch", „antwortstrukturierend", „metakommunikativ", „textverknüpfend" (nach Zifonun [u.a.] 1997, 904; dort auch die entsprechenden Literaturverweise).

Angesichts dieser Vielfalt kann eine gewisse Ratlosigkeit aufkommen und es scheint sinnvoll, die Suche nach einer klassenkonstituierenden Grundbedeutung der Partikeln zunächst zurückzustellen und sich weiterhin auf Einzelanalysen zu konzentrieren, wie dies in Ickler (1994, 381) vorgeschlagen wird. Ich denke jedoch, daß es durchaus möglich ist, eine abstrakte Bedeutungskomponente zu isolieren, die allen Partikeln und ihren Verwendungen zugrunde liegt. Diese gemeinsame Basis liegt in einer relationalen Struktur, durch die die partikelhaltige Äußerung mit einer anderen, vorgegebenen Einheit verknüpft wird, so daß die partikelhaltige Äußerung als zweiter, d.h. reaktiver Gesprächszug in einer unterstellten dialogischen Sequenz erscheint.

Auf das Vorhandensein einer solchen relationalen Struktur wurde in der Forschung schon mehrfach hingewiesen. So spricht Hentschel (1986, 31) von der „metakommunikativen Deixis" der Modalpartikeln; Franck (1979, 8) hebt, allerdings nur für einige Partikeln, hervor, daß sie „rückwärtsgerichtet" sind und „spezifische Voraussetzungen [...] über den Argumentations- und Interaktionszusammenhang" machen. Und auch Ickler (1994, 377) beschreibt im Grunde diese relationale Komponente wenn er festhält, daß die „Modalpartikeln [...] bestimmte Äußerungen in größere, grundsätzlich dialogisch zu interpretierende Textzusammenhänge ein[passen]" (vgl. hierzu auch König 1977, 129, Franck 1980, 82ff. u. 252ff., Doherty 1985, 15, Abraham 1990, 129, Petrič 1995).

Auf diesen Beobachtungen aufbauend wird im folgenden ein Modell zur Beschreibung der relationalen Grundstruktur der Modalpartikeln vorgestellt (hierzu ausführlich Diewald 1997 und Diewald/Fischer 1998).

2. Die relationale Bedeutungsstruktur der Modalpartikeln

Die relationale semantische Basis besteht im wesentlichen aus zwei Elementen: erstens aus einer allen Partikeln gemeinsamen indexikalischen Struktur, die die Verbindung zwischen der partikelhaltigen Äußerung und dem Bezugselement herstellt und zweitens aus lexemspezifischen semantischen Merkmalen, durch die die relationale Struktur in ihrer Art bestimmt wird, also z.B. als adversative, iterative oder konzessive Relation. Die folgenden Ausführungen befassen sich schwerpunktmäßig mit dem ersten, verweisenden Aspekt, da dieser die Grundlage für die dialogische Funktion der Partikeln darstellt. In einer ersten Annäherung kann diese verweisende Komponente folgendermaßen gefaßt werden (MP = Modalpartikel):

(1) Bezugselement außerhalb der Äußerung ← (MP & Äußerung im Skopus der MP).

Die Partikel verknüpft also die Äußerung, in der sie sich befindet, mit einem weiteren Element außerhalb der Äußerung. Aufgrund dieser relationalen Struktur gleichen die Partikeln konjunktionalen und anderen grammatischen Elementen ebenso wie Diskurspartikeln (vgl. Diewald/Fischer 1998). Das Spezifikum der Modalpartikeln gegenüber anderen Relatoren besteht jedoch in der Art des Bezugselements. Die Modalpartikeln kodieren keine syntaktischen oder semantischen Relationen zwischen Satzgliedern oder Teilsätzen, noch bringen sie deiktische Relationen zwischen Zeichenbenutzer und Sachverhaltsdarstellung zum Ausdruck. Stattdessen verknüpfen die Modalpartikeln die Äußerung mit einem Sachverhalt, den der Sprecher als relevant, als im Raum stehend, betrachtet und auf den er die partikelhaltige Äußerung bezieht. Dies sei durch den Vergleich einer Äußerung ohne Modalpartikel mit ihrer modalpartikelhaltigen Entsprechung (hier mit der Modalpartikel *aber*) illustriert:

(2) Das ist keine gute Konstruktion.

(3) Das ist aber keine gute Konstruktion. (Sagerer [u.a.] 1994)

Während Satz (2) eine bezüglich modaler Inhalte neutrale Sachverhaltsdarstellung ist, drückt Satz (3) aus, daß der durch die partikelhaltige Äußerung dargestellte Sachverhalt von der ursprünglichen Sprechererwartung abweicht. Die Partikel zeigt an, daß der Sprecher die Proposition *daß das eine gute Konstruktion ist* als vorgegeben betrachtet, daß die aktuelle Situation jedoch von der Vorgabe abweicht.

Die zentrale Funktion aller Modalpartikeln kann daher folgendermaßen beschrieben werden: Indem Modalpartikeln einen Verweis auf Vorgebenes enthalten, markieren sie die Äußerung, in der sie stehen, als nicht-initial.

Diese Beschreibung deckt sich weitgehend mit der Auffassung von Foolen (1989, 312f.), der bezüglich der gemeinsamen Grundbedeutung der Modalpartikeln folgendes feststellt:

> Als Klassenbedeutung für Modalpartikeln gilt, daß sie immer auf eine implizite, im Kontext relevante Proposition hinweisen. Diese implizite Proposition ist immer eine logische Variante der explizit ausgedrückten Proposition.

Der vorgegebene Sachverhalt ist typischerweise nicht im Vortext genannt, die Modalpartikeln sind also keine textverknüpfenden Elemente im engeren Sinn. Der Inhalt der Vorgabe, auf die der Sprecher Bezug nimmt, wird somit erst durch die partikelhaltige Äußerung selbst explizit (vgl. Franck 1979, 11). In (3) wird durch die partikelhaltige Äußerung gekennzeichnet, daß es um die Proposition *daß das eine gute Konstruktion ist* geht. Diese wird vom Sprecher aufgenommen und entsprechend der lexeminhärenten Partikelsemantik modifiziert. Bei *aber* ist diese eine adversative Relation, so daß die Grundbedeutung dieser Partikel paraphrasiert werden kann als ‚Indizierung einer adversativen Relation zwischen pragmatischem Prätext und in der Äußerung dargestellter Situation'. Diagramm (1) kann somit für Satz (3) folgendermaßen konkretisiert werden:

(4) Schema der relationalen Grundstruktur der Modalpartikeln:

nicht versprachlichte Vorgabe:		Äußerung:
Proposition 1	←	MP & modifizierte Proposition 1'
Daß das eine gute Konstruktion ist		*das ist aber keine gute Konstruktion*

Die vorgegebene Proposition wird hier der *pragmatische Prätext* genannt. Dieser Begriff soll die wesentlichen, d.h. definierenden Aspekte der Modalpartikelfunktion andeuten. Es sind dies folgende drei Punkte:

1. Die Vorgabe, auf die sich die Partikel bezieht, ist typischerweise nicht versprachlicht (daher *pragmatisch*).
2. Die Vorgabe besteht aus einer Proposition, die versprachlicht werden kann (daher Prä*text*).
3. Bei dem Bezugselement handelt es sich um Vorausgehendes (daher *Prä*text).

Aus obigen Überlegungen läßt sich ein Schema für die Bedeutungserfassung der Modalpartikeln ableiten, das die beiden Bezugspunkte der Relation, also den pragmatischen Prätext und die aktuelle Gesprächssituation, sprachlich expliziert. Dieses Beschreibungsschema ist angelehnt an Wierzbickas Konzept der universalen semantischen Metasprache (*natural semantic metalanguage* = NSM; s. Wierzbicka 1986 und 1991), das eine kleine Gruppe natürlichsprachlicher Ausdrücke als semantische Primitive definiert, mit Hilfe derer Wortbedeutungen ebenso wie ihre spezifischen Gebrauchsbedingungen notiert werden können. Durch diese Art der Bedeutungsparaphrase ist es möglich, illokutive und situative Komponenten systematisch und einheitlich zu notieren und gemeinsam mit der Kernproposition, also der Sachverhaltsdarstellung, die in der partikelhaltigen Äußerung thematisiert wird, in einem Schema darzustellen. Ein erster Vorschlag für das Grundschema der Bedeutungsbeschreibung der Modalpartikeln ist in (5) dargestellt:

(5) Allgemeines Bedeutungsschema der Modalpartikeln (s.a. Diewald/Fischer 1998):

Pragmatischer Prätext:	im Raum steht: Proposition
relevante Situation:	Sprechereinstellung bezüglich der im Raum stehenden Proposition
→ Äußerung:	modifizierte Proposition mit Partikel

Die erste Zeile des Schemas formuliert den pragmatischen Prätext, die zweite Zeile die aktuelle Gesprächssituation (die relevante Situation), die dritte Zeile nennt die partikelhaltige Äußerung, durch die die relevante Situation mit dem pragmatische Prätext verknüpft wird. Dieses Schema muß für jedes Partikellexem und für die verschiedenen Verwendungsweisen konkretisiert werden. Für die Beschreibung der Bedeutung von *aber* in (3)

(3) Das ist aber keine gute Konstruktion (Sagerer [u.a.] 1994)

zum Beispiel wird das Grundschema folgendermaßen konkretisiert:

(6) Bedeutungsschema der Modalpartikel *aber* in (3):

Pragmatischer Prätext:	im Raum steht: daß das eine gute Konstruktion ist
Relevante Situation:	ich denke: das ist keine gute Konstruktion
→ Äußerung:	*Das ist aber keine gute Konstruktion!*

Bei der Darstellung einzelner Verwendungen wird also in allen drei Zeilen die Kernproposition eingefügt. Daneben können die erste Zeile, der pragmatische Prätext, und die zweite Zeile, die relevante Situation, mit spezifischeren Beschreibungen aufgefüllt werden. In (6) steht in der Zeile des pragmatischen Prätextes die Formulierung „im Raum steht". Dies ist die neutralste und allgemeinste Ausprägung des pragmatischen Prätextes. Sie deutet an, daß hier nicht festgelegt ist, wer die Vorgabe macht, wer also die Proposition „in den Raum gestellt" hat. Der Sprecher bezieht sich in diesem Fall auf generell gültige Standardvoraussetzungen. Wird dagegen – um eine weitere Möglichkeit zu nennen – die Vorgabe dem Dialogpartner zugeschrieben, wird also eine echte dialogische Struktur impliziert, dann kann dieser spezifische Ausgangspunkt in den pragmatischen Prätext aufgenommen werden, und zwar mit der Formulierung „durch das, was du gesagt hast, steht im Raum, daß p".

Auch in der zweiten Zeile, der relevanten Situation, sind Modifikationen möglich, die sich auf die Auswahl der Illokution beziehen, die der Sprecher in der relevanten Situation trifft. Dies wird im Schema durch unterschiedliche Hypersätze wie „ich denke", „ich will", „ich sage" zum Ausdruck gebracht. Im obigen Beispiel (3) wird durch „ich denke" angezeigt, daß die relevante Situation so beschaffen ist, daß der Sprecher einen assertiven Sprechakt vollzieht. Wird *aber* dagegen als Modalpartikel in direktiven Sprechakten verwendet (die allerdings nur als indirekte Sprechakte direktive Funktion haben, als Strukturtyp liegt ein Aussagesatz vor), wie in

(7) Das ist echt alles ein klappriger Kram. Mußt aber gucken, ob da auch zwei Gewinde aneinander sind (Sagerer [u.a.] 1994),

dann erscheint diese Sprecherintention, die die relevante Situation bestimmt, in der zweiten Zeile der Bedeutungsbeschreibung in Form von „ich will". Dies ist in (8) illustriert:

(8) Bedeutungsschema der Modalpartikel *aber* in direktiven Sprechakten:

Pragmatischer Prätext:	im Raum steht: du mußt nicht gucken, ob da auch zwei Gewinde aneinander sind
Relevante Situation:	ich will: du mußt gucken, ob da auch zwei Gewinde aneinder sind
→ Äußerung:	*Mußt aber gucken, ob da auch zwei Gewinde aneinander sind*

Soweit zum Prinzip der Darstellung der Partikelbedeutung und der Notierung von Varianten. Im folgenden Abschnitt werden weitere Konkretisierungen besprochen.

Inwiefern ist diese relationale Grundstruktur der Modalpartikeln nun dialogisch? Durch den immer vorhandenen Bezug auf den pragmatischen Prätext wird, wie ausgeführt, die partikelhaltige Äußerung als nicht-initial markiert. Sie ist eine Folgeäußerung, die sich jedoch nicht direkt auf den Inhalt der vorhergehenden Äußerung des Dialogpartners oder des Sprechers bezieht. Die partikelhaltige Äußerung hat keinen sprachlich explizierten „Vorgängerausdruck", d.h. die Verknüpfungsfunktion der Modalpartikeln ist nicht anaphorisch. Stattdessen bezieht sich die partikelhaltige Äußerung auf den pragmatischen Prätext. Dieser wiederum wird im mündlichen Dialog typischerweise als impliziter, d.h. dem Partner unterstellter Gesprächsschritt präsentiert. Indem sich die partikelhaltige Äußerung auf einen dem Partner unterstellten, vorhergehenden Gesprächszug bezieht, erscheint sie nicht nur als *nicht-initial*, sondern als *reaktiv*. Die relationale Struktur der Modalpartikeln evoziert eine dialogische Sequenz aus zwei Zügen (deren erster Zug implizit ist) und läßt so eine Art Nebenschauplatz zu dem, was explizit geäußert wird, entstehen.

Ein treffendes Beispiel dafür, daß diese dialogische Komponente der Modalpartikeln nicht von einer real gegebenen dialogischen Struktur abhängt, sondern – in Form der relationalen Struktur – inhärenter Bestandteil der Partikelsematik ist, findet sich in Zifonun [u.a.] (1997). Dort wird ein Satz aus dem Bürgerlichen Gesetzbuch (Beispiel 9) mit der Modalpartikel *ja* versehen (Beispiel 10):

(9) Für die Kosten eines Rechtsstreits haftet das Gesamtgut auch dann, wenn das Urteil dem Gesamtgut gegenüber nicht wirksam ist. (Bürgerliches Gesetzbuch § 1438,2 nach Zifonun [u.a.] 1997, 909)

(10) Für die Kosten eines Rechtsstreits haftet ja das Gesamtgut auch dann, wenn das Urteil dem Gesamtgut gegenüber nicht wirksam ist. (Zifonun [u.a.] 1997, 910)

Selbst in einem stark situationsentbundenen, schriftsprachlichen Satz wie (9) genügt die Einfügung einer Modalpartikel, in diesem Fall *ja*, um einen dialogischen Effekt zu erzeugen. Der partikelhaltige Satz (10) erscheint als zweiter Zug einer dialogischen Sequenz. Man könnte sich – so Zifonun [u.a.] (1997, 910) – z.B. vorstellen, daß er in einer Gruppe von Studierenden im Rahmen der Vorbereitung auf eine juristische Prüfung fällt.

Im folgenden Abschnitt werden einige typische Verwendungsweisen der Partikel *denn* im Dialog erläutert und mittels des erarbeiteten Schemas dargestellt. Daß die Wahl auf *denn* fiel, hat folgenden Grund: *Denn* tritt als Modalpartikel nur in Fragesätzen auf, und Fragen sind geradezu der Prototyp initiierender Gesprächszüge (Franck 1979, 5). Wenn sich selbst an ihnen die hier vertretene Auffassung, daß Modalpartikeln die Äußerung in der sie stehen, als nicht-initial und reaktiv bestimmen, erhärten läßt, dann erhöht dies deren Plausiblität. Die reaktive Komponente kommt dann eindeutig, weil gegen die anders gerichtete Tendenz des Satztyps bzw. der Illokution, durch die Partikel zustande.

3. *Denn*-Fragen im Dialog

Durch die Verwendung von *denn* in Fragsätzen wird die Frage als derjenige Sprechakt markiert, der sich als Konsequenz aus der Relation zwischen pragmatischem Prätext und relevanter Situation ergibt. Die Frage erscheint als „extern motiviert" und „nicht der Willkür des Sprechers entsprungen" (Ickler 1994, 383). Durch *denn* wird also eine konsekutive Beziehung zwischen dem pragmatischen Prätext und der aktuellen Gesprächssituation hergestellt: Die Modalpartikel *denn* dient der Indizierung einer konsekutiven Relation zwischen dem pragmatischen Prätext und der in der Äußerung dargestellten Situation (Diewald 1997; vgl. auch König 1977, 123, Franck 1980, 222ff., Wegener [demn.] 12ff.).

Anders als bei *aber* umfaßt der pragmatische Prätext hier nicht nur die Kernproposition, sondern auch die illokutive Ebene: Die Komponente des Frage-Stellens ist bereits Bestandteil des pragmatischen Prätexts und wird in der ersten Zeile des Schemas notiert. Als allgemeines Schema für *denn*-Fragen ergibt sich damit (11):

(11) Allgemeines Bedeutungsschema für *denn*:

Pragmatischer Prätext:	im Raum steht: ich frage: p?
Relevante Situation:	ich frage: p?
→ Äußerung:	*denn & p?*

Dieses Grundschema kann im Dialog in unterschiedlicher Weise spezifiziert werden, was nachfolgend anhand einiger Varianten dargestellt wird. Die verwendeten Dialoge sind der von Redder und Ehlich (1994) herausgegebenen Textsammlung entnommen.

Bei der ersten Variante schließt die partikelhaltige Frage direkt an den vorhergehenden Gesprächsschritt des Partners an, d.h. der pragmatische Prätext läßt sich aus der Vorgängeräußerung ableiten. Ein Beispiel ist:

(12) Zeuge: Und wir fahren, nich wahr, und dann mit der Geschwindigkeit achtzig bis hundert.

Richter: Warum fahren Sie denn so schnell? (Hoffmann 1994, 61, Z. 53ff.)

Mit Hilfe von *denn* stellt der Richter seine Frage als durch die Partneräußerung motiviert dar. Obwohl er also eine neue Sequenz einleitet, vollzieht er gleichzeitig einen reaktiven Gesprächszug, so daß man solche *denn*-Fragen geradezu als „Gelenkfragen" bezeichnen könnte. Das Schema für diesen Fall ist in (13) dargestellt:

(13) Schema für *denn* in (12):

Pragmatischer Prätext:	durch das, was du sagst, steht im Raum: ich frage: Warum fahren Sie so schnell?
Relevante Situation:	ich frage: Warum fahren Sie so schnell?
→ Äußerung:	*Warum fahren Sie denn so schnell?*

Gelegentlich finden sich hier auch eingeschobene Verständnisfragen, was die *denn*-Frage in die Nähe einer Hörerrückfrage, d.h. einer Variante der Hörerrückmeldung bringt (vgl. Henne/Rehbock 1982, 179 und Franck 1980, 225). So im folgenden Beispiel (Unterstreichung markiert simultan geäußerte Passagen):

(14) Zeuge: Und öh/ also es gab denn keine V/ Verbindung ö mit der/also mit denen wir uns unterhalten könnten. A/

Richter: Ham Sie denn mit dem Fahrer nicht gesprochen?

Zeuge: Ja: und dann ungefähr ein/n/eine Minute oder was ä anderthalb Minuten, und ich habe ihm gesagt [...] (Hoffmann 1994:57, 17ff.)

Der Richter geht zunächst davon aus, daß der Zeuge mit dem Fahrer gesprochen hat. Die Äußerung des Zeugen läßt beim Richter Zweifel an dieser Annahme aufkommen und darauf hin stellt er die *denn*-Frage, die der Zeuge positiv beantwortet, bevor er in seinem Gesprächszug fortfährt. Durch diese Rückfrage klärt sich, daß der Zeuge mit seiner Äußerung *es gab denn keine V/Verbindung ö mit der/also mit denen wir uns unterhalten könnten* keineswegs sagen wollte, daß er nicht mit dem Fahrer gesprochen hat, sondern daß er damit auf den betrunkenen Zustand des Fahrers anspielt, der ein sinnvolle Verständigung verhinderte. *Denn*-Fragen der Variante I dienen insgesamt, ob als eigener Gesprächsschritt oder als Hörerrückfrage, der regulären, schrittweisen Weiterführung des Dialogs. Sie tun dies, indem sie qua Partikel eine Rückwärtsverknüpfung an den pragmatischen Prätext herstellen, während sie qua Frage eine Vorwärtsverknüpfung erzeugen (vgl. Franck 1980, 222).

Eine zweite Variante von *denn*-Fragen knüpft wie Variante I direkt an den vorhergehenden Gesprächsschritt des Partners an. Allerdings handelt es sich hier um tendenziöse Fragen im Sinne von Franck (1979, 4), wobei der Sprecher eine negative Antwort voraussetzt. Ein Beispiel ist (15):

(15) Richter: Und ich weiß jetzt nich, warum Sie versuchen, die Sache jetzt äh so etwas schwierig darzustellen. Ob Sie Angst haben oder weil Sies nich mehr wissen, ich weiß es nich.

Zeuge: Wieso? Wovor/ warum soll ich denn Angst haben, und dann [...] (Hoffmann 1994, 85, Z. 10ff.)

Der Zeuge wehrt hier die Unterstellung ab, er könnte Angst haben. Seine *denn*-Frage hat eine deutlich negative Antwortpräferenz. Da diese Antwortpräferenz ebenfalls Bestandteil des pragmatischen Prätext ist, wird die erste Zeile des Schemas bei diesem Typ komplexer; dies zeigt Diagramm (16):

(16) Bedeutungsschema für *denn* in (15):

Pragmatischer Prätext:	durch das, was du sagst und durch das, was ich denke, steht im Raum: ich frage: Warum soll ich Angst haben?
Relevante Situation:	ich frage: Warum soll ich Angst haben?
→ Äußerung:	*Warum soll ich denn Angst haben*?

Die Funktion solcher tendenziöser *denn*-Fragen geht von Ironie, über Abwehr bis zum Gegenangriff.

Bei einer dritten Variante von *denn*-Fragen besteht der pragmatische Prätext aus einer Standardannahme, die der Sprecher als für die aktuelle Gesprächsphase relevant und seine Frage motivierend darstellt. Der pragmatische Prätext ergibt sich also nicht direkt aus einer vorhergehenden Partneräußerung. Hierher gehört die schon häufig diskutierte Verwendung von *denn*-Fragen in der Gesprächseröffnung (vgl. Kosaka 1989, 161, König 1977, 120f.). Ein Beispiel ist Satz (17), die gesprächseröffnende Frage eines Sachbearbeiters im Versicherungsamt bei einer Klientenberatung:

(17) Sachbearbeiter: So, was kann ich denn für Sie tun? (Becker-Mrotzek/Fickermann 1994, 110, Z. 1)

Der pragmatische Prätext besteht hier aus dem Standardwissen bzw. dem situativen Rahmenwissen über verschiedene Arten der Gesprächseröffnung (vgl. König 1977, 121). Durch die Verwendung einer *denn*-Frage wird ein im doppelten Sinn „verbindlicher" Ton angeschlagen, indem ein vorhergehender Zug unterstellt wird, wodurch der erste Zug als nicht-initial und reaktiv erscheint. Auf diese Weise wird die Grenze zwischen Nicht-miteinander-Sprechen und Miteinander-Sprechen verwischt und der Übergang erleichtert. Nummer (18) zeigt das semantische Grundschema kann für diesen Fall:

(18) Bedeutungsschema für *denn* in (17):

Pragmatischer Prätext:	durch das, was alle über diese Situation wissen, steht im Raum: ich frage: Was kann ich für Sie tun?
Relevante Situation:	ich frage: Was kann ich für sie tun?
→ Äußerung:	*Was kann ich denn für Sie tun*?

Schließlich sei noch eine vierte Variante angeführt, die der dritten darin gleicht, daß sich auch hier der pragmatische Prätext nicht aus dem vorhergehenden Gespächsschritt ableiten läßt. *Denn*-Fragen dieses Typs befinden sich meist am Ende eines aus mehreren Propositionen bestehenden Gesprächsschritts des Sprechers. Der pragmatische Prätext bezieht sich auf gemeinsames Wissen aus weiter zurückliegenden Passagen des aktuellen Dialogs oder auf allgemeines Standardwissen. Ein Beispiel für den ersten Fall, Bezug auf weiter zurückliegende Gesprächsteile, ist (19); das Schema ist in (20) gegeben:

(19) Staatsanwalt:	Also is auch egal. Sie haben „in der Nähe der Stichstraße" gesacht.
Angeklagter:	Jaja.
Staatsanwalt:	Öf/ja Nochmal, mit welchem Fahrzeuch sind Sie denn hingefahren? (Hoffmann 1994, 75, Z. 211ff.)

(20) Bedeutungsschema für *denn* in (19):

Pragmatischer Prätext:	durch das, was wir bisher gesagt haben, steht im Raum: ich frage: Mit welchem Fahrzeuch sind Sie hingefahren?
Relevante Situation:	ich frage: Mit welchem Fahrzeuch sind Sie hingefahren?
→ Äußerung:	*Mit welchem Fahrzeuch sind Sie denn hingefahren?*

Als letztes Beispiel sei (21) angeführt, bei dem der pragmatische Prätext auf Standardwissen Bezug nimmt. Das Bedeutungsschema ist in (22) gegeben.

(21) Verteidiger:	Sie haben jetzt hier ausgesacht, daß äh Sie sozusagen nicht ausgestiegen sind. Immerhin wars ja inner Nacht. Wie konnten Sie denn sehen, daß die Augen gerötet sind? (Hoffmann 1994, 76, Z. 217ff.)

(21) Bedeutungsschema für *denn* in (21):

pragmatischer Prätext:	durch das relevante Standardwissen (Nachts sieht man nicht gut) steht im Raum: ich frage: Wie konnten Sie sehen, daß die Augen gerötet sind?
relevante Situation:	ich frage: Wie konnten Sie sehen, daß die Augen gerötet sind?
→ Äußerung:	*Wie konnten Sie denn sehen, daß die Augen gerötet sind?*

Die Frage erscheint hier als ein aus Standardannahmen hergeleiteter neuer Gesprächszug. Dabei wird unterstellt, daß auch der Partner diese Standardannahmen teilt, so daß der in dieser Frage ausgedrückte Zweifel des Sprechers an der Richtigkeit der Aussage des Partners als intersubjektiv nachvollziehbar und nicht willkürlich erscheint.

In solchen Fällen zeigt sich im übrigen die Nähe zwischen der Modalpartikel *denn* und dem Temporaladverb *dann/denn*, auf die auch Wegener ([demn.], 13f., 16) hinweist. So könnte man die obige Passage reformulieren als:

(23) Wenn es in der Nacht war, wie konnten Sie dann sehen, daß die Augen gerötet sind?

Diese Nähe zu adverbiellen und konjunktionalen Elementen, deren rückwärtsverknüpfende Funktion ja unbestritten ist, ist m.E. ein stützendes Element für die hier vorgeschlagene Bedeutungsstruktur der Modalpartikeln (vgl. Diewald 1997, Diewald [demn.]).

Die Liste der möglichen Funktionen von *denn*-Fragen ist mit den in diesem Abschnitt vorgestellten Varianten mit Sicherheit nicht abgeschlossen. Doch ging es hier in keiner Weise um Vollständigkeit, sondern darum, zu zeigen, wie das im zweiten Abschnitt dargelegte Bedeutungsschema in systematischer und leicht handhabbarer Weise für verschiedene Partikelverwendungen modifiert werden kann.

4. Zusammenfassung

Die Modalpartikeln bringen zum Ausdruck, daß die Äußerung, in der sie stehen, nicht initial ist, sondern an ein in der kommunikativen Situation vorgegebenes Element, den pragmatischen Prätext, anknüpft. Die Modalpartikel weist auf den pragmatischen Prätext zurück und bringt ihn mit der geäußerten Sachverhaltsdarstellung in Beziehung. Diese relationale Struktur kann anhand eines Bedeutungsschemas expliziert werden, das die beiden Endpunkte der Relation, also den pragmatischen Prätext und die relevante Situation, mit Hilfe einer kleinen Anzahl metasprachlich definierter Lexeme formuliert. Die partikelhaltige Äußerung erscheint so als das Ergebnis der Einbeziehung und Komprimierung des pragmatischen Prätextes in die aktuelle Situation.

Die dialogische Struktur der Modalpartikel ergibt sich aus der Tatsache, daß der pragmatische Prätext typischerweise als dem Hörer unterstellter, wenngleich nicht versprachlichter Gesprächszug erscheint. Indem der entsprechende initiierende Zug als vorgegeben impliziert wird, erscheint die modalpartikelhaltig Äußerung als ein reaktiver Zug. Diese dialogische Komponente ist je nach aktuellem Kontext unterschiedlich deutlich ausgeprägt, woraus sich, wie am Beispiel von *denn*-gezeigt, verschiedene Varianten der Partikelverwendung im Dialog erklären.

Literatur

Abraham, Werner (1990): Zur heterogenen Entfaltung der Modalpartikel im Ahd. und Mhd. – In: Anne Betten (Hg.): Neuere Forschungen zur historischen Syntax des Deutschen: Referate der Internationalen Fachkonferenz Eichstätt 1989. Tübingen: Niemeyer (RGL 103), 124-138.

Becker-Mrotzek, Michael und Ingeborg Fickermann (1994): Versicherungsamt. – In: Redder/Ehlich (Hgg.) (1994), 110-135.

Diewald, Gabriele (1997): Grammatikalisierung. Eine Einführung in Sein und Werden grammatischer Formen. Tübingen: Niemeyer (GA 36).

Diewald, Gabriele [demn.]: Die Entwicklung der Modalpartikel *aber*: ein typischer Grammatikalisierungsweg der Modalpartikeln. – In: Hans Otto Spillmann und Ingo Warnke (Hgg.), Akten des 32. Linguistischen Kolloquiums vom 17. bis 19. September 1997, Universität Kassel. Frankfurt/Main: Lang.

Diewald, Gabriele und Kerstin Fischer (1998): Zur diskursiven und modalen Funktion der Partikeln *aber, auch, doch* und *ja* in Instruktionsdialogen. In: Linguistica 38, 75-99.

Doherty, Monika (1985): Epistemische Bedeutung. Berlin: Akademie-Verlag (studia grammatica 23).

Foolen, Ad (1989): Beschreibungsebenen für Modalpartikelbedeutungen. – In: Weydt (Hg.) (1989), 305-317.

Franck, Dorothea (1979): Abtönungspartikel und Interaktionsmanagement. Tendenziöse Fragen. – In: Weydt (Hg.) (1979), 3-13.

Franck, Dorothea (1980): Grammatik und Konversation. Königstein/Ts.: Scriptor (Monographien zur Linguistik und Kommunikationswissenschaft 46).

Henne, Helmut und Helmut Rehbock (1982): Einführung in die Gesprächsanalyse. 2., erw. u. verb. Aufl. Berlin, New York: de Gruyter.

Hentschel, Elke (1986): Funktion und Geschichte deutscher Partikeln: *Ja, doch, halt* und *eben*. Tübingen: Niemeyer (RGL 63).

Hoffmann, Ludger (1994): Eine Verhandlung vor dem Amtsgericht. – In: Redder/Ehlich (Hgg.) (1994), 19-90.

Ickler, Theodor (1994): Zur Bedeutung der sogenannten ‚Modalpartikeln'.– In: Sprachwissenschaft 19, 374-404.

König, Ekkehard (1977): Modalpartikeln in Fragesätzen. – In: Harald Weydt (Hg.): Aspekte der Modalpartikeln. Studien zur deutschen Abtönung. Tübingen: Niemeyer, 115-130.

Kosaka, Koichi (1989): Abtönungspartikel *denn* und Satznominalisierung. – In: Weydt (Hg.) (1989), 160-170.

Petrič, Teodor (1995): Indexikalische Leistungen der Modalpartikeln und ihre natürlichkeitstheoretische Bewertung. – In: Linguistica 35, 245-259.

Redder, Angelika (1990): Grammatiktheorie und sprachliches Handeln: *denn* und *da*. Tübingen: Niemeyer (LA 239).

Redder, Angelika und Konrad Ehlich (Hgg.) (1994): Gesprochene Sprache. Transkripte und Tondokumente. Tübingen: Niemeyer (Phonai 41).

Sagerer, Gerhard, Hans-Jürgen Eikmeyer und Gert Rickheit (1994): Wir bauen jetzt ein Flugzeug. Konstruieren im Dialog. Arbeitsmaterialien. Tech. Report, SFB 360 Situierte künstliche Kommunikatoren, Universität Bielefeld.

Wegener, Heide [demn.]: Zur Grammatikalisierung von Modalpartikeln. – In: Irmhild Barz und Günther Öhlschläger (Hgg.), Zwischen Grammatik und Lexik. Tübingen: Niemeyer.

Weydt, Harald (1969): Abtönungspartikel. Die deutschen Modalwörter und ihre französischen Entsprechungen. Bad Homburg, Berlin, Zürich: Gehlen.

Weydt, Harald (Hg.) (1979): Die Partikeln der deutschen Sprache. Berlin, New York: de Gruyter.

Weydt, Harald (Hg.) (1983): Partikeln und Interaktion. Tübingen: Niemeyer.

Weydt, Harald (Hg.) (1989): Sprechen mit Partikeln. Berlin, New York: de Gruyter.

Wierzbicka, Anna (1986): A Semantic Metalanguage for the Description and Comparison of Illocutionary Meanings. – In: Journal of Pragmatics 10, 67-107.

Wierzbicka, Anna (1991): Cross-cultural Pragmatics. The Semantics of Human Interaction. Berlin, New York: de Gruyter.

Zifonun, Gisela [u.a.] (1997): Grammatik der deutschen Sprache. 3 Bde. Berlin, New York: de Gruyter.

Robert Maier

Dialogic Characteristics of Political and Public Debates

1. Introduction

In this contribution I would like to introduce an approach how one can identify, analyze and evaluate fragments of dialogue in political and public debates. The general idea is quite simple. In public debates, the different parties engaged are individuals, who represent in general social groups or institutions. These parties use discourses in their contributions to public debates. In these discourses, the parties elaborate in particular social identities and social relations between these identities and also a specific representation of the world. The elaborated social identities are sometimes individualized in different ways: on the one hand the author of a contribution will represent a specified social identity in his/her discourse and situate the auditorium, or in other words the reader or listener in given social space, and on the other hand there will an elaboration of at least another social identity which can be identified by name, for example the director of a well-known organization, or by a generic figure, such as Mr. Smith, who stands for a specific social identity. Between these individuals, who stand for specified social identities, fragments of dialogue can appear in the discourse.

To begin with, I will suggest a working definition of public debates. In a following section I will introduce some criteria how to analyze discourse, and I will apply these criteria in analyzing the discourses of globalization to illustrate this approach. After having distinguished five discourses of globalization, I shall present some example of fragments of dialogue in these discourses.

2. Public debate

Public debates in modern times presuppose a public sphere which can only exist if formally or *de facto* there are conditions of public discussion of issues of general interest. As the point of public debates is not restricted to discuss matters of general interest but also to influence decisions of general interest, some form of democracy will be needed in order to enable the full development of public debates. The existing forms of democracy in present time do not really match the various ideal models of democracy which have been formulated by philosophers and social scientists. Held (1987) offers a good overview of models of democracy.

The model of deliberative democracy is particularly interesting when considering public debates, because a large participation of citizens in decisions is one of the main features of this ideal model. Deliberative democracy presupposes that all citizens participate in one way or another in the process of formulation of standpoints of policy. This participation does not mean that all citizens will directly influence the decisions, but it offers at least the possibility to do so. Any citizen or group of citizens should be able to bring his/her standpoints and arguments in the public sphere. These standpoints and arguments may be rejected in a public debate, but they may sometimes influence to some extent the opinions of others and in the long run have some impact on decisions of policy of general interest.

Public debates can be understood as social arenas where different parties formulate and discuss issues with the aim to influence the other parties and general decisions. The arenas have various forms, to begin with there were rather small – but in principle open for everybody – gatherings of people in cafes discussing issues of general interest. With the development of the media quite different forms of arenas exist at the present (Habermas 1990). With the Internet a new type of medium starts to play an important role.

The parties which participate in public debates can be individuals or groups. But groups are always represented by individuals. These individuals participate in their quality of citizens, in other words they have in principle equal rights, and their wealth, race or other particularities should not play any role. However, equal participation is an ideal which is far from being realized in practice.

Recent studies of the public sphere and of public debates (Gutmann and Thompson 1996, Van Kersbergen and Propper 1995, and the special numbers of the journals "Raisons Pratiques" and "Hermes") permit to characterize public debates as open, dynamic and heterogeneous.

Public debates are open in the sense that the parties participating can change. There may be individuals and groups which did not take part in any discussion for a long time who can at one moment start to participate. For example, the participation of women was marginal for a long time, but in recent decades a growing number of women does play a role in the public sphere.

Public debates have also a quite dynamic character, because not only the participants can change but also the issues which are discussed. Even a single issue or problem can over time be transformed quite radically, for example by being related to other issues or by being split in several distinct problems.

Moreover, public debates are quite often heterogeneous, which indicates the fact that one given issue can be discussed at the same time in several arenas, for example in different media, with various accents and by different parties.

There are three criteria of successful participation in public debates. These criteria are generally acknowledged because they formulate in fact only general preconditions. The first one simply specifies that a party succeeds to get in the public sphere. To get in means that a party will be able to formulate a standpoint and to present it in one or the other arena where public debates take place. This criterion involves that a party is well informed and able to analyze critically complex states of affairs, to formulate critical arguments and alternatives and finally to present these arguments and alternatives in a way which fits into the habits of a given arena of debate.

The second criterion goes a step further. It involves acknowledgement of a given contribution. A simple formulation would be: getting discussed. Once a party succeeds to get in the public sphere with a standpoint the game is not over. Other parties which were already present can simply ignore this new contribution. This contribution can only play a role in the public debate if at least one party acknowledges this new contribution, for example by discussing it or by rejecting it partially or completely. This second criterion means that a contribution in a public debate is taken seriously, that is discussed in a critical way. By being discussed, even if the discussion will lead to partial rejection, a standpoint of a party can exercise some influence.

The third criterion of success in the public sphere points to the possibility to influence the issues of general interest and to participate to some extent in the process of decision making. This criterion presupposes that the first two have been successfully completed. Simply put it means to participate in decision making. By influencing issues of general interest a party can contribute to maintain and transform dominant forms of discourse or in other words values, norms and themes which are considered as important by a majority of the participants in the public sphere. Decisions can be taken either formally, by changing laws or institutions, or informally by establishing new standards of conduct concerning norms, values and customs.

3. How to analyze discourse

Contributions in public debates have a discursive nature. A discourse is a social form of action by which a text, written as well as spoken, is produced, distributed and consumed in a specific way. As a social form of action, discourse is goal-oriented, but can as any social action also produce unintended consequences. A good overview of discourse theories is offered by Fairclough (1992).

With this definition one can identity a certain number of criteria which permit to classify different discourses. For the purpose of this article it is sufficient to use the following criteria:

(1) the source of the discourse; This can be an individual author who writes as an autonomous person, but that is rather an exception. In general, the author is clearly situated socially and politically, as a member of a political movement or as working for a certain institution or as representing a social movement.

(2) the constructed auditorium, or in other words the intended addressee of the discourse. A discourse can be addressed to all reasonable individuals, or specifically to scientists or to citizens of a certain Nation State.

(3) the form of distribution; a given discourse can be distributed in the specific form of a book, or as more or less explicit presuppositions in a variety of news items in different media or other arenas of public debates.

(4) the main characteristics of the discursive object; Any discourse presents a representation of some part of the world, and this representation as a discursive object has specific characteristics.

(5) the social identities shaped with the help of the discourse and the social relations between these identities; in any discourse appear social actors, such as the social classes, Nation States or politicians in the discourses of globalization, actors which are related to each other in specific ways. An examination of the actors put on the scene by the different discourses of globalization, for example, permits to distinguish families of such discourses which introduces different actors or at least different types of relationships between them.

(6) the explicit aims formulated by the discourse and the actions which are supposed to be successful for reaching these goals. Discourses of globalization, for example, formulate quite different aims. On the one hand, globalization as a process can be depicted as almost natural, which should not be hindered at all, or on the other as a very undesirable tendency which has to be stopped or which should be controlled.

With the help of these criteria I will suggest in the following section a classification of the main discourses of globalization. However, it should be noted, that the use of these criteria is not altogether an innocent and neutral affair, because the use of these criteria implies that in what follows I will not be concerned with a quest of what is true or not in the various discourses. With these criteria one can only describe the reasons offered and the arguments formulated by the different discourses of globalization without any possibility to reject one or more of these discourses. For this goal, other instruments will be needed (Maier, 1996).

4. Discourses of globalization

I will now apply the criteria established in the last section and examine the discourses of globalization in order to establish a classification. Five families of discourse can be distinguished clearly with the help of these criteria.

(1) A first family of discourses of globalization can be identified as originating from the New Right movements or parties in various European countries. These discourses are addressed to all the citizens of a Nation State who feel threatened by some of the transformations which are considered as being brought into being by globalization. This discourse is distributed mainly by speeches and pamphlets. The central themes of this discourse are 'flows' of migration and the threat of a deterioration of working, housing and living conditions in the given Nation State. In other words, globalization or at least some of its consequences undermine according to this discourse the national identity and culture and the national well-being. Three social identities play a central role: the good, national citizens, the cosmopolists, linked to financial capital who have no consideration for national identity and well-being and the migrants who threaten the working and living conditions of the good citizens. In other words, the good, the bad and the ugly.

The explicit aim of this discourse consists in the defence of national identity and well-being. Barjon (1996) offers a good analysis of the French situation.

(2) A second family of discourses depicts globalization as a quasi-natural consequence of technological and/or economic developments. The authors of this discourse are international organizations, such as the IMF (International Monetary Fund) or the WTO (World Trade Organization), many politicians and managers. These authors belong to

what is called the neo-liberal tendency. The discourse is addressed to 'reasonable' and 'rational' citizens of the world. The discourses are distributed through books (see for example Krugman, 1996), by declarations, reports, interviews, etc. Globalization is represented as a natural consequence of technological and/or economic factors.

According to this discourse the new technological possibilities of production, ranging from financing, the distribution of production and its management to the technical procedures involved push the production and consumption of goods and values in a more global order.

In this discourse three main social identities are set up. First of all, the responsible managers of this globalizing venture. In the second place one encounters the 'world citizens' who in the long run will all profit from this global extension. However, the discourse distinguishes between two sub-categories of this social identity: one sub-category of well qualified producers can profit immediately from the new opportunities offered, whereas a second sub-category, generally called the 'uneducated' or 'unqualified' face eventually more or less serious problems in the short run. However, there is no need to deplore them because in the long run they will also profit from the globalizing venture. Finally, a third category is introduced, which is formed by persons and groups who do not understand what is going on. They try to negate the natural course by resisting the changes and opportunities offered by the new technological form of production, by being attached to quite conservative values and forms of life. The relationships between these three social identities are quite peculiar, because the first one is just a specific designation of the first sub-group of the second identity, whereas the third type of identity may correspond with parts of the second sub-group of the second identity.

The explicit aim of this discourse is to point out the pointlessness of throwing sand in the machine. If globalization is the automatic consequence of new technological possibilities, any resistance or artificial attempt to stop the ongoing tendencies will only have problematic effects for everybody. Or in other words, trying to stop time is either a sign of madness or of total irresponsibility.

At present, this rich family of discourses occupies a rather dominant position, which is evident as well by the social position of its producers as by the powerful means of distribution involved.

(3) A third family of discourses of globalization is based on a fundamental distinction: there are on the one hand technological and economic structures with their own laws, and on the other hand social relations which are and can be regulated by idealistic principles. This type of discourse is produced by intellectuals and politicians who accept on the one hand economic laws, but who consider that a certain quality of social relationships is and should be independent of economy. This discourse is addressed to the

responsible citizens of the world, who are supposed to be accountable for the quality of social relations. This discourse is distributed by books, appeals, declarations, news items, etc.

The main theme of this discourse is about the possible dangers of the ongoing forms of globalization for the quality and conditions of social relations. This discourse does not negate the possible positive effects of globalization which offer new opportunities for human individuals and groups, nor does it reject globalization *en bloc*. However, globalization considered basically as an economic enterprise may disturb and eventually destroy the acquired qualities of social relations. In the first place, democracy appears as threatened, but good candidates – in the sense of being disturbed – are also the environment, the Nation State, international negotiations, etc.

This discourse introduces the following social identities: on the one hand there are the managers of the global economy and on the other hand are the responsible world citizens. The first ones are blindly concerned with the economic affairs, whereas the second ones are mainly concerned with the preservation of the quality of social relations. There is a possible third form of identity, constituted by persons who are either excluded and marginalized or who are not conscious of the effects of the ongoing waves of globalization. These groups have not at all a fixed membership, members of the first and of the third group can join forces with the second, responsible one. This is also the explicit aim of this discourse which is directed against the unnecessary and destructive influences of globalization by trying to set up political forms of management and control of the problematic consequences of globalization.

A typical example of this discourse can be found in the work of the group of Lissabon (1994); in their book they suggest that a certain number of new international contracts concerning democracy and the environment have to be concluded in order to preserve the quality of life, which is seriously threatened by the consequences of globalization. Other authors are Martin and Schumann (1996).

(4) A fourth family of discourses of globalization is formulated by some post-marxists, sometimes called regulation theorists, such as Lipietz (1996), Went (1996) and Hirsch (1995). The authors are academics or critical intellectuals. They address the general public, but the fact that this discourse is only distributed by books and articles in scholarly journals imposes a serious limitation on the real auditorium.

This discourse attempts to integrate a structural approach with a genetic, historical one. According to this discourse, there are socio-historical periods, and in each of these periods one can find a specific form of economic activities and of social-political forms. In other words, economy and politics are not conceived as independent entities of a different nature. They are interdependent, and in each period there will be a new structure which specifies the boundaries of the economic and the of the political domain as well as their interdependencies. This structure is called a regime of regulation. In our century, there was a dominant regime of regulation, called 'fordism' up to the seventies. For several reasons this regime could not function any more, and in the last twenty years we are according to this discourse in a phase of transition characterized by the emergence of new forms of production and above all by struggles about the new definition of what belongs to the economic domain and what to the social and political one. Globalization designates these transformations. These movements and struggles have not yet produced a new regime of regulation.

In this discourse one finds many social identities, related to the various events and actions which are part of the ongoing, very much disputed, construction of a new regime of regulation. The aim of this discourse is mainly directed at a clarification of what is going on, in order to understand and to orient practical interventions.

> (5) A fifth type of discourse on globalization attempts to offer an original interpretation of globalization. Globalization as a general tendency or as a basic process is rejected as a substantialist illusion. In fact, what we encounter is an ever increasing mix of traits and aspects of activities from all over the world. This discourse is produced by some intellectuals (Nederveen Pieterse, 1995) and cultural agents. It is addressed in principle to the general public, but the actual auditorium is mainly constituted by young people. Its distribution occurs by articles and declarations in the fora of the cultural avantgarde.

The main theme of this discourse are the ever-increasing and ever-changing forms of mix of elements of practice (information, clothing, food, articles, music, activities, etc.) from all over the world. According to this discourse there are not only more intercultural encounters, but there is a general tendency to break down global practices in bits and pieces and to recombine them in various ways. Through these fortuitous encounters and recombinations new, rather unstable and fragmented identities (Gergen, 1990) are constituted, which can be called hybrids. This discourse rejects the substantialist illusions of other discourses of globalization and underlines the value of the playful, open combinations of hitherto separated blocks of practices.

5. Fragments of dialogue

With the help of one example I would like now to illustrate how one can identity and analyze fragments of dialogue in public debates.

Duclos (1996), assuming a social identity as critical citizen belonging to the third family of discourses on globalization identifies in his articles some of the dangers of globalization. In his article we can read the following reasoning passage (Duclos, 1996, 14):

> Let's consider Mr. Smith, working in a private enterprise (or – why not? – a public one, because they resemble each other more and more). This person will be more or less forced to make plans for old age, for sickness, for incapacity, by contributing to various funds. These funds cannot but play games on the financial markets, in the movements of financial capital looking for the highest returns. These financial games force enterprises to reduce costs, because if the enterprise does not make any profit, it will be eaten up and eventually destroyed by speculative movements. But in order to make more profit, costs have to be reduced, and this reduction will also effect labor costs, by reducing the labor force or by fragilizing it. A possible consequence can be that Mr. Smith, with all his efforts, will contribute to be kicked out of his job.

Mr. Smith is a typical representative of another social identity of the third family of discourse, who is not conscious of the devastating effects of globalization. The author, Denis Duclos, engages a critical dialogue with the reader, who is not supposed to share the social identity of the author, using Mr. Smith as an example. With this example Duclos attempts to convince the reader that being unconscious about the consequences of globalization can be personally self-destructive and more in general that globalization brings into being social relations which are self-destructive.

This fragment of dialogue involves three personal instances, the author, the reader and Mr. Smith, each with a clear social identity. Between social identities no dialogue is possible, they are after all only discursive constructions. But between the personalized representatives of these social identities bits and pieces of dialogue can be elaborated in a discourse. These fragments of dialogue have in general an argumentative character, they serve to formulate critical arguments about social identities and social relations.

With the help of the formulated criteria concerning discourse one can identity the social identities and the social relations, and analyze contributions in public debates in terms of personifications of these social identities. If moreover, fragments of dialogue between the personalized instances can be identified, we have reached our goal.

6. Concluding remarks

The approach I have suggested for identifying and analyzing fragments of dialogues in public debates is not really new. Dialogue analysis has been used extensively for this purpose. On the other hand, discourse analysis has contributed a critical approach for analyzing social identities and social relations. What I suggest here is nothing more than a combination of aspects of dialogue analysis and of discourse analysis.

This combination can be useful for the following three reasons:

(1) With this approach it will be possible to identify certain fragments of dialogue in public debates. But that is nothing much.

(2) More important is the fact that with the help of this approach one can analyze the identified fragments of dialogue using the combination of dialogue and discourse analysis. Indeed, with this approach relations will be established between personal instances on the one hand and social identities on the other hand. The personal instances can be the author, the reader or listener, a clearly identified person occupying a well-known social function or a paradigmatic figure – such Mr. Smith – standing for a certain social identity.

Between the social identities hold certain social relations, which are defined by the social distribution of goods, power, knowledge or certain capacities. For example in the second family of discourses of globalization one can find the responsible managers, but also the persons attached to tradition who block the natural development and who are therefore irresponsible. Responsibility stands here for power and knowledge.

To the social identities correspond the personal instances, and to the social relations between the social identities correspond the dialogic interactions between the personal instances. But this correspondence does not mean that the personal instances and the dialogic interactions are only passive reflections of the social identities and the social relations. They do not just mirror the social reality. On the contrary, the personal instances and their dialogic activity are in general at odds with the stereotyped social identities and relations.

As a personal instance they can reveal in their dialogic interventions tensions and unsuspected contradictions of the social identities and the "normal" social relations between these identities. The example of the last section clearly illustrates this possibility. Mr. Smith standing for the normal, responsible individual, appears as being involved in a diabolic process in which he may destroy himself by being responsible. This means that something is profoundly problematic with the social identities and social relations in which Mr. Smith is involved.

Contributions to public debates are in general critical and polemic. Therefore, we should not be astonished that authors use the fragments of dialogues between personal instances in order to point to the tension lines and contradictions in the more stereotypical social identities and social relations they elaborate also in their discursive contributions to public debates.

(3) This approach permits also to evaluate in a certain way the dialogic fragments. Discourse analysis does not permit to evaluate elements of discourse by comparing them with "objective" reality. But it is possible to distinguish with the help of discourse analysis different types of discourses, such as for example the five families of discourse on globalization. One cannot say with discourse analysis that one of this discourses is true and the other false, but one can compare these discourses with each other.

This comparison offers the following possibility. If in given discursive contribution to a public debate, a fragment of dialogue has been identified and analyzed, it is possible to ask if there are other types or families of discourse with a comparable discursive object. If one can find other families of discourse, it will be possible to ask the question if for comparable social identities and personal instances similar tensions and contradictions will hold. In short, this form of evaluation permits to adopt new perspectives by switching from one family of discourse to another.

These remarks, I hope, show the richness of the approach suggested here.

References

Barjon, C. (1996): Enquête sur les réseaux Le Pen. – In: Nouvel Observateur, 1669, 30/10/1996.

Bohman, J. (1996): Public deliberation. Pluralism, Complexity and Democracy. Cambridge-Mass: MIT Press.

Bourdieu, P. (1982): Ce que parler veut dire. Paris: Fayard.

Duclos, D. (1996): L'autophagie, grande menace de la fin du siècle. – In: Monde Diplomatique, Août 1996.

Eemeren, F.H. van (1987): Argumentation studies=five estates. – In: J.W. Wenzel (ed.): Argument and critical practice. Proceedings of the Fifth SCA/AFA Conference on Argumentation, Annandale, VA: Speech Communication Association, 9-24.

Fairclough, N. (1992): Discourse and social change. Cambridge: Polity Press.

Foucault, M. (1972): L'histoire de la folie à l'âge classique. Paris: Gallimard.

Gergen, K. (1990): The saturated self. Dilemmas of identity in contemporary life. New York: Basic Books.

Groep van Lissabon, Petrella, R. (1994): Grenzen aan de concurrentie. Brussel: VUB Press.

Gutmann, A. & D.F. Thompson (1996): Democracy and disagreement. Cambridge-Mass.: Belknap Press of Harvard UP.

Habermas, J. (1981): Theorie des kommunikativen Handelns. Frankfurt: Suhrkamp Verlag.

Habermas, J. (1990): Strukturwandel der Öffentlichkeit. Frankfurt: Suhrkamp Verlag.

Held, D. (1987): Models of democracy. Cambridge: Polity Press.

HERMES (1995), Special issue on Communication et Politique, – In: Hermes, 17/18, Paris: Editions CNRS.

Hirsch, J. (1995): Der nationale Wettbewerbsstaat. Staat, Demokratie und Politik im globalen Kapitalismus. Berlin: Edition ID-Archiv.

Hirschman, A.O. (1991): The rhetoric of reaction. Cambridge-Mass: The Belknap Press of Harvard UP.

Kersbergen, K. van & I.M.A.M. Propper (eds.) (1995): Publiek debat en democratie. Den Haag: Sdu Uitgeverij.

Krugman, P. (1996): De Borreltafeleconomie. Drogredenen over Globalisering. Utrecht: Het Spectrum.

Lipietz, A. (1996): La société en sablier. Le partage du travail contre la déchirure sociale. Paris: Editions La Découverte.

Maier, R. (1996): Forms of identity and argumentation. – In: Journal for the theory of social behaviour, 26, 1, 35-50.

Martin, H.P. & H. Schumann (1996): Die Globalisirungsfalle. Der Angriff auf Demokratie und Wohlstand. Hamburg: Rowohlt.

Nederveen Pieterse, J. (1995): Globalization as hybridisation. – In: Featherstone, M., Lash, S. and Robertson, R. (eds.): Global modernities. London: Sage, 45-68.

Prittwitz, V. von (1996): Verhandeln und argumentieren. Dialog, Interessen und Macht in der Umweltpolitik. Opladen: Leske + Budrich.

RAISONS PRATIQUES (1992): Special issue on Pouvoir et Légitimité. Figures de l'espace public. – In: Raisons Pratiques, 3, Paris: Editions de l'École des Hautes Etudes en Sciences Sociales.

Ramonet, I. (1997): Régimes globalitaires. In: Monde diplomatique, janvier 1997.

Robertson, R. (1995): Globalization: time-space and homogeneity-heterogeneity. – In: Featherstone, M., Lash, S. and Robertson, R. (eds.): Global modernities. London: Sage, 25-44.

Went, R. (1996): Grenzen aan de globalisering? Amsterdam: Het Spinhuis.

Ileana Vântu

The Head-Line and its Function in Press Interviews

1. The Oral Press-Interview as a Special Form of Dialogue

The analysis of press interviews makes it evident that the head-line is an interesting topic, no matter how long the respective interview is.

From the very beginning, we are going to formulate some general remarks on the press interview in its oral form, as a special form of dialogue.[1]

Thus, it is obvious that an interview takes place between two persons. The first one, designated by us with the general term of reporter is the speaker who formulates the first turn of the interview.

During an interview, both speakers act as two equal partners or, at least, try to act in such a way. It is obvious that the reporter usually makes an effort to lie at the same social level with the interviewer's. The professional speaker represented by the reporter has in mind to get more information about a person with a high social status. The interviewee is an important person in his (or her) community, because of his (or her) personality or social status. This is the reason why the community where he (or she) lives wants to know more about his (or her) life. The reporter acts like a barometer: feeling the curiosity of the respective community, he takes the interview aiming to make a certain person speak openly about himself, about another person or special event, about a certain opinion a.s.o. All this news makes more complete the general information already present in the mind of the members that constitute the community to which the interviewee belongs.

During this special type of dialogue, the interviewee behaves in two possible ways, according to his or her intention to co-operate or not with the reporter. It is interesting to notice that the refuse to co-operate occurs in a limited number of interviews. The refuse is, frequently, dissimulated under the form of turns carrying under-dimensional[2] information.

An important feature of an interview is the fact that both speakers are aware of the presence of a third interlocutor namely the reader – for the press interviews – and the listener and TV viewers – for radio and TV interviews. In our opinion, this basic property must be taken into account during any investigation concerning the head-line of any interview.

2. The Form and Function of Written Press-Interviews

The aim of our paper is to present some remarks on the way the head-lines of press interviews, in their written form, are built up as well as on their function.

We use a corpus of interviews published in some Romanian newspapers during the years following 22 December 1989[3]: *România liberă, Adevărul, Cotidianul, Evenimentul zilei, Ziua.*

2.1. The Linguistic Form of the Head-lines

The first problem raised for discussion refers to the linguistic form of the head-lines. Thus, we could notice that, no matter how long the interview is, the head-line is represented by means of a sequence with diverse forms:

a) a sequence present "tale-quale" in a turn built up by the interviewee;
b) a sequence that can be found partially in a turn built up by the interviewer; the sequence used as a head-line is the result of a sequence from the text, partially changed by the reporter;
c) a sequence formulated by the reporter.

We mention the following examples for each type of sentence:

a) *Abia acum România are un program care încurajează investitorii*[4] "Only now does Romania have a programme that stimulates the investors" (România liberă, no. 2102, 25.02.1997, p.8); *Nu vor fi două categorii de ţări candidate*: "There will not be two categories of candidate countries" (România liberă, no. 2398, 16.02.1998, p. 5); *Dacă nu este acoperit în fapte artistice de înaltă calitate, banul este un ban ticălos* "If money is not converted into artistic events of high quality, then we have dirty money" (Adevărul, no. 2401, 14-15.02.1998, p. 3).

b) *Cred că aş putea să mai spun...* "I think that I could also say..." (Cotidianul, no. 53 (218), 18.03.1992, p. 4); *Spre sfârşitul lui 1998, [românii]*[5] *ar putea avea sentimentul că au ieşit din necaz* "By the ned of 1998, [Romanian peoole] should have the feeling that they are out of trouble" (România liberă, no. 2143, 14.04.1997, p. 3).

Both head-lines quoted under b represent sequences with a form partially changed by the reporter. The original forms of these sequences are: *Cred că aş putea să mai spun, dar trebuie să-mi ordonez imaginea cu documentele, să le punem cap la cap* "I think I could also say some things, but I must coordinate the images in my mind with the documents"; *Eu sper că, spre sfârşitul anului 1998 – începutul lui 1999, românii ar trebui să aibă sentimentul nu neapărat că o duc cumsecade, dar că au ieşit din necaz"* "I hope that, by the end of 1998, beginning of 1999, Romanians should have a feeling if not of a decent life, at least of relief".

c) *Interviu cu dl. Alexandru Piru* "An interview with Mr. Alexandru Piru" (Cotidianul, no. 25, 13.06.1991, p. 3); *Emil Constantinescu a cerut liderilor occidentali să ajute România* "Emil Constantinescu requested for support in favor of Romania from Western leaders" (România liberă, no. 2038, 6.12.1996, p. 2); *Un înalt ierarh ortodox rupe tăcerea: IPS Nicolae Corneanu, mitropolitul Banatului, face un act exemplar de penitenţă publică, mărturisind că a colaborat cu Securitatea*[6] "An important orthodox priest puts an end to his silence: His Holyness Nicolae Corneanu, the bishop of Banat, makes an exemplary public repentance, admiting that he has co-operated with the Security" (România liberă, no. 2113, 10.03.1997, p. 11); *Se vor limpezi apele în PDSR*[7]*? se întreabă, înaintea Conferinţei Naţionale , deputatul Iosif Buda, fostul şef de campanie electorală a lui Ion Iliescu* "Will the situation in PDSR become more clear, asks himself Iosif Boda, the former head of the electoral campaign for Ion Iliescu before the National Conference to start" (Adevărul, no. 2072, 16.01.1997, p. 2); *Ion Iliescu condamnă încercarea actualei puteri de a porni totul de la zero!* "Ion Iliescu blames the present political power for its attempt to have a new start" (Evenimetul zilei, no. 1627, 30.10.1997, p. 3); *Două task 'forces' româno-americane pe urmele marilor infractori* "Two Romanian-American task forces tracking big delinquents" (România liberă, no. 241, 7.03.1998, p. 9).

As concerns the last mentioned head-lines, it is interesting to notice that the reporter uses a supplementary sequence situated graphically on top of the title: *Ca să nu devenim o spălătorie pentru bani negri* "In order to prevent our transformation into a laundry for dirty money".

All these three classes of head-lines settled by us have interesting featurs regarding their inner communicative intention. Thus, if we compare a head-line like *Emil Constantinescu a cerut liderilor occidentali să ajute România* "Emil Constantinescu requested for support in favor of Romania from Western leaders" to a second one, namely *Un înalt ierarh ortodox rupe tăcerea; IPS Nicolae Corneanu, mitropolitul Banatului, face un act exemplar de penitență publică, mărtusisind că a colaborat cu Securitatea* "An important orthodox priest puts an end to his silence: His Holyness Nicolae Corneanu, the bishop of Banat, makes an exemplary public repentance, admiting that he has co-operated with the Security" the difference is obvious. Formulating the first head-line, the reporter intents only to communicate an item of information to his readers. But for the second head-line, we can detect a "double" intention from the reporter's side: to convey information and, at the same time, to evaluate a situation.

A second remark concerning, this time, the class c only, is the following: a head-line formulated exclusively by the reporter, is expressed by means of a single sequence or of a set of sequences which are graphically disposed in various ways. We have already mentioned a "super head-line": *Ca să nu devenim o spălătorie de bani negri* "In order to prevent our transformation into a laundry for dirty money". This sequence is graphically disposed on top of the head-line.

But, one can often notice sequences placed below the head-line, sequences that can be designated by the term "sub-head-line". Sometimes the "sub-head-lines" are used in the text of the interview, dividing it into several segments.

2.2. The Connections of the Head-line to the Text of the Interview

Another crucial problem concerning the head-line of an interview is the form of its connections to text of the interview.

As concerns the semantic and syntactic connections, we have noticed the existence of two situations.

The first situation is illustrated by the head-lines included in the *a* and *b* classes namely head-lines identical or just partially identical to sequences of the interview. It means that the repetition – total or partial – of a sequence does not act upon its semantic and syntactic relations with the rest of the text. The respective head-line has the same semantic and syntactic connections with the sequences constituting the text – of the interview – as the sequence whose repetition it is.

The second situation is represented by head-lines formulated exclusively by the reporter.

If we adopt a syntactical perspective, these head-lines, included in the *c* class are not connected to the text of the interview.

As concerns the semantic connections, we think that they are, obviously, necessary.

These semantic connections represent the subject of our following remarks.[8]

First of all, we noticed the existence of a common correspondent in the real universe for both the head-line and the sequences included in the interview. It can be even admitted the presence of the same semantic field. This is the reason why the reporter can make a choice and select, from various possible forms, the most adequate to his (her) purpose. In our opinion, the reporter's aim is to draw the reader's attention and to make him read the interview.

These numerous possible forms that can be selected by the reader are expressed, as we have already pointed out, by a single sequence with the status of head-line or by multiple sequences with the status of head-lines, "super-head-lines" and "sub-head-lines".

From a pragmatic point of view, the head-line is closely connected to the text of the interview and can be compared to a fr. *macrodidascalie*. We adopt the opinion formulated by the American linguist of Romanian origin Sanda Golopenţia on the characteristics of a fr. *didascalie,* in general, and, implicitly, of a general *didascalie* designated with the term of fr. *macrodidascalie*. These characteristics are the following:

- it constitutes an agreement or a contract between the author of the play on one hand, and the director, the actor and the spectator or reader on the other hand;
- it defines, in time and space, the frame of the agreement or contract;
- it constitutes an fr. *embrayeur pragmatique*, namely a device used to start an action.[9]

Thus, if we apply these characteristics of the scenic indications named fr. *didascalie* or fr. *macrodidascalie* to the head-line of a press interview, one can make the following remarks:

- the agreement is settled between the reporter and the interviewee and consists in the intention of both speakers to transmit news to the social community in which they live;
- the frame proper to the head-line of the interview in its written form is the following: as regards the spatial coordinate, the agreement mentioned before is placed on a secondary plane; as concerns the temporal coordinate, the agreement is expressed *a posteriori* in comparison to the moment when the interview ends.
- the head-line as an *embrayeur pragmatique* indicates that the reporter begins his action to communicate new information to the readers and the reader begins, also, his action to acquire news.

The last aspect we are going to analyze concerns the relations between the head-lines and their "super" or "sub" head-lines.

Usually, there are no syntactic connections. From a semantic perspective they are obviously connected, because they have the same correspondent in the real universe. This correspondent is formed by numerous elements with multiple relations between them.

The "sub head-lines" are situated by the reporter in lines placed graphically just below the head-line included into the text of the interview. But the syntactic and semantic connections remain unchanged, as we have already mentioned.

It is interesting to emphasize that, in some cases, these semantic connections are not explicitly expressed. Then, the reader must "discover" the respective connections, in order to understand in detail the whole interview.

For instance, an interview published in *Cotidianul* – no. 91(256), 13.05.1992, p. 4 has the head-line *Cred că în viața publică trebuie să ai o linie etnică* "I think that as a politician you must have an ethical way of acting". The "sub-head-lines" are the following:

1. *N-am căutat măriri politice, vă spun drept*
   "I have not sought for important political functions, I assure you";
2. *Cu cei mai în vârstă s-a întâmplat ceva. A intrat frica în ei*
   "Something happened to the older ones. They have been overcome by fear";
3. *Interesul obştesc trece înaintea interesului partizan*
   "The public interest leaves behind the private interest";
4. *Dacă suntem mocani, de ce să-mi fie ruşine? Sunt mândru!*
   "If we are shepherds why should I be ashamed of? I am proud of it!"
5. *Nu fac decât să mă străduiesc să reîntregim Convenția*
   "I do nothing but try to unify the Convention"[10].

Between the head-line and the five "sub-head-lines " the reader can suppose the existence of the following semantic entities[11].

1. "and that is why", "and, in order to be honest to myself";
2. "and that is why I do not agree with the fact that";
3. "and that is why I believe that";
4. "as well as in the private life, for instance", "fact that makes me say";
5. "and that is why".

3. Conclusion

Our remarks on the head-line of a press interview in its written form constitute, of course, a first attempt to analyse its structure and function. But we hope that the preceding paragraphs made evident the basic pragmatic characteristic of this type of head-line: it is an fr. *embrayeur pragmatique* and relies on the co-operation of three actants namely, the reporter, the interviewee and the reader, this last one represented by a large group of persons.

As concerns its structure, the head-line is formulated in such a way as to draw the reader's attention and even to communicate him a certain amount of information. As a consequence, the reporter hopes that the reader will become eager to know more about the topic suggested by the head-line and will proceed to read he interview.

Notes

1) In our articles, already published, or in press, the main subject we have discussed concerns the coherence and the cohesion of the interview; cf. *Semantic aspects of the Interview*, in "Journal of the Romanian-American Academy, 1993, *Cohérence et cohésion dans une interview*, RRL XXXIX, 1994, no.2, p. 199-202, *Cohérence et cohésion dans une interview. Analyse de texte*, Proceedings of the XXL International Congress for Romanic Linguistics and Philology, Palermo, 1995, in press.
2) We think that the information is "under-dimensional" in the cases when the respective turn-usually an answer-offers a reduced amount of information in comparison with the requirements formulated by the other speaker.
3) The 22 of December 1989 is the day when the totalitarian communist state was abolished in Romania.
4) The head-line represents the identical repetition of a sequence included in a turn built up by the interviewee, although it is not situated between quotation marks.
5) The noun *românii* "Romanians" has been added by us, in order to make the meaning more clear.
6) *Securitate* "Security" was the name for the politic policy in communist Romania.
7) PDSR is the abreviation of Romanian Socialist Democratic Party; this was the political party that ruled Romania between 1992-1996.
8) Head-lines having the form *Interviu cu* "Interview with" + the proper name of the interviewee do not illustrate the respective remark, their referent being extremely general.
9) Cf. Sanda Golopenţia and Monique Martinez Thomas, *Voir les didascalies*, CRIC Ibericas, no.3, 1994, p. 51-52.
10) The late liberal politician that gives the interview refers to the Romanian Democratic Convention, a political association including parties and civic organizations. The respective politician – his name was Vintilă Brătianu – member of an important liberal family, considers that he has a moral duty to support the Convention. We must point out that, at the moment when he was giving the interview, some liberal leaders decided to cancel the status of the National Liberal Party as a member of this Convention.

Magareta Manu-Magda

Der Dialog zwischen den nationalen Minderheiten und der Bevölkerungsmehrheit in den Medien (Das Beispiel Rumäniens)

1. Vorbemerkung

Der Dialog, im wesentlichen als kooperative soziale Interaktion erfaßt, (Stati 1988, 13), wird heute als Hauptlösung für die zeitgenössischen gesellschaftlichen Probleme angesehen. Deshalb wurden in den letzten Jahren dem Terminus „Dialog" (im Sinne eines reellen, authentischen Dialogs) zahlreiche, mehr oder weniger passende, Bestimmungen hinzugefügt, wie, zum Beispiel: „sozial", „politisch", „interkulturell", „interethnisch", „zwischengemeinschaftlich", „interpersonell" etc. Alle aufgezahlten Bezeichnungen dienen dazu, den Rahmen der Zusammenarbeit durch Dialog zu definieren.

Das vorliegende Referat bezieht sich auf eine besondere Art von „sozialem Dialog" (siehe Gutu-Romalo 1991): den „interethnischen Dialog". Wir werden versuchen, die spezifischen Modalitäten des argumentativen Diskurses, mit dem sich die nationalen Minderheiten an die Bevölkerungsmehrheit richten, zu analysieren.

Grundlage sind die Texte der Sendungen in deutscher und ungarischer Sprache des rumänischen Rundfunks und Fernsehens.

2. Was ist der soziale Dialog?

Der soziale Dialog wurde als dialogale Varietät mit folgenden Besonderheiten definiert (siehe Gutu-Romalo 1991, 438-439):

a) der Gruppencharakter der Teilnehmer: das Individuum wird in der dialogalen Tätigkeit durch eine Gemeinschaft ersetzt; jede Einzelperson, die der erwähnten Gruppe angehört, verwandelt sich in einen Repräsentanten der Gruppe, einen Wortträger.
b) die Existenz einer Hierarchie auf drei Ebenen, welche außer des Diskursuniversum des Individuums auch zwei Varietäten von gemeinschaftlichen Universen miteinbezieht – das von der Gruppe dargestellte Universum und das der Teilnehmer.
c) die Dominanz des Lösungsdialogs ("solving problem dialogue") und des Klärungsdialogs ("clarification of assumed or actual misunderstandings dialogue" - vgl. McGuire/Lorch 1965, 242-244) in sozialen Debatten.

Hinsichtlich der linguistischen Organisation charakterisiert sich der soziale Dialog durch:

a) das Auftreten von Repliken von beträchtlichem Volumen (sehr ausgedehnt), welche häufig konvergente Meinungen ausdrucken. Somit können Stagnationsmomente in der diskursiven Tätigkeit erscheinen, ohne daß die Regeln des Dialogs gebrochen werden.
b) die Abwesenheit von Phänomenen von dialogaler Syntax.
c) die Notwendigkeit des Gebrauchs von expliziten Indikatoren für die Sicherung des kongruenten Charakters der Repliken.
d) die Seltenheit von Interferenzphänomenen zwischen gleichzeitigen Repliken.
e) der Beitrag von schriftlichen und mündlichen Texten zur Abwicklung des Dialogs.

3. Der interethnische Dialog – ein Sonderfall des sozialen Dialogs

Der interethnische Dialog ist eine interaktionelle Beziehung, die sich zwischen Gruppen, die unterschiedlichen, zusammenlebenden Ethnien angehören, entwickelt, im allgemeinen in „geographischer Proximität", im Rahmen desselben Staates oder an der zwischenstaatlichen Grenze. Diese Beziehung ist dazu bestimmt, gemeinsame Probleme des Zusammenlebens zu lösen.

Die Ethnie (im engen Sinne des Wortes) konnte als ein stabiles Populationsaggregat definiert werden (vgl. Molino 1981, 243), welches auf einem gegebenen Territorium historisch ansässig ist, relativ konstante sprachliche und kulturelle Besonderheiten gemeinsam hat, das Bewußtsein der eigenen Identität besitzt und dieses Bewußtsein durch einen Namen hervorhebt, der die beschriebene Gemeinschaft kennzeichnet.

Die essentielle Bedingung für die Einhaltung des Kooperationsprinzips (Conditio sine qua non des Dialogs) besteht darin, die ethnische Identität der in den Dialog miteinbezogenen Teile nicht anzurühren.

Die Rücksichtnahme auf die Sensibilität bezüglich der nationalen Identität ist direkt mit der strategischen Verhaltensweise der Gesprächspartner verbunden (keine Aggression im Verhältnis zur positiven und negativen „face", d.h. Einhaltung von Höflichkeitsprinzipien – vgl. Brown/Levinson 1978).

Die Strategie als verbale Interaktion (Landowski 1983, 5-7) wird als eine interaktive Konfrontation erfaßt, die dazu bestimmt ist, das Polemische in ein kontra-aktuelles Gleichgewicht umzuwandeln; sie setzt sowohl eine asymmetrische Situation (Interessenkonflikt, Kenntnisse), als auch ein, vom semiotischen Standpunkt aus, kompetentes Subjekt voraus (ein Subjekt das fähig ist, den Schein des Antiagenten zu konstruieren und dessen Kontrastrategien gedanklich vorwegzunehmen)

4. Der interethnische Dialog – argumentatives Vorgehen

Das Spezifische des interethnischen Dialogs, als argumentatives Vorgehen, ergibt sich aus der gerade erwähnten essentiellen Bedingung: die Unabsetzbarkeit der ethnischen Identität der Gesprächspartner. Demzufolge ruht diese Art von Diskurs, im Vergleich zu anderen, hauptsächlich auf „Indirektheit" und einem hohen Grad von „Implizität".

Bei der Konstruktion des interethnischen Dialogs verläßt man sich auf das komplexe Inventar der diskursiven Manipulationen, auf das Miteinbeziehen der intersubjektiven Dimension (Argumentation, sozio-kulturelle und rhetorische Normen, Kommunikationsakte) und intersemiotischen Dimension (Redundanz und Interferenz der verbalen und nonverbalen Formen). Somit wird jeder Diskurs als ein Konglomerat von Diskursen angesehen.

Der „Andere" ist immer im Diskurs anwesend, er stellt die stumme Präsenz dar, die sowohl die Wahl der diskursiven Einheiten als auch den Diskurstyp, den Kommunikationsmakroakt bestimmt. Die lineare, telegraphische Auffassung des Diskurses (von Empfänger zu Empfänger) wird durch eine poliphonische Logik des Diskurses ersetzt, in welcher Sprechen eigentlich Voraussehen der interpretativen Erwartungen des Gesprächspartners bedeutet (Flahault 1978, 77 apud Roventa-Frumusani 1995, 197).

5. Der mediatisierte politische Diskurs – heute die Hauptform des interethnischen Dialogs

Die Typologisierung ist in der Diskursanalyse eine notwendige Bedingung und Resultante, Effekt der Verschließung eines diskursiven Raumes, also der Konstruktion des Korpus.

Da die linguistische Organisierung jedes Diskurses von der „diskursiven Instanz" abhängt (die konkreten Bedingungen der Kommunikation) kann man eine, auf den erwähnten Komponenten basierende Typologie vereinbaren, und zwar: der Kommunikationskanal, das Verhältnis Sprecher-Aussage, das Verhältnis zwischen den Gesprächspartnern (vgl. Roventa-Frumusani 1995, 30-31).

Ohne detaillierte Beschreibung dieser Typologie müssen wir jedoch erwähnen, daß wir uns im Folgenden auf den mediatisierten politischen Diskurs (im Fernsehen), mit einigen ausgewählten Unterkategorien, auf Grund der oben angegebenen Parameter beziehen werden, und zwar:

- der Kanal: Fernsehen (mit verschiedenen Unterarten: Vortrag – frei oder gelesen –, Reportage, Interview, Debatte, etc.)
- das Verhältnis Sprecher – Aussage: der Zeitabstand zwischen Aussagen (die Häufigkeit des Zitierens), die Distanzierung zwischen Sprecher und Aussage (der übernommene/nicht übernommene Diskurs – in der ersten oder dritten Person), der Abstand zwischen Diskurs und Intertext (konstruktiver oder polemischer Diskurs).
- Beziehungen zwischen Gesprächspartnern: die Anwesenheit oder Abwesenheit des Gesprächspartner (Dialog oder Erzählung), die Anzahl der Gesprächspartner (Konversation oder Vortrag), die zwischenmenschlichen Beziehungen (autoritärer Diskurs oder egalitärer Diskurs).

Die Rolle des politischen Diskurses wird immer wichtiger, da die Lösung der Grundprobleme der nationalen Minderheiten heute meistens in die politische Sphäre verlegt wird und sich der Schwerpunkt des politischen Raumes aus dem Parlament zunehmend zu den Medien verlagert. Die nationalen Minderheiten fühlen das Bedürfnis einen starken Verbündeten für die Lösung ihrer spezifischen Probleme zu gewinnen: die öffentliche Mehrheitsmeinung.

Im Folgenden werden wir versuchen, einige der oben dargestellten Ideen anhand der Analyse eines Sonderfalls von Dialog (der interethnische Dialog) zu veranschaulichen: der Dialog zwischen den nationalen Minderheiten und der Bevölkerungsmehrheit in den Medien (das Beispiel Rumäniens).

6. Durchführungsmodalitäten des interethnischen Dialogs in den Sendungen des Rumänischen Fernsehens (TVR) für die ungarische und deutsche Minderheit

In der Organisationsstruktur des TVR existieren drei eigene Abteilungen, die den nationalen Minderheiten gewidmet sind: die Abteilung in deutscher Sprache, die Abteilung in ungarischer Sprache und die Abteilung für andere Minderheiten. Die Existenz dieser Abteilungen illustriert eine Form der Auswirkung des in der rumänischen Verfassung verankerten Rechts der nationalen Minderheiten, sich in ihrem Streben zur Bewahrung und konstruktiver Betonung der nationalen Identität frei auszudrücken.

Auf dem Hintergrund dieses offiziellen programmatischen Ziels wenden sich die Sendungen in ungarischer und deutscher Sprache hauptsächlich an die Ethnien die einen beträchtlichen Prozentsatz der Bevölkerung Rumäniens darstellen (Im Jahre 1997 bildeten die Magyaren einen Anteil von 7,917% und die Deutschen 1,664% der Gesamtbevölkerung – die zweitgrößte mitwohnende Nationalität nach den Magyaren), Ethnien, in deren Sprache die betreffenden Programme ausgestrahlt werden. Die Sendungen wollen sich auch an die Zuschauer der Gesamtbevölkerung wenden, die sich für die dargestellte Problematik interessieren (durch die in rumänische Sprache simultan übersetzten Untertexte, die nach stillschweigender Übereinkunft die Programme begleiten).

Die erwähnten Sendungen (deren Zeitdauer proportionell zum Prozentsatz der Minderheit im Vergleich zur Mehrheit steht) verkörpern mediatisierte „Mikrouniversen" und sind im Kleinen ähnlich wie das Gesamtprogramm des Rumänischen Fernsehens. Gegenwärtig gibt es keine spezifischen Vorschriften mehr was die Programmpolitik für die Minderheiten betrifft. Die Redakteure der Sendungen sind verpflichtet, die Vorschriften der Nationalen Kommission für Audiovision in Rumänen zu respektieren und sind für ihre professionelle Arbeit selbst verantwortlich. Zu vermeiden sind Parallelismen mit anderen Sendungen.

Aus Zeitmangel werden wir uns im vorliegenden Referat nur auf die Sendung in ungarischer Sprache des Rumänischen Rundfunks beziehen; bei anderer Gelegenheit werden wir die heute nur teilweise erörterten Schlußfolgerungen vervollständigen.

In der Analyse der dialogalen Strategien werden wir uns besonders auf die politischen Komponenten im Rahmen dieser Programme beziehen – ohne daß das Politische selbst das Thema unseres Vorgehens darstellt.

Den Titel des klassischen Artikels von J.A.Fishman (1965) paraphrasierend "Who Speaks, what Language, to Whom and When?", versuchen wir zu unterscheiden:

7. "Who Speaks, what Language, to Whom and When?"

"Who Speaks?"

Die Sendungen in ungarischer Sprache, ähnlich denen des ganzen Rumänischen Rundfunks und Fernsehens, zu dem sie gehören, nehmen eine neutrale Position im Verhältnis zu den aktuellen politischen Formationen ein, und setzen sich als Ziel dem Zuschauer objektive Informationen vorzutragen.

Die magyarische Ethnie, der diese Sendungen gewidmet sind, steht unter der Protektion der Union der Magyaren in Rumänen (UDMR), die einzige auf ethnischen Kriterien basierende Formation der Magyaren, die auch als politische Partei registriert ist und seit den Wahlen im Jahre 1996 Teil der Regierungskoalition ist.

Das Regierungsprogramm dieser Partei enthalt die Forderungen der magyarischen Ethnie, und zwar: lokale Autonomie, Gebrauch der ungarischen Sprache in der Verwaltung, zweisprachige Tafeln mit den Namen der Ortschaften (in den Gebieten, in denen die ungarische Bevölkerung in der Mehrzahl ist), Schulen auf allen Ebenen, in denen in der Muttersprache unterrichtet wird etc. Diese Forderungen treffen auf keine Zustimmung bei der Bevölkerungsmehrheit. Somit werden sie zu einem „casus belli", sowohl im Parlament, als auch in einigen offiziösen Zeitungen politischer Oppositionsparteien und auch in den Veröffentlichungen der unabhängigen Presse. Die UDMR, und somit die gesamte ungarische Minderheit in Rumänen, werden des Extremismus und Irredentismus bezichtigt und die gesamte rumänische Bevölkerung in den Gebieten, in denen mehrheitlich Ungarn wohnen, wird viktimisiert.

In dem Maße, in dem das erklärte Thema der Programme in ungarischer Sprache dem oben erwähnten entspricht, ist es üblich, daß die Stimme der OTMAR, als gewählte Vertretung der Ungarn in diesem mediatischen Raum die Hauptstimme ist. Man kann sie sowohl direkt, als auch indirekt, polyphonisch eingestreut in den verschiedenen mediatisierten Arten fühlen:

- DIE DIREKTE REPLIK – polemische Antwort auf verschiedene unpassende, klagende Behauptungen; diese Art von Replik wird häufig während der Sendung direkt von markanten Persönlichkeiten der Partei oder selbst vom Präsidenten der OTMAR gegeben.
- DIE NACHRICHT (scheinbar neutral) – die aus der Gesamtheit der aktuellen Neuigkeiten gewählte Nachrichtengruppe ist in einer solchen Weise zusammengestellt, daß sie die Stellung der OTMAR im Verhältnis zu den diskutierten Ereignissen wiedergibt.

- DAS INTERVIEW (unterstützt die These) – Meinungsumfrage oder Interview mit Persönlichkeiten (dient als Autoritätsargument).
- DIE REPORTAGE (veranschaulicht die These), in verschiedenen Formen: bedeutende Aspekte des täglichen Lebens, die Vorstellung von historischen Dokumenten als schriftliche Zeugen, andere Elemente mit Überzeugungskraft.
- DIE POLITISCHE DEBATTE (institutionalisierte Konversation die sich als Ziel den Angriff und die Verteidigung einer vorher festgelegten Aussage setzt und eine vielfältige Botschaft weitergibt, die sich einerseits an den direkten Gesprächspartner und andererseits an die Zuschauer richtet).

"What Language?"

Der Code, mit dem die Kommunikation in diesen Sendungen stattfindet ist die ungarische Sprache. Die Texte werden simultan in rumänische Sprache übersetzt und im unteren Teil des Fernsehbildes wiedergegeben.

Die zwei parallelen Texte funktionieren „stereophonisch" und haben unterschiedliche illokutive Objektive.

Die ungarische Textvariante hat folgende Funktion: sie muß die ungarische Ethnie darüber informieren, wie die OTMAR ihre Auftrage erfüllt hat. Die Funktion der rumänischen Textvariante besteht darin, die Probleme der Magyaren in einer solchen Weise darzustellen daß sie die Unterstützung der Bevölkerungsmehrheit gewinnt (dies beruht auf einer bemerkenswerten mediatischen und argumentativen Komponente).

Die Möglichkeit einer solchen gleichzeitigen Kommunikation erlaubt der OTMAR sowohl einen reaktiven politischen Diskurs (dargestellt durch explizite und implizite Repliken im Rahmen eines Dialogs, der dazu dient, übernommene oder zufällige Mißverständnisse zwischen den zwei Ethnien zu klaren) als auch einen initiativen politischen Diskurs zu führen (dargestellt durch einleitende Repliken eines zwischenethnischen Dialogs, der zur praktischen Lösung der Probleme dienen soll).

"To Whom?"

Nach der Art, in der die Sendungen in ungarischer Sprache zusammengestellt sind, kann man leicht die Konfiguration des potentiellen Publikums, an das sich die OTMAR wendet, voraussehen:

- die unstrukturierte Masse der sicheren Unterstützer (grundsätzlich die magyarische Ethnie)

- die Gegner (diejenigen, die während der Sendung angegriffen werden oder denen man polemisch antwortet) – Individuen oder bekannte Massen (die aber nicht unbedingt genannt werden) von „Verleumdern", eine Zeitung oder eine politische Fraktion.
- die unstrukturierte Masse der Unterstützer der Gegner.
- die unstrukturierte, neutrale Masse der Zeugen, potentielle Verbündete als Folge des argumentativen Vorgehens.

"When?"

In der gewählten Diskurssituation (der mediatisierte politische Diskurs) baut man hauptsächlich auf Indirektheit, und zwar auf:

A. Repräsentationsstrategien (mit denen der Redner seine eigene interpretative Version durchzusetzen versucht, indem er den evaluativen-subjektiven Diskurs unter einem faktuellen, objektiven Diskurs versteckt).
B. Die strategische Verwendung der impliziten Inhalte (vgl. Larrue-Trognon 1994) – minimales Risiko für den Redner, der jederzeit die implizite Aussage verneinen kann – maximaler Vorteil, was den lateralen Empfang (das Publikum) betrifft.

Zur Veranschaulichung unserer Behauptungen werden wir im Folgenden ein Beispiel vorstellen: kennzeichnende Aspekte aus der Sendung in ungarischer Sprache vom 9. März 1998, 16-17.30 Uhr.

Die Sendung hat zwei, scheinbar nicht miteinander verbundene Komponenten politischen Inhalts:

1. eine Nachrichtengruppierung; die Hauptnachricht bezieht sich auf das Treffen zwischen dem Staatspräsidenten und den OTMAR Repräsentanten und auf die Ergebnisse dieses Treffens.

Der Nachrichtensprecher kündigt am Anfang, in neutralem Ton das Ereignis an:

> Am 3. März 1998 hatte Präsident Emil Constantinescu ein, einige Stunden dauerndes Treffen mit einer von Marko Bela gefuhrten Delegation der OTMAR.

Anschließend erscheint auf dem Bildschirm Marko Bela, Parteichef der OTMAR und faßt kurz den Inhalt des Gesprächs mit dem Präsidenten zusammen. Damit wird eigentlich, versteckt die These der Sendung dargestellt:

> Während des Gesprächs im Schloß Cotroceni lobte der Präsident die Tätigkeit der OTMAR sehr. Er schätzt die Tatsache, dass die OTMAR, obwohl sie eine Organisation zur Verteidigung der Rechte der magyarischen Ethnie ist, die Interessen des Staates vor die Parteiinteressen setzt und

die Lösung der allgemeinen ökonomischen und sozialen Probleme des Landes übernommen hat. Meine Kollegen hatten die Möglichkeit, ihre Meinung im Verhältnis zu einigen allgemeinen Problemen auszudrücken und haben sich selbstverständlich auch auf die Probleme bezogen die uns direkt angehen; solche Probleme sind eigentlich Probleme der gesamten Gesellschaft und sind eng mit den Bemühungen zur euroatlantischen Integration verbunden, und zwar: das Problem der Minderheiten, die Lösung des nationalen Problems, das Anwachsen in letzter Zeit nationalistischer Akzente und antimagyarischer Manifestationen und der Angriffe gegen die OTMAR; die Tatsache, daß alles was die Regierung in der ersten Phase ihrer Arbeit für die nationalen Minderheiten getan hat, allmählich in Frage gestellt wird. Wir haben den Präsidenten gebeten die nationalistischen und extremistischen Positionen mit Entschlossenheit zu bekämpfen.

2. Die zweite interessante Komponente, die erst später in der Sendung erscheint, ist eine komplexe Montage von Reportagen und Interviews die die vorher abgekündigte und von dem Reporter reformulierte These versteckt veranschaulichen. Wir fassen den Kommentar des Reporters zusammen: die Tendenz zur Vereinigung der Welt kann sich nur dann entwickeln, wenn langfristig Diversitäten beibehalten werden; diejenigen die gegenwärtig die Integration der osteuropaischen Länder in ein gemeinschaftliches Europa vorbereiten, müssen unbedingt das Bedürfnis zur Beibehaltung der Identität der nationalen Minderheiten in Betracht ziehen.

Im Kommentar (pro domo) des Reporters, der als ein Plädoyer für die Lösung der scheinbar gemeinsamen Probleme der 17 Minderheiten in Rumänen vorgestellt wird, sind Fragmente von Interviews (in rumänische Sprache) mit Repräsentanten der nationalen Minderheiten – Zigeuner, Tataren, Polen – vermengt, die konzertiert (mit Beispielen aus dem täglichen, gemeinsamen Leben der Minderheiten und der Mehrheit, das in der mündlichen oder schriftlichen Presse häufig falsch beschrieben wird) die Idee aus dem zentralen Interview (in ungarischer Sprache, mit dem Präsident des parlamentarischen Komitees für Nationale Minderheiten, Bartunek Istvan) unterstützen, und zwar: Der Versuch zur Erhaltung der eigenen Identität stellt keinen Versuch zur Beschlagnahme der Rechte der Mehrheit dar. Das ist die Wahrheit, die die Stimme der OTMAR durchsetzen möchte, nicht nur unter den eigenen Wählern, sondern auch in den Reihen der Bevölkerungsmehrheit (mittels der Übersetzung).

8. Schlußfolgerungen

In den vorliegenden Seiten haben wir versucht, von einem gesonderten Fall ausgehend einige Charakteristiken des „interethnischen Dialogs“ festzuhalten:

1. Wir haben den „ethnischen Dialog" als einen Sonderfall des "sozialen Dialogs" beschrieben, der als spezifische Bedingung der dialogalen Kooperation die Respektierung des unwidersprochenen Charakters der ethnischen Identität der Gesprächspartner hat.
2. Wir haben erwähnt, daß um die Unterstützung der öffentlichen Meinung für die Lösung der spezifischen Probleme der nationalen Minderheiten zu gewinnen, die beschriebene Art von Dialog hauptsächlich durch mediatische Kanäle stattfindet.
3. Wir haben festgestellt, daß die diskursiven Strategien, die innerhalb des interethnischen Dialogs erscheinen, im Grunde auf Indirektheit und Implizitheit beruhen.

Literatur

Brown, P./St. Levinson (1978): Universals in Language Politeness Phenomena. – In: Goody, E.N.: Questions and Politeness. Strategies in Social Interaction Cambridge, 56-289.

Fishman, J. A. (1965): Who Speaks, what Language, to Whom and When?. – In: La Linguistique 2, 67-87.

Flahault, F. (1978): La parole intermédiaire, Paris.

Gutu-Romalo, V. (1991): Considérations sur le „dialogue social". – In: Dialoganalyse III, Referate der 3. Arbeitstagung, Bologna, 1990, Teil 2, Tübingen, 433-439.

Landowski, E. (1983): De quelques conditions de l'interaction. – In: Actes semiotiques– Documents V, 30.

Larrue, J./A. Trognon (1994): Introduction a la pragmatique du discours politique, Paris. McGuire, M.T./St. Lorch (1965): Natural Language Conversations Modes. – In: Journal of Nervous and Mental Disease 146, 3.

Molino, J. (1981): Ethnolinguistique et sémiologie: pour une ethnosémiologie. – In: Ethnolinguistique: contributions théoriques et méthodologiques, Paris, 237-249.

Roventa-Frumusani, D. (1995): Semiotica discursului stiintific, Bucuresti.

Stati, S. (1988): Il dialogo. Considerazioni di linguistica pragmatica, Napoli.

Dieter D. Genske/Ernest W.B. Hess-Lüttich

Conflict, Crisis, and Catastrophe
Cultural Codes and Media Management in Environmental Conflicts: the Case of Water

1. The challenge

This is a short report on a new research project based on a joint initiative of the recently installed chair for *génie sanitaire* at the Institut du Génie de l'Environnement (IGE/GS) of the École Polytechnique Fédérale de Lausanne (EPFL) and the chair for *Textwissenschaft* at the Department of Germanic Studies of the University of Berne. It aims to bring together at least six different perspectives of research hitherto operating in entirely separate fields: media studies, intercultural communication, conversation analysis, environmental studies, sanitary engineering, public relations analysis. The focal point where these perspectives meet is discourse. It starts a dialogue on an issue of vital importance to ecology world wide: water. It serves as an example for key questions such as how environmental conflicts are communicated in the mass media, how environmental awareness can be awakened by the media, how media can be used to change everyday behavioural routines with respect to sustainable development, how intercultural instruction can be enhanced by technology and face-to-face interaction.

One of the major ecological problems of the near future will be the global water shortage, already today responsible for many political conflicts all over the world, as well illustrated by a recent German television series on the issue ("Wasser", ZDF July-August 1998, focusing especially on the situation in Africa, Mexico, Turkey, Syria, Israel, etc.). Our main research interest, therefore, is to look at the increasingly important rôle of media in communicating ecological problems caused by water shortage and sustainable solutions to fight their consequences. If such solutions for sustainable management of water resources cannot be communicated effectively, water problems may not only deteriorate into environmental crises but also political conflicts and even regional catastrophes which in the last resort will affect our First World societies in one way or another (e.g., migration, international relations, developmental policies, crisis intervention, etc.: cf. Hess-Lüttich 1997).

So far, sanitary engineering has proposed a number of solutions, even if predominantly technical ones, i.e. solutions dealing with preserving water quality and reducing water consumption. The communicators involved in the complex dialogue process (from finding the solution and inventing the necessary technology to its local implementation and effective application) are institutions and organisations on one hand, local project workers and their addressees on the other. Thus, the attempt of analysing this complex dialogue process means taking systematically into account aspects of (i) *institutional communication* (mass media, help organisations, local communication networks), (ii) *interpersonal communication* (face-to-face conversation, instructional discourse, behaviour routines), and (iii), due to the manifold cultural differences involved, *intercultural communication* (cross-cultural dialogue, cultural stereotypes, international relations).

The research project sketched out in the following aims to design of a theoretical framework for transdisciplinary analysis of the interface between the three main communication axes (institutional, intercultural, interpersonal), and establishment of a model derived from that analysis for application "in field work", allowing us to implement, harmonise, and optimise communication patterns in local cross-cultural instruction processes as well as in campaigning on environmental issues through critical media reports, public relations concepts, and the like (cf. Hess-Lüttich 1992 a, b). The findings could, and should, be applied, for instance, to the field of sanitary engineering where the IGE/GS has established a close co-operation with the École Inter-Etats d'Ingénieurs de l'Équipement Rural (EIER) and the Centre Régional pour l'Eau Potable et l'Assainissement (CREPA) in Burkina Faso, for francophone West Africa, on one hand, and on the other to the field of communication studies and public health where the Berne Institute is about to establish contacts with the Centre for Cultural and Media Studies (CCMS) at the University of Natal, Durban, for anglophone eastern and southern Africa.

2. Risk research and communication conflict

In modern "risk society" (Beck 1996), everybody is obliged to deal with uncertainties and their consequences. Facing risks has become part of everyday life nowadays (Blanke 1990:

135). The term *risk society* refers to social institutionalisation of accepting risks within contemporary societies (Beck 1996). Special interest groups conducting their initiatives no matter whether they contradict the interests of other groups typically take the risk of *conflict*. If conflict cannot be resolved by negotiation, this may lead to a *crisis*. A crisis marks the turning point at which the balance of power is re-considered, re-discussed, re-evaluated by all parties involved. If all negotiations fail, i.e., if the conflicting parties insist on questioning and re-defining the existing equilibrium, the crisis may become a *catastrophe* in the sociological sense of conflict research (Apitz 1987: 13).

What would the scenario for a *global* catastrophe look like in a post-war age? What would its crucial issues be? When would it occur? Meadows et al. recently revised their famous 1972 report to the Club of Rome, entitled *The limits of growth*, which gave a prognosis on the increase in resource consumption with growing world population. In their second report 20 years later, *Beyond the limits*, it is clearly stated that within a few decades many natural resources will be exhausted, the first being *water*. People need water to drink, to prepare meals, to wash their laundry, to produce products, to enable agriculture.

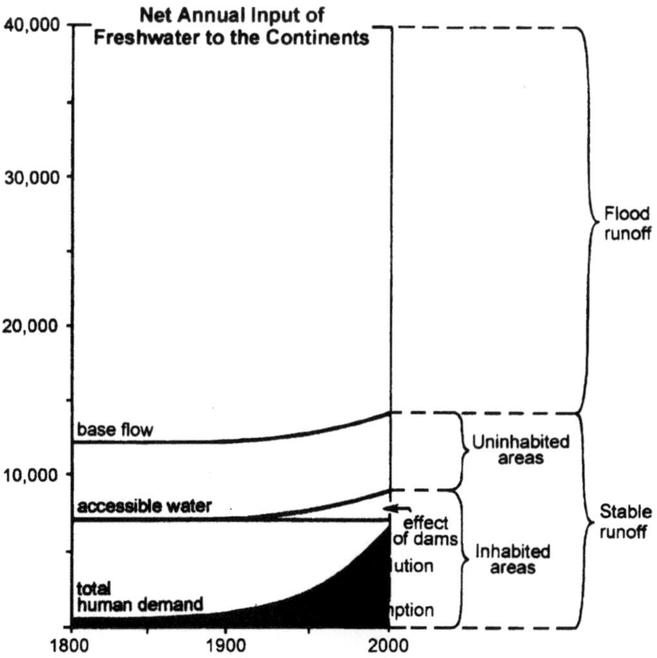

According to the prognosis published in Meadows et al. 1992, water will be the first primary resource to become exhausted.

People not only consume water; they also contaminate it, thus causing remarkably high *passive* water consumption. To remediate contaminated groundwater resources is such a complex and costly problem that only highly developed countries can afford it if there is a clearly defined need. While Europeans today enjoy an average water consumption of some 250 litres per person per day, and Americans of more than 600 litres, peri-urban population in cities like, say, Ouagadougou, Burkina Faso, has to cope with some 20 litres per person per day, way below the absolute minimum defined by the WHO for developing countries. Critical water shortage is already reality and part of everyday life in many countries today. There are many conflicts on water rights; many areas are frequently plagued by crises in water supply; some are on the verge of being exposed to regional catastrophes caused by water shortage.

Liquid waste from a hospital enters an open channel. About 100 meters downstream water is collected from wells neighbouring the channel to water vegetables to be sold on the local market. When water wells have run dry, water has been taken directly from the channel (Burkina Faso, photo by Karin Linxweiler, 1998).

But why on earth should we in central Europe think about these problems? Take Switzerland, for instance, a country as rich in water as it could be, where it is abundantly available. That is exactly the point forcing us to think about a global water crisis and its possible consequences. According to Brand (ed. 1997), the pressure of migrating people seeking space, resources, and water, will increase considerably as compared to those fleeing from civil wars and political or religious suppression. Any ecological crisis will have a negative impact on the economy, on social structure, probably even on the internal social peace the rich countries have been enjoying for such a long period (cf. Joas 1992: 325 et passim; Scharping & Görg 1994).

Management and resolution of crises normally starts with their prevention before the crisis breaks out, i.e. in the phase of conflict (when crisis management comes too late – as described e.g., in *UNESCO Courier* 10 (1997) – it slides into the phase of catastrophe). Although there are numerous international organisations dealing with the exploitation of water resources in regions of water need, the demand has increased. Although an International Water Decade (1980-1990) was proclaimed by the UN, the number of military conflicts over water resources is growing. Although the technology is available to resolve water shortage, global water management has deteriorated. And finally (although the Rio de Janeiro World Summit in 1992 passed the well-known Agenda 21 including the now almost proverbial notion of sustainable development) the concept of careful resource consumption for the benefit of future generations – as clear and simple as it sounds – has yet not been sufficiently implemented. Could it be that it has not found the right communication path through administrations, organisations, and institutions down to those affected by these resource shortages? It is this very question we want to raise in this multidisciplinary dialogue (cf. Welford 1995; Breitmeier 1996: 132-145; Joussen & Hessler eds. 1995; Brand ed. 1997).

One of the key aspects of understanding and explaining conflicts with respect to primary resources such as water seems to be a failure in communication due to mismanagement of down-to-consumer information and control. Socio-cultural, political, and economical characteristics of the population targeted must already be taken into consideration in the planning phase of a crisis communication project. This has been common ground in all disciplines dealing with communicating technical information between cultures since the 1950s (Clyne 1996; Scollon & Scollon 1995). In the late 1980s, however, when an integrated theory of intercultural technology transfer had still not been achieved, Kievelitz (1988) outlined a theory of development ethnology ("Entwicklungsethnologie"). From a pragmatic viewpoint, he pointed at weaknesses and contradictions in communication models to date and called for combined ethnological theory and practice in order to improve communication strategies in projects of technical co-operation across cultures (Kievelitz 1988: 99):

> Technische Zusammenarbeit spielt sich stets in einem fremden Kulturraum ab. Dabei macht die Kooperation und Interaktion zwischen Einzelpersonen, Gruppen und Vertretern von Institutionen den überwiegenden Teil jeglicher Projektarbeit aus. Die Zusammenarbeit zwischen Menschen ist die wichtigste aller Aufgaben im Projekt; über Personen wird jeglicher Erfolg in der Arbeit erreicht, ganz unabhängig davon, ob ein Projekt auf Regierungsebene angesiedelt ist oder unmittelbar bevölkerungsnah, und gleichgültig, ob es sich dabei um ländliche Regionalentwicklung, Institutionenaufbau oder Regierungsberatung handelt.
>
> [Technical co-operation always takes place in a foreign culture. The co-operation and interaction between individuals, groups or representatives of institutions represents the main part of any project work. Co-operation between people is the most important of all tasks of a project; via people every success of the work is achieved, regardless if the project is launched at the governmental level or directly close to the population, and despite the type of development project, be it regional, institutional, or governmental.]

Recent studies agree that these findings remain to be tested empirically and applied in field work (cf., e.g., Prochnow 1996: 63). Although the traditional intervention philosophy has meanwhile shifted towards a participative concept of *empowerment*, many reports show that, in practice, inefficiency and cost ineffectiveness prevail in intercultural communication (Weiland 1984; IEZ 1994), and that misunderstanding and even social conflicts are quite often provoked (Gnägi 1995: 361-368).

Facing the existing trends towards globalisation, the empirical investigation of intercultural communication should not be restricted to what has been dealt with so far within the framework of *cultural studies*, and it should be linked with the expanding research field of *international communication*. Meckel & Kriener (eds. 1996) propose a systematic division of the research on international communication into four segments: (i) technical and infrastructural development on a global scale, (ii) the institutional dimension of internationalisation, (iii) the institutional context of media products (including journalism, instruction), (iv) the textual dimensions of media products (including content analysis, media semiotics). Given the background of newly emerging structures for global communication and new technical developments in the media system, the authors take a close look at recent political, economical, social, and journalistic implications of international communication, thereby not only introducing aspects of journalism and communication theory into discussion on international communication, but also strongly suggesting change in the clearly eurocentric direction of traditional analysis of mass media impact in developing countries – especially those with resource shortages (cf. Grossenbacher 1988, Grossenbacher & Saxer 1987).

All this is of direct relevance to analysis of crisis communication: for companies and organisations, crisis communication has primarily economical dimensions; a *crisis* interferes with the standard routine; it disturbs the normal processes and negatively affects the economy of an organisation. Many examples of attempts of ecological crisis management, some of them not very successful, are still in the public conscience, for better or worse linked with catchwords such as Bophal, Seveso, Tschernobyl, Brent Spar, and Schweizerhalle, to name only a few. Instances such as these have been analysed from various perspectives: from a primarily economical viewpoint by, e.g., Weber (1980), from a strictly communicative perspective by Apitz (1987) or Heintzel, Kunczik & Zipfel (eds. 1995), and, most recently, from an integrated standpoint combining economical analysis of ecological crisis management with its communication theoretical implications by Scherler (1996).

The overall communication structure of a typical reaction of organisations (companies) having caused a severe ecological accident is characterised by the initial phase of internal discussion of the social and thus economical impact of this accident on the organisation or company. At the next stage, press releases are prepared by the organisation's public relations department (for a more detailed discussion of the term *public relations* and its research tradition, introduced into German already by Oeckl 1950 as "Öffentlichkeitsarbeit" (Oeckl 1993), cf. Barthenheier, Haedrich & Kleinert eds. 1982; Flieger 1986; Böckelmann 1991; Becher 1996). At this stage, the functioning of the internal communication is crucial for a successful positive presentation of the organisation to the public. All board members must know the complex structure of their organisation and their communication pathways, allowing them to communicate efficiently within their infrastructure and through all levels of hierarchy as a prerequisite of full feedback to staff members working out a public relations strategy (cf. Kalmus 1994; Armbrecht 1992). Internal business communication ("Unternehmenskommunikation", cf. Bungarten ed. 1994 a, b) is a vital factor in the organisation's attempt to socialise its staff members and make them identify with their company and its corporate identity. Public relations training is considered to play an important part in this process. So far, however, a unifying concept of the public relations function does not exist (Ronneberger & Rühl 1992: 11).

Since the late 1980s, public relations has also been recognised as an ample field of research in communication science and its neighbouring disciplines in the German-speaking countries. Whereas research on public relations carried out in the United States remained more or less empirical with a strong focus on application (Armbrecht & Avenarius eds. 1992), European studies clearly emphasised also theoretical desiderata. Having diagnosed a "defizitäre wissenschaftliche PR-Lehre und -Forschung" [insufficient academic teaching and research in public relations] in Germany, Ronneberger & Rühl (1992: 10) called for a theory of public relations and submitted "a first draft". It gives an outline of the few existing theoretical approaches and of recent developments. But it also indicates certain contradictions in fundamental concepts and methodology of these approaches. Alternatively, it offers a new approach based on communication science, bridging the gap between the theory and practice of public relations.

The gap is still wide. Interest in practical public relations tools is still dominant, reflecting the prevailing underestimation of PR's external relevance of for the organisation's image in the media. The same applies to internal business communication: its structure is hardly influenced at all by public relations concepts (cf. Broghs 1994; Armbrecht 1992; Theis 1994). There are very few attempts to analyse the fundamental relationship between communication, decision, organisation, and marketing. The management function is only one among many other public relations functions (Ronneberger & Rühl 1992). These also include scrutinising the demands of the organisation, rules of external markets, and the social environment of an organisation; in particular, they include provision of complex decision strategies for changing daily routines and for adjustment and/or optimisation of communication. Following the lines of system theory, the authors distinguish between three levels of public relations: (i) at the *macro* level the functional relationship between public relations and society as a whole, (ii) at the *meso* level the performance of public relations in relation to other functional systems in society (such as mass media, pressure groups, lobbying, etc.), and (iii) at the *micro* level the public relations tasks and internal as well as external communication structures of an organisation, including, e.g., face-to-face interaction in project work (Ronneberger & Rühl 1992: 183-193 and 249-280). In this sense, public relations theory can be understood as one possible starting point to provide the supporting pillars for a bridge between mass communication and individual communication, between institutional and interpersonal communication, as the most relevant frameworks for crisis communication. As far as we can see, the interface of these two frames of conflict communication has not been investigated in a synoptic approach so far (cf. new proposals in Fiehler ed. 1998). A concept for an integrated theoretical model remains a desideratum (an early exception is Richter 1979). However, empirical case studies in various fields seem to indicate the necessity of a more complex approach and an in-depth analysis of this relationship.

For instance, in a field study dealing with installation of a municipal waste incineration plant, Wiedemann, Schütz & Peters (1991) conclude that an open information policy might trigger interactive participation of target groups concerned. Hence, public relations could well serve as a key issue in fostering *empowerment* of groups facing conflict situations.

Modern societies call for new ecological quality. It is more and more regarded a core dimension of freedom. For many years, conservation or restoration of an intact environment was believed to be a task of solid engineering. This exclusively technical approach has been shattered considerably in recent years (cf. Joussen & Hessler eds. 1995): modern ecology favours transdisciplinary co-operation between engineering sciences, social and political sciences, psychology and semiotics, natural science and humanities. Only such a dialogue between all the disciplines involved can provide the basis for fruitful discussion on how to respond to environmental degradation in an effective manner, i.e.one publicly acceptable. However, the manifold facets involved make it difficult to develop an integrated theoretical strategy for communicating ecological concepts through media and across cultures. The core function of communication in this process is still scarcely acknowledged (cf. Aurand, Hazard & Tretter eds. 1993). It remains widely ignored by communication science which seems absorbed by investigating headline journalism and media scandals, text design, and media ethics.

One rare exception is a recent study by Meier & Schanne (eds. 1996) sponsored by the Swiss National Science Foundation. Devoted to the "Rolle des Journalismus bei der Wahrnehmung und Bewältigung gesellschaftlicher Risiken" [rôle of journalism in realising and mastering social risks], it presents an in-depth survey of media performance on ecological issues in general and on environmental risks in particular. According to these findings, it appears that mass media often serve as a mouth-piece for promoting the interests of industries, companies, and business organisations. The key role of public relations plays in this process is therefore an important object of research (cf. Grossenbacher 1989). Astonishingly, the water crisis – as one of the most urgent environmental problems to be dealt with globally – was not even mentioned, let alone been defined as an object for further case studies.

On the other hand, an aspect investigated thoroughly in communication sciences is the mutual dependency and resulting rôle conflict between journalists and public relations agents, the mass media, and business organisations (cf. Baerns 1985). Business organisations, institutions, and companies, facing an increasingly critical and ecologically aware public, are more than ever confronted with problems of legitimising and justifying procedures. This again holds a strong potential for further rôle conflicts (Becher 1996). But topical studies applying this to the water crisis are still lacking to date, just as systematic investigation into instruments and types of public relations such as open-house and information days, poster campaigns (as launched by the pharmaceutical industry), TV commercials (e.g., combat AIDS-campaigns), cultural events (e.g., the August 1 floating candle campaigns for Swiss-Aid), or cross-cultural campaigns of relief agencies (e.g., Red Cross).

3. Water talk – an African field study

Water is a case in point. International experts and environmental organisations do not hesitate to speak of a global water *crisis*. This indicates that the very complex implications of such a crisis will not only affect arid areas of the world but also in one way or other the so-called water-rich countries in the northern hemisphere. The problem can only be tackled with a combination of international and interdisciplinary approaches extending across traditional academic boundaries. In the light of this understanding, the EPFL has allocated a seed budget to the IGE/GS to finance preparation of a research project focusing on communication problems with respect to the water crisis (7/98 - 12/98: Karin Linxweiler helped with preparing relevant data). This is why two research groups have decided to co-operate which normally would be protected against any contact with each other by the high barriers of scientific cultures: the chair for *génie sanitaire* at the Institut Génie de l'Environnement of the EPFL and the chair for *Textwissenschaft* at the University of Berne (see above), both strongly motivated by an unconventional understanding of the social responsibility of scientific endeavours.

The premises were optimal for a pilot field study. The IGE/GS has been co-operating for many years with the École Inter-États d'Ingénieurs de l'Équipement Rural (EIER) and the Centre Régional pour l'Eau Potable et l'Assainissement (CREPA) in francophone Africa. The CREPA was founded as an international organisation based in Ouagadougou, Burkina Faso, dealing with problems of water supply and sanitary engineering. Branches ("antennes nationales") of the CREPA are located in more than 15 French-speaking countries in western and central Africa.

Ecological problems dominate daily life all along the sub-sahelian zone. Of special interest here are peri-urban zones, since these are the fastest growing in population but have at the same time the weakest infrastructure. The UN Summit Habitat II in Istanbul 1996 published an assessment projecting that two out of three inhabitants of our planet will be living in cities in less than one generation (quoting a prognosis of the World Resource Institute in Washington carried out in collaboration with the World Bank). Neither water nor electricity is available in the fast-growing peri-urban zones of poorer countries. Clean water has to be collected at water points which have been installed with the help of international organisations in co-operation with local institutions and authorities. The health situation is hazardous in the peri-urban zone. Insufficient waste management causes multiple diseases connected with the lack of sanitary installations.

Our pilot field study was devoted primarily to the peri-urban quarters of Ouagadougou, the capital of Burkina Faso, during an intensive two-week survey in June 1998. But for comparison, the much smaller city of Ouahigouya in the north – a so-called "ville secondaire" – and the rural village of Roumtenga were also included in this survey. Its main interest was to analyse attempts of international aid organisations, such as CREPA, to communicate concepts of water supply and sanitation to the local population.

On-site discussions with delegates of CREPA, municipal officers and administrators, local water point committees, 'water masters' and traders, and target groups of the local population yielded an insight into the most complex communication pattern developed in a pragmatic way by those sharing the common interest in getting and providing water. These communication efforts – which include not only the transfer of technical and social issues but aim at the same time to change traditional behaviour patterns for vital reasons of mere survival – have not been analysed so far.

The instructional concept of CREPA concentrates on how the quality of clean water collected at the well point can be maintained until the moment of consumption. The quality of water may already degrade during transport to the huts if not carried in closed containers, and later in the huts if not stored in especially designed jars. If the water quality degrades due to insufficient sanitary precautions, water-related diseases are the inevitable consequence. In the poor quarters of the towns – which are mainly located in the peri-urban zone – the mortality rate of infants exceeds 30%.

Women gather at the local water distribution points: the starting points of the *water communication path* (Burkina Faso, photo D. Genske 1998)

CREPA decided some time ago – probably somewhat intuitively – to start with sanitary education efforts at the water points since these are the locations the local women visit every day to satisfy their families' water demands. It was certainly a wise decision, by the way, to designate water points as optimal locations for implementing educational campaigns: utilising the water distribution path as a communication path is a strategy with a long tradition. It has been used for ages by magicians, churches, and mosques, especially in the more arid regions of the world.

The CREPA task, however, was complicated by the fact that an educational programme dealing with issues of sanitation has to address delicate questions of the private sphere and maybe even intrude into intimate behaviour patterns. In order to communicate these issues, CREPA has adopted the SARAR-concept developed by the Indian ministry of Education in the 1970s. SARAR is an acronym for the concept's five basic principles: Self-esteem – Associative strength – Resourcefulness – Action planning – Responsibility. An important aspect of the SARAR approach adopted is that local representatives from the quarter in which the water point was installed are recruited and trained to communicate sanitary concepts. They are referred to locally as 'animateurs' and 'animatrices'. The locals have confidence in them since they live in the same quarter and are familiar with their local culture and their particular problems. The 'animateurs' and 'animatrices' are based at the water points to contact the locals on their daily walk for water. They talk with the women in their language and go with them to their huts to discuss problems of sanitation *face-to-face*. This personal procedure has proven far more successful than any other approaches such as public slide shows or videos or hypertext computer instruction. These are consumed passively, if at all, without triggering any change of behaviour, besides the fact that these methods of instruction are more expensive and demand a certain technical infrastructure which normally cannot be provided in underdeveloped peri-urban zones.

Another specific complication is that, as a rule the locals in peri-urban zones migrated from rural areas. Many of them cannot read or write, and often they speak different dialects. This is not a problem for sociolinguistics or language policy but one of cultural semiotics. To overcome the communication barrier, CREPA adopted the strategy of the "boîte d'images" first introduced in connection with projects financed by the World Bank. This approach works with pairs of iconic illustrations in the form of cartoon sequences representing the *before* and *after* status as traditional everyday routines vs. new behaviour patterns. The former are interpreted as dangerous to health and therefore marked as undesirable while the latter – indicating an improved sanitary standard – are explained as to how people will benefit from them. All illustrations are semiotically adapted to the local culture and to situations of the people's everyday experience, depicting typical huts of the quarter inhabited by local people wearing typical clothes. Therefore, the target person can easily identify herself (or himself) with the situation depicted and recognises certain behavioural patterns, realises their consequences, and understands how to improve the situation. The "boîte d'images" is repeatedly discussed with the locals and commented upon in order to ensure success in individual education during this instructional discourse.

The SARAR method works with images depicting undesirable behaviour patterns juxtaposed with the improved situation (Burkina Faso, photo by Karin Linxweiler 1998)

Benefitting from this experience, CREPA has realised that communicating water related problems cannot be left to the engineers who develop technologies to ensure minimal sanitary standards such as special water jars or transport equipment. Any technical innovation which makes it necessary to change traditional behaviour patterns in situations of intercultural contact calls for the contribution of sociologists, ethnographers, and communication experts, turning this educational task into a transdisciplinary challenge.

The water and sanitation project visited in Burkina Faso offers a textbook example for the specific intercultural communication problem that we are interested in: a message developed within an organisation (such as CREPA) has to be communicated – by means of public relations procedures and based on cultural semiotics – to a target group, in triangular intercultural dialogue (expert – animateur – local) and face-to-face conversation (animateur – local, animateur – expert for feedback and re-evaluation), supported by culture-specific and locally adjusted instructional material that requires no technical infrastructure, in order to initiate the change of behaviour patterns detrimental to those exercising them.

Our focus is the very interface between these two axes of communication. We aim to giving it a theoretically integrated basis for empirical analysis which in turn may be of interest for the conceptual advancement of both dialogue analysis and theory of intercultural communication. Another long-term perspective for further research may be to try and transfer those communication strategies observed to be successful in getting people to practically change the way they deal with water and to apply them in carefully adapted ways to other educational issues of equally vital importance. For instance, the Agence Canadienne de Développement International (ACDI), which we contacted during our field study and which conducts a $ 14 million (Can) project to fight the AIDS crisis in the French-speaking countries of Africa (Projet d'appui à la lutte contre le SIDA en Afrique de l'Ouest), was not aware of the communication strategies utilised by CREPA, let alone of its proven efficiency. Ironically, the head office of ACDI in Ouagadougou is located just some 100 meters away from the CREPA and EIER offices. This, we believe, illustrates more than anything else the need for further research and mutual co-operation across academic boundaries in this scientific endeavour.

4. Objectives

In a world with ever-increasing international communication links and at the same time degrading primary resources, ecological crisis communication is a challenge for all parties involved, be they natural scientists offering technical solutions, public relations agents of organisations prompting concepts, or project workers *in situ* initiating changes in behaviour face-to-face. The danger of misunderstanding is high since language differences and cultural contrasts complicate the approach. Differences in forms of communication as well as the locally varying interpretation of standards and status add fundamental problems to the analysis of communication processes in this particular context. When dealing with issues of water quality and sanitation, diverging ethnical traditions, moral beliefs, and magical rituals open up further dimensions of the problem. There is not much use in developing sustainable technological solutions fighting the water shortage if they cannot be communicated. Communication failures with regard to essential primary resources easily lead from conflict to crisis, and from there to catastrophe.

For reasons of reducing the complexity of the problem, we suggest focusing on the two main frames of communication which we associated with a multiplicity of perspectives in the first section:

- the intercultural-institutional perspective: media communication
- the intercultural-interpersonal perspective: face-to-face interaction.

The first frame raises questions as to the codes of cross-cultural media campaigns of First World organisations with the objective of alerting people for ecological issues, the second to the codes of cross-cultural instructional discourse with the objective of initialising changes in individual everyday behaviour routines in Third World areas of ecological crisis (or even catastrophe, if you think, e.g., of Sudan).

Our research project will follow both perspectives in drawing a systemic model for integrated analysis of heterogeneous facets of semiosis or communication processes involved, paradigmatically illustrated by those concerning the water crisis. The already established co-operation of IGE/GS with CREPA/EIER offers a real world reference case. It could, and indeed should, be complemented by a similar constellation of problems (African culture, peri-urban zones, water crisis) in a different (i.e. anglophone) area of the continent. Therefore, contacts were also established with the Durban Centre for Cultural and Media Studies (CCMS, University of Natal), where similar lines of transdisciplinary research on crisis communication have been followed (sponsored, e.g., by state departments of education and of health; cf. Tomaselli 1992; Parker 1994; Tomaselli 1996).

Objectives of the project include

- information on conflicts or crises due to water shortage
- participants in the dialogue on water shortage conflicts
- a rôle model of these participants according to the perspectives given above
- content analysis of technical information communicated in the dialogue
- content analysis of social, cultural, and organisational information
- dialogue analysis of fallacies and misunderstandings
- a model of the interface between institutional and interpersonal communication
- public relations strategies to prevent conflict leading to crisis and catastrophe
- application of the model to case studies in African peri-urban zones

With these objectives we hope to bridge the gap between not only cultures in the empirical analysis of cross-cultural communication on issues concerning us all but also scientific cultures (in the sense of C.P. Snow) in co-operation of disciplines which normally take no notice of each other, the methodological hinge joint being dialogue analysis of conflict communication in intercultural settings (Fiehler ed. 1998).

References

Anderson, Alison (1997): Media, Culture and the Environment, New Brunswick/N.J.: Rutgers University Press.

Apitz, Klaas (1987): Konflikte, Krisen, Katastrophen. Präventivmassnahmen gegen Imageverlust, Wiesbaden: Gabler.

Armbrecht, Wolfgang (1992): Innerbetriebliche Public Relations. Grundlagen eines situativen Gestaltungskonzepts, Opladen: Westdeutscher Verlag.

Armbrecht, Wolfgang & Horst Avenarius (eds.) (1992): Ist Public Relations eine Wissenschaft? Eine Einführung, Opladen: Westdeutscher Verlag.

Aurand, Karl, Hazard, Barbara P. Hazard & Felix Tretter (eds.) (1993): Umweltbelastungen und Ängste. Erkennen, Bewerten, Vermeiden, Frankfurt a.M.: Westdeutscher Verlag.

Baerns, Barbara (1985): Öffentlichkeitsarbeit und Journalismus. Darstellung latenter Beziehungen durch Ermittlung von Einflüssen im Mediensystem. – In: Heribert Schatz & Klaus Kange (eds.): Massenkommunikation und Politik, Frankfurt a. M.: Haag & Herchen.

Barthenheier, Günter, Günther Haedrich & Horst Kleinert (eds.) (1982): Öffentlichkeitsarbeit. Dialog zwischen Institutionen und Gesellschaft, Berlin/New York: De Gruyter.

Becher, Martina (1996): Moral in der PR? Eine empirische Studie zu ethischen Problemen im Berufsfeld Öffentlichkeitsarbeit, Berlin: Vistas.

Beck, Ulrich (1996) [[1]1986]: Risikogesellschaft. Auf dem Weg in eine andere Moderne, Frankfurt a.M.: Suhrkamp.

Blanke, Thomas (1990): Zur Aktualität des Risikobegriffs. Über die Konstruktion der Welt und die Wissenschaft von ihr. – In: Leviathan 18.1: 134-143.

Böckelmann, Frank (1991): Journalistische Berufsfeldforschung ‚Pressestellen', München: Ölschläger.

Böckelmann, Frank (1998): Die Gelben, die Schwarzen, die Weissen, Frankfurt a.M.: Eichborn.

Bonfadelli, Heinz & Werner A. Meier (eds.) (1993): Krieg, Aids, Katastrophen. Gegenwartsprobleme als Herausforderung für die Publizistikwissenschaft, Konstanz: Universitätsverlag.

Brand, Karl-Werner (ed.) (1997): Nachhaltige Entwicklung. Eine Herausforderung an die Soziologie, Opladen: Leske + Budrich.

Breitmeier, Helmut (1996): Umweltforschung im Schlepptau der Politiker? Abschied vom Konzept der ‚Nachhaltigen Entwicklung' und Aufbruch zu mehr Effektivität in der internationalen Umweltpolitik. – In: Elmar Altvater (ed.): Globale Krisen und europäische Verantwortung, Baden-Baden: Nomos, 132-145.

Broghs, Horst P. (1994) [[1]1991]: Einordnung der Öffentlichkeitsarbeit in die Unternehmensstruktur. – In: Gero Kalt (ed.): Öffentlichkeitsarbeit und Werbung. Instrumente, Strategien, Perspektiven, Frankfurt a.M.: Institut für Medienentwicklung und Kommunikation, 63-68.

Bungarten, Theo (ed.) (1994 a): Sprache und Kultur in der interkulturellen Marketingkommunikation, Tostedt: Attikon.

Bungarten, Theo (ed.) (1994 b): Unternehmenskommunikation. Linguistsiche Analysen und Beschreibungen, Tostedt: Attikon.

Clyne, Michael (1996) [[1]1994]: Inter-cultural communication at work. Cultural values in discourse, Cambridge: Cambridge University Press.

Dettmar, Erika (1989): Rassismus, Vorurteile, Kommunikation. Afrikanisch-europäische Begegnung in Hamburg, Berlin/Hamburg: Erich Reimer.
Fiehler, Reinhard (ed.) (1998): Verständigungsprobleme und gestörte Kommunikation, Opladen/ Wiesbaden: Westdeutscher Verlag.
Flieger, Heinz (1986): Public Relations als Profession. Informationen zum Berufsfeld Öffentlichkeitsarbeit, Wiesbaden: Verlag für deutsche Wirtschaftsbiographien.
Gnägi von Bellmund, Adrian (1995): Entwicklungszusammenarbeit und sozialer Wandel im Südwesten Malis. Überlegungen zur Struktur und den Auswirkungen der populistischen Interventionspraxis, Diss. U Bern.
Grossenbacher, René & Ulrich Saxer (1987): Medien und Entwicklungsprozess. Eine empirische Studie im westafrikanischen Benin, Köln: Böhlau.
Grossenbacher, René (1988): Journalismus in Entwicklungsländern. Medien als Träger des sozialen Wandels?, Köln: Böhlau.
Grossenbacher, René (1989) [[1]1986]: Die Medienmacher. Eine empirische Untersuchung zur Beziehung zwischen Public Relations und Medien in der Schweiz, Solothurn: Vogt-Schild.
Heintzel, Alexander, Michael Kunczik & Astrid Zipfel (eds.) (1995): Krisen-PR. Unternehmensstrategien im Umweltsensiblen Bereich, Köln/Weimar/Wien: Böhlau.
Hess-Lüttich, Ernest W.B. (1992 a): Medienkultur – Kulturkonflikt. – In: Hess-Lüttich (ed.) (1992): 9-19.
Hess-Lüttich, Ernest W.B. (1992 b): Interkulturelle Kommunikation – Medienkommunikation. – In: Hess-Lüttich (ed.) (1992): 23-40.
Hess-Lüttich, Ernest W.B. (ed.) (1992): Medienkultur – Kulturkonflikt. Massenmedien in der interkulturellen und internationalen Kommunikation, Opladen: Westdeutscher Verlag.
Hess-Lüttich, Ernest W.B. (1997): Reden über die Fremden: Zum schweizerischen Migrationsdiskurs in der öffentlichen und institutionellen Kommunikation. – In: Bernd Scheffer (ed.): Medien und Fremdenfeindlichkeit, Opladen: Leske + Budrich, 193-224.
IEZ (1994): Interdisziplinäres Forschungsinstitut für Entwicklungszusammenarbeit der Universität Linz (ed.)1994: Nord-Süd-Beziehungen. Entwicklungspolitische Aspekte in Wirtschaft, Ökologie und Kultur, Frankfurt a.M.: Brandes & Apsel.
Joas, Hans (1992): Die Kreativität sozialen Handelns, Frankfurt a.M.: Suhrkamp.
Joussen, Wolfgang & Armin G. Hessler (eds.) (1995): Umwelt und Gesellschaft. Eine Einführung in die sozialwissenschaftliche Umweltforschung, Berlin: Akademie.
Kalmus, Michael (1994) [[1]1991]: Innerbetriebliche Kommunikation. – In: Gero Kalt (ed.): Öffentlichkeitsarbeit und Werbung. Instrumente, Strategien, Perspektiven, Frankfurt a.M.: Institut für Medienentwicklung und Kommunikation, 69-73.
Kievelitz, Uwe (1988): Kultur, Entwicklung und die Rolle der Ethnologie. Zur Konzeption einer Entwicklungsethnologie, Bonn: Politischer Arbeitskreis Schulen.
Mansell, Robin & Uta Wehn (eds.) (1998): Knowledge Societies: Information Technology for Sustainable Development, Oxford: Oxford University Press.
Meadows, Dennis H. et al. (1972): The limits of growth, New York/N.Y.: Universe Books.
Meadows, Dennis H. et al. (1992): Beyond the Limits, London: Earthscan Publications.
Meckel, Miriam & Markus Kriener (eds.) (1996): Internationale Kommunikation. Eine Einführung, Opladen: Westdeutscher Verlag.

Meier, Werner A. & Michael Schanne (eds.) (1996): Gesellschaftliche Risiken in den Medien. Zur Rolle des Journalismus bei der Wahrnehmung und Bewältigung gesellschaftlicher Risiken, Zürich: Seismo.

Oeckl, Albert (1993): Geschichte der Public Relations. – In: Dieter Pflaum (ed.): Lexikon der Public Relations, Landsberg am Lech: Verlag Moderne Industrie.

Parker, Warren (1994): The Development of Community-Based Media for AIDS Education and Prevention in South Africa: Towards an Action-Based Participation Research Model, Durban: U of Natal.

Prochnow, Martina (1996): Entwicklungsethnologie. Ansätze und Probleme einer Verknüpfung von Ethnologie und Entwicklungshilfe, Hamburg: LIT.

Richter, Helmut (1979): Konflikte in Dialogen. – In: Wilfried Heindriche & Gerhard Charles Rump (eds.): Dialoge. Beiträge zur Interaktions- und Diskursanalyse, Hildesheim: Gerstenberg, 39-65.

Ronneberger, Franz & Manfred Rühl (1992): Theorie der Public Relations. Ein Entwurf, Opladen: Westdeutscher Verlag.

Scharping, Michael & Christoph Görg (1994): Natur in der Soziologie. Ökologische Krise und Naturverhältnis. – In: Christoph Görg (ed.): Gesellschaft im Übergang. Perspektiven kritischer Soziologie, Darmstadt: Wissenschaftliche Buchgesellschaft, 179-201.

Scollon, Ron & Suzanne Wong Scollon (1995): Intercultural Communication. A Discourse Approach, Oxford: Blackwell.

Scherler, Patrick (1996): Management der Krisenkommunikation. Theorie und Praxis zum Fall Brent Spar, Basel/Frankfurt a.M.: Helbing & Lichtenhahn.

Theis, Anna Maria (1994): Organisationskommunikation. Theoretische Grundlagen und empirische Forschungen, Opladen: Westdeutscher Verlag.

Tomaselli, Keyan (1992): The role of the media in promoting intercultural communication in South Africa. – In: Communicatio 18.1: 60-68.

Tomaselli, Keyan (1996): Approaching Images. The Semiotics of Visual Representation, Højbjerg: Intervention Press.

UNESCO Kurier (1997): Naturkatastrophen. Vorbeugen und informieren 38.10.

Weber, Philipp (1980): Krisenmanagement, Organisation, Ablauf und Hilfsmittel der Führung in Krisenlagen, Diss. Univ. Zürich, Bern: Peter Lang.

Weiland, Heribert (1984): Unvorhersehbare Folgekosten durch Vernachlässigung sozio-kultureller Gegebenheiten. – In: Walter A.S. Koch (ed.): Folgekosten von Entwicklungsprojekten, Berlin: Duncker & Humblot, 129-150.

Welford, Richard (1995): Environmental Strategy and Sustainable Development. The Corporate Challenge for the 21st Century, London: Sage.

Wiedemann, Peter M., Hans Schütz & Hans Peter Peters (1991): Information Needs Concerning a Planned Waste Incineration Facility. – In: Risk Analysis 11.2: 229-237.

Bei Fragen zur Produktsicherheit wenden Sie sich bitte an:
If you have any questions regarding product safety,
please contact:

Walter de Gruyter GmbH
Genthiner Straße 13
10785 Berlin
productsafety@degruyterbrill.com